Searching for Sovereignty

By Dr. Anab Whitehouse

Publisher: Bilquees Press

In conjunction with the

Interrogative Imperative Institute

Table of Contents

<u>Introductory Note</u>

Although chapter 1 of this book might appear to be just about Canada's attempt to rework its constitution during the 1980s, in reality, the first chapter is a general exploration into the idea of constitution-making considered from a variety of perspectives. The particular backdrop against which the commentary in Chapter 1 might be developed is Canadian, however, the nature of the issues being discussed in that chapter, as well as the form that the specific principles and guidelines take in the second chapter -- these two, together, -- constitute a fully delineated way of approaching the problems entailed by trying to formulate a constitution – Canadian, American, or otherwise.

This book as a whole should be seen as a complement to other writings of mine that address related issues but from a different direction. For example: *Democracy Lost and Regained* -- as well as: *Shari'ah, 2nd Edition, Beyond Democracy, Final Jeopardy: Sovereignty and the Reality Problem (Volume V), and Final Jeopardy: Education and the Reality Problem (Volume VI)* -- all serve to extend and lend added depth to the discussion given expression in the present work.

As odd as it might seem to some, I see the problems facing western constitutional democracies and the problems of governance confronting the Muslim world as being very resonant with one another. The principles and ideas being espoused through this book, along with the thoughts and considerations of the other three books mentioned above, form – I believe – a repository of ideas through which the problems of governance involving both west and east might be addressed in a constructive fashion.

Chapter 2 and 3 examine the idea of leadership from two different perspectives: East and West. More specifically, the western approach to leadership is examined through the lenses of both classical and modern theories involving the idea of leadership. On the other hand, the 'eastern' approach to leadership entails a critical look at the ideas of a small number of "revolutionary" figures in Muslim history.

Finally, Chapter 4 takes an extended journey through the terrain of the American Constitution in relation to several investigations (namely, those conducted by the 9/11 Commission and NIST – National Institute of Standards and Technology) into the tragic events of 9/11. The analysis of this chapter develops the perspective that there were a variety of unconstitutional activities entangled with the work of both the 9/11 Commission and the NIST studies.

There is no need to read the book in sequence. The chapters are complementary to each other, but they do not presuppose one another.

Anab Whitehouse

Chapter 1:<u>Some Basic Issues</u> (Part 1)

<u>Introduction</u>

The extended essay that follows is not intended to be an exhaustive, definitive treatment of the issues that it explores. Obviously, many of the topics with which this document deals are quite complex and far-ranging in scope. Moreover, there are many different perspectives one could choose as a means of engaging and examining such topics.

The present chapter is intended as a discussion paper that delineates a way of looking at various facets of the current Constitutional problems besetting Canada (this essay was written around 1990 during the time when the Constitutional debates that were being conducted in Canada). It offers a critical analysis of a number of the themes that I believe have played a fundamental role in creating and shaping the crisis facing Canadians.

The ensuing discussion also puts forth a variety of suggestions that, if implemented, might go a long way toward helping Canada resolve many of its constitutional problems. However, irrespective of whether any of the proposals contained in this document are realized in practice, I believe the essay's critical perspective and proffered proposals should become part of the discussion process that surrounds and permeates the present constitutional crisis.

From a certain vantage point, the exploration that follows is not for the politically faint-hearted. Both the analysis and proposals put forth in this chapter are rigorous in nature, and, as such, neither of these two aspects leaves much to the reader's imagination concerning how I feel about various issues or where I stand on different matters.

As an interested observer and participant in the social/political fabric of Canadian life, I, to borrow the vernacular of sports, have tried to call things as I see them. I realize some of these judgment calls might well upset some segments of Canadian society.

The intention underlying such judgment calls is neither to insult nor to vilify any group. In fact, to continue with the analogy of sports, by citing apparent infractions concerning the spirit and substance of democratic principles, I, somewhat like a referee, am not making any moral judgments about the integrity of the people or groups to whom some of the remarks are addressed.

These remarks are directed at drawing attention to the inappropriateness of the behavior involved, according to our understanding and interpretation of the rules and character of the democratic game. As will be readily apparent at various points in our discussion, I believe some sorts of behavior to be far more inappropriate than other kinds of behavior.

Like a referee, I have a love for, and commitment to, the game in which I am involved, and also, like a referee, I want to see the game played well, cleanly and fairly. Everyone enjoys the game more when it is played under such conditions.

In addition, like a referee, I acknowledge the possibility that some of our calls might be shown to be, under the hindsight of instant-replay, questionable. Nonetheless, I believe we have a duty, as participants in the democratic game, to put forth our judgments to the best of our ability and let the chips fall where they may.

Indeed, in the foregoing sense, all Canadians are assuming the role of so many referees during this constitutional debate. In this regard, we all have a duty to call things as we see them, with the hope that, in doing so, the quality of the game will improve.

As a Canadian, I subscribe to the general idea of democracy. Furthermore, the present document is dedicated to putting forth a framework that is thoroughly consistent with democratic ideals and principles.

At the same time, the document has been written because I believe many of the political practices, institutions and processes that exist in Canada fall far short of the promise and potential that democratic theory has for meeting the social and political needs of a truly multi-cultural society. Consequently, the proposals advanced in the current document could be construed to be an exercise in democratic thinking that is intended to tap into, or unlock, more of the potential of democratic theory than we believe is taking place in Canada at the present time.

The present document is presented with the understanding that mere tinkering with the Canadian Constitution will not serve the best interests of Canada or Canadians. Radical reconstruction is necessary, but such reconstruction must be built upon a thoroughly democratic foundation.

Multiculturalism cannot survive in an environment that pays only lip service to the underlying principles and values of that philosophy. The principles and values of multiculturalism must be put into everyday practice.

The only way the philosophy of multiculturalism can be translated into a lived reality is for people in Canada to come to terms with the different levels of meaning inherent in the idea of, on the one hand, unity in diversity, and, on the other hand, sovereignty. Both of these ideas are given expression in a variety of ways during the course of the present document.

A word of caution should be mentioned in relation to the idea of sovereignty. This cautionary note might prevent much misunderstanding during the discussion that follows.

More specifically, sovereignty is a structurally complex idea. Many people have different ideas about its character and scope. However, as used in the current document, it must always be understood to be a relative and not an absolute term.

Sovereignty might best be construed in terms of having a certain degree of control over, or autonomy in, one's life. Underwriting this control or autonomy is some form of direct, unmediated access to real power on some given level of scale.

The shape that sovereignty assumes in any given socio-political context must always be a function of the dialectic between the rights and duties of care of the participants in that context. Consequently, the sovereignty of one individual must be balanced against the sovereignty of other individuals.

Moreover, the sovereignty of one level of government must be harmonized with the sovereignty of other levels of government. The same holds true with respect to the sovereignty association of communities and various levels of government.

Therefore, nothing in the ensuing discussion of sovereignty or related ideas should be construed as advocating either some form of anarchy or the break-up of Canada. Canada must remain whole and united, and it can accomplish this, I suggest, through the combination of constraints and degrees of freedom permitted by the principles and proposals put forth in this document.

The appendix at the end of the main discussion provides a synopsis of the principles and proposals that have been introduced at different junctures during the discussion. In some cases, the appendix contains specific recommendations that were not discussed in the main text.

Whenever this occurs -- which is not often -- the recommendations have been added as concrete expressions of the principles at work in our perspective. As such, these extra suggestions are consistent with the spirit of the democratic framework being proposed in this document.

I have included this appendix in order to facilitate understanding for those people who would like to get an overall idea of the democratic framework being proposed without having to search through the various arguments that stand behind such proposals. Nonetheless, I strongly urge readers to study the entire document and not limit oneself to the appendix. I believe that a great deal will be missed and, therefore, misunderstood if one restricts one's interaction with this document to the appendix alone.

The Electrified Constitution

A number of years ago, Martin Seligman, a psychologist, performed a rather gruesome experiment. However, it is an experiment that might provide considerable insight into certain aspects of the constitutional problems with which Canada is confronted at the present time.

Consequently, despite the rather dark nature of the experiment, the general character of Seligman's work will be summarized below. Essentially, the experiment is quite simple in design. First, one constructs a small, two-room structure.

The rooms have an adjoining doorway between them that can be left closed or open. One of the two rooms has a floor of wire mesh that can be electrified at the whim of the investigator.

Next, one takes an animal with the right sort of intellectual capabilities- namely, not too much and not too little. A dog seems to have been the animal of choice.

The dog, then, is placed in the room with the wire mesh floor. In the interests of science, the doorway leading to the second room-the one without a wire mesh floor is closed so as to eliminate an unwanted variable such as the dog's being able to escape.

The third facet of the experiment calls for a constant, non-lethal, but quite painful electrical current to be administered through the wire mesh floor of the first room. Naturally enough, the dog objects to this sort of treatment.

However, the dog can do nothing about the situation except to howl in pain and run around the room trying to escape from the painful stimuli. Unfortunately for the dog, there is no escape. Everywhere the dog runs involves coming into contact with some aspect of the wire mesh floor.

Through the courage and dedication of the scientists involved in the experiment, the process is allowed to continue on unabated. Eventually, the dog retires to one or another of the four corners of the room, lies down, and just continues to whimper in pain.

After some suitably lengthy period of time, this aspect of the experiment is brought to a close. The second stage of the proceedings discloses the raison dìtre, such as it is, for the experiment as a whole.

In this facet of the experiment, the doorway to the second, "safe" room is opened, permitting an avenue of escape for the dog. At this point, dogs that were 'run' in the first part of the experiment are placed back in the room with the wire mesh floor.

Once again the floor is electrified. Once again, most of the dogs retire to a corner and just whimper in pain. There is no attempt on the part of the majority of dogs to make use of the open doorway to the non-electrified room.

In fact, even when the experimenters manually take the dogs through the doorway and show the animals that the second room is safe, nonetheless, when the dogs are placed back in the first, electrified room, most of them (roughly two-thirds of the dogs) simply return to their "favorite" corner and continue to whimper in pain. This pattern of behavior will persist (for two-thirds of the dogs) even after the experimenters have shown the dogs -- on scores of different occasions -- that there is an avenue of escape open to them' should they choose to avail themselves of it.

Martin Seligman referred to this phenomenon as "learned helplessness". Interestingly enough, the learned helplessness phenomenon has been shown to hold for human subjects who, like the dogs, were initially exposed to irritating stimuli (but not shocks) from which the human subjects could not escape in the first part of the experiment.

In the second part of the experiment, two-thirds of the human subjects, again like the experiments with dogs, will not even try to escape from the irritating stimuli, despite being given the opportunity to stop, or escape from, the unpleasant stimuli.

There seem to be a number of features of the above summarized experiment that might be applicable to the constitutional crisis that besets Canadians at the present time. In fact, this crisis really has been in existence since Confederation began, and the implications of the aforementioned experiment also have been present since the beginning of Confederation. The major difference between then, and now is that the people of today have had a lot longer to become shaped by the forces at work in learned helplessness.

The Canadian Constitution is like a complex, intricately woven, wire mesh floor with a potential to be electrified. Canada can be likened to a room that surrounds that wire mesh floor, and the people of Canada are analogous to the experimental 'subjects' that are introduced into the space enclosed by the room of nationhood. The Prime Minister, the legislators, the Premiers and the courts are akin to the experimenters who, according to their mood and whim, deem it proper and fitting to apply various kinds of shocks of varying voltage- some political in character, others economical, and still other species of voltage involving issues of morality, ideology, education, religion, ethnicity, race and/or gender.

For some time now, Canadians desperately have been seeking a second, safe room-a room free of the pain that has come, over the years, from the repeated shocking that have been administered by those in power. However, although the various species of shocks are <u>administered</u> by people of power, the shocks themselves <u>have been made possible</u> by the intricately woven character of the constitutional wire mesh that makes up the political and legal floor on that Canadians are forced to walk whether they like it or not.

Eventually, after being exposed to a situation from which there appears to be no escape, many people begin to exhibit some of the symptoms of learned helplessness. For example, a great many Canadians, apparently, have decided to lay-down in their corner of choice and do nothing but whimper as they continue to be the victims of one set of shocks after another.

When one juxtaposes the phenomenon of learned helplessness next to the constitutional crisis tends to lead to two very important questions. (a) How much time will pass before the vast majority of Canadians begin to exhibit more and more characteristics of the above mentioned sort of learned helplessness due to constant exposure to an authoritarian rigidity and unresponsiveness of governments that insist that Canadians must go on suffering for the glory of democracy, as presently practiced, rather than be provided with one or more constitutional escape routes? (b) Even if some escape routes are found that lead to, relatively speaking, safe, or at least far less painful, circumstances, will the people of Canada be so far ensconced in the human version of learned helplessness that they would choose to continue to suffer in the wired room of the Constitution, as presently conceived, rather than seek relief in some alternatively structured room of constitutionality?

<u>Representational Democracy</u>

What would be required in order for Canada to be a participatory democracy? Some people might wish to argue that Canada already satisfies the requirements of a participatory democracy.

After all, voting is considered to be a fundamental expression of participation. Moreover, people are free to run for public office, or to help out in their riding association of choice, or to try to shape the policy platforms adopted by a political party. All of these count as acts of participation.

While conceding the point that there are a number of avenues through which Canadians can participate in the political process, nonetheless, the idea of a participatory democracy need not be limited to the foregoing sorts of possibilities. For example, once elections take place, the opportunities for most Canadians to continue participating in the political process often become severely curtailed.

This is the case because Canada operates according to the values of representational democracy. These values tend to place very determinate limits on the extent to which non-elected or non-governmental officials can participate in the political process.

There are, in general terms, two methods of putting into practice the concept of representational democracy. One approach construes the idea of representation to mean that the elected official must be faithful to the wishes, desires and interests of the electorate. Therefore, the elected official assumes the responsibility of actively seeking to convert such wishes, desires and interests into a governmental policy that is realized in various sorts of laws, social programs, economic measures, environmental activity and so on.

In taking on this sort of responsibility, the elected official acts as an agent for the electorate. As such, the elected individual's personal views concerning policy issues, social programs and legal standards are far less important than the wishes of the electorate. The elected official serves as a resource person for the electorate and tries to find potentially acceptable or feasible ways of implementing the desires of the electorate, as well as lobbying for, and negotiating on behalf of, the electorate's interests.

The other general approach to the notion of representational democracy, which might be labeled the "visionary model", holds a very different picture of the role of an elected official. From the perspective of the second approach, the elected official's primary responsibility is not necessarily to serve, or actualize, or be an agent for the wishes, desires and interests of the electorate. The task of the elected official is to seek to implement what such an individual believes is in the best interests of all of the electorate, even if these beliefs run, partially or entirely, contrary to the wishes, desires of the electorate.

Under such circumstances, campaign platforms become the blueprint or vision that drives the political activities of the elected official. Indeed, being elected is interpreted by people who adopt this "visionary" approach to representational democracy as a mandate from the electorate to pursue the various planks in the campaign platform during their tenure of office.

In practice, what occurs is a sort of mixture of the two aforementioned, general approaches to representational democracy. Although one does find elected individuals who are purists with respect to one approach or the other, usually elected officials try to combine the roles of agent/resource person for the electorate with the role of political visionary.

In this way, some of the wishes, desires, and interests of the electorate are realized precisely in the way for which the electorate -- or some of them -- had hoped. At the same time, the elected official also has pursued the realization or implementation of policies and programs that he/she believes to be in the interests of the electorate even if the latter do not share that belief.

Irrespective of which sort of approach to representational democracy one takes, there are problems. For example, the visionary perspective tends to be colored by some very questionable assumptions concerning the significance to be attached to the electorate's voting patterns. Very rarely, if ever, do members of the electorate as a whole vote for a particular individual in order to endorse the entire platform of the party for which the individual is standing as a candidate.

Some portions of the electorate, of course, are committed to a given party's platform, from beginning to end. However, even within the core members of a party, not all aspects of the platform are deemed to be equally important or fundamental.

Consequently, once in office, some planks of the platform might be more readily sacrificed than are other planks of the platform. In fact, elected representatives of the same party might be differentially committed to various facets of their party's platform and will seek to influence the political process accordingly, once they gain office.

Like most everything else in politics, the party platform constitutes a compromise amongst the competing factions of the party. Therefore, what occurs, once the members of a party get into power, will reflect the dialectic that transpires as different members seek to influence, orient, color and slant the position of the leader of the party. Indeed, the disaffection or alienation experienced by various factions of an elected party usually emerges as the actions of the leaders of that party go in directions that appear to marginalize the concerns, interests and wishes of such factions.

Aside from the foregoing issues, there are a wide variety of reasons why members of the electorate vote for a given individual that have little or nothing to do with a party's platform. These reasons range from: the charisma of the person vying for office, to: the looks of the candidate, and from: which candidate has the slickest campaign machinery, to: which candidate for which one has the least disliking.

Furthermore, during the course of office, issues that were not anticipated by anyone have a way of emerging. Elected officials with a visionary bent might take stands with respect to these problems. The stands they take might, or might not, be done in consultation with members of the electorate, but irrespective of which might be the case, there is no guarantee that the official's final position is going to reflect the beliefs, attitudes or feelings of the electorate.

The bottom line for the visionary approach to representative democracy is the belief that one has been elected for one's leadership qualities and one's ability to guide the country in a direction that is somehow "best" for everyone. What qualifies as being "best" is a function of the structural character of the vision held by these sorts of individuals.

This commitment to the bottom line remains firm even if one's leadership should involve decisions that are unpopular with those who vote for one. The visionary believes he or she has an obligation to impose these values onto society since such a person tends to believe this is the reason why people voted for that individual.

As such, they have reduced everyone's interests down to their own. They believe that their values/beliefs have more legitimacy and are more defensible than the values/beliefs of other people.

On the other hand, these people who advocate a 'give-the-people-what-they-want' approach to representative democracy are not without their problems. The reason for this is quite simple. One cannot possibly satisfy all of the wishes of all of the people all of the time.

Sometimes what people want is too costly. Or, the wants of some people might be exploitive or abusive of other people. Moreover, the wants of different groups of people might conflict with one another and, therefore, cannot be satisfied simultaneously.

Consequently, those who pursue the GTPWTW approach to representative democracy often end up serving the needs of only certain segments of the electorate. More often than not, the needs being served are the ones with which the individual's own likes and dislikes are most congruent. Therefore, those members of the electorate whose needs and interests do not fall within the sphere of interests of this sort of elected official will be marginalized, whether rightly or wrongly.

Both approaches to representative democracy have their strengths and weaknesses. Furthermore, both approaches permit participation of a limited nature.

Some people might wish to argue that the political opportunities provided by the foregoing alternatives represent the most that can be accomplished, or hoped for, within the context of a democratic society. However, there are those who would argue for a form of democracy that gives a much stronger emphasis to the idea of participation than does representational democracy in either of its two alternative forms.

Participatory Democracy and the Process of Recall

When people talk about the desire to have participation in the governing process, the discussion is often couched in terms of having a direct, active, unmediated contact with the governing process. Their desire is to have more autonomy over their political lives in the sense that they do not want their point of view to be marginalized, shunted aside or ignored by politicians.

They are seeking some way to have options open to them that offer the hope of circumventing, within limits, the traditional access to power -- namely, the politician. In other words, the spirit of participation is rooted in the desire to have access to a form of real power that is beyond the control of politicians and that will make politicians more responsive to the needs of the electorate than does the prospect of holding elections every four or five years.

In short, the sort of participatory power being sought is that which enables one to make political choices that have substantive impact. Such power is not dependent on having to curry the favor of, or having to plead one's case to, politicians who might not really be interested in helping one and who even might have a vested interest in placing obstructions in the way of some of those who are seeking their assistance or trying to have a point of view taken seriously by such politicians.

There are a number of ways of providing the electorate with a sense of having the direct, substantive, unmediated participatory power that they seek. For instance, the power of recall is one such possibility. The mechanism of recall can assume several forms.

The first variety would be the right of a suitably sized group of the electorate of a given riding, region or province to force elected officials to answer their questions, criticisms and so on in a face-to-face interchange. Such a form of recall does not occur at the whim, convenience or mood of the elected official.

It is an obligation of office that must conform to the requirements of the electorate's convenience, mood and needs. If necessary, the elected official would have to undertake a series of such interchanges when the size of the recall group is not capable of being handled in one meeting.

A second form of recall would be the right of a suitably sized group of the electorate to remove an elected official from office prior to the expiry date of a person's term of office. Presumably, after being permitted to perform in office for some minimum length of time-such as one year-the electorate would have the right to take the appropriate procedural steps to: (a) remove the person from office, and (b) proceed with a by-election to replace the person who has been removed. The idea is to provide the electorate with a mechanism of access to power that is responsive without being unnecessarily intrusive and obstructionist in practice.

If a recall vote is taken but does not generate the requisite proportion of ballots against the elected official, that individual could not be subjected to another recall vote for one year. Furthermore, one might wish to argue for some sort of quorum conditions that require that a minimum number of the eligible voters must cast ballots in order for the vote to be considered valid in the event of a recall vote that goes against the elected official. This quorum condition might be different in the two kinds of recall votes outlined earlier.

If one liked, one could even establish some combination of the two forms of recall. For example, if the need should arise, after having served one year, an elected official could be subject to recall by the electorate in order to respond to the latter's dissatisfactions with the official's performance. If the question of a second recall action became necessary, the electorate would be entitled to seek the official's removal from office.

Referendum Issues

Another sort of power that would enable the electorate to have direct, substantive and unmediated access to the process of governing is linked with the idea of a referendum. There is almost nothing that is more conducive to a sense of helplessness than to see policies, programs or changes that are being instituted and over which one has no control, despite feeling very much opposed to such activities of the government.

Many people would like to have an opportunity to counter some of the decisions made by government. The referendum does represent a mechanism that provides the electorate with a potentially powerful way to affect the governing process in a fundamental manner.

One does not have to propose a government by referendum in order use this form of people power. Some sort of balance needs to be sought that, on the one hand, will permit those elected to govern, yet, which, simultaneously, places constraints on the sorts of liberties elected officials can take with the "mandate" they presume the electorate has given them. Moreover, in addition to providing the electorate with a meaningful, pro-active method of imposing constraints on the way in which they are governed, the process of referendum also provides the electorate with a substantial set of degrees of freedom that permit it to participate in the machinery of government and, thereby, invests political choice with real power.

Three arguments often are cited against the use of referenda. These arguments emphasize: (a) the expense of running a referendum; (b) the potentially complicated or unwieldy nature of a referendum; and (c) referenda subvert the parliamentary process. Let's explore each of these in turn.

The basic issues underlying the expense of running a referendum is not a function of cost, per se. The real problem focuses on, firstly, whether or not the cost can be justified by the advantages secured through such expenditure, and, secondly, even if the costs can be justified, whether or not one can afford those costs.

Perhaps the best way to address the aspect of justification is to ask the following question: putting aside all issues of cost, what possible reason could a democracy offer that would deny its people the entitlement to decide their fate in a direct, unmediated fashion, at least some of the time? Seemingly, any attempt to usurp the people's entitlement to request referenda from time to time would violate the very spirit to which democracies are supposed to be dedicated. In short, the desire to prevent people from having sufficient autonomy over their lives such that they are not afforded an avenue (i.e., referenda) to express their political will directly as citizens, rather than through political surrogates, is inimical to the democratic process.

Let's assume for the moment, therefore, that costs, whatever they might be, can be justified in light of the benefits that are obtained by citizens through the referendum mechanism. The question then, becomes: can we afford such costs?

Part of the answer to this question is clouded by our lack of knowledge about the frequency of the referendum event. A determinate answer to the foregoing question is also hard to establish because we don't know if the referendum would be a solitary affair or whether it would be run in conjunction with other events, such as elections, which would reduce costs relative to running a referendum on its own.

For the sake of argument, let's arbitrarily suppose that referenda are limited to a maximum of two per year for any given level of government. Let's further suppose that these referenda are unconnected with any other ongoing event such as an election.

There are a number of possibilities that come to mind with respect to the matter of underwriting the costs of a referendum. To begin with, costs could be cut considerably by requiring every citizen above a certain age to be required to volunteer time if called upon to help organize and operate a referendum.

Just as people are selected for jury duty, one could be selected for other forms of civic duty that are crucial to the health of a democracy. Democracy is not merely about rights of the individual. It is also about duties of care that the individual owes to society. In any event, once one has served such a duty on a given level of governmental activity, then, one would not be eligible to be called again for volunteer duty on that level for some specified period of time.

Secondly, people are prepared to make political contributions in order to promote and support political activities that serve their interests. The individual's interests are served in a fundamental way when one is provided with an opportunity to vote directly for, or against, issues that have the potential to affect one's life in a substantial way. Consequently, to contribute to a referendum fund would be a way of actively supporting, as well as participating in, a process that was not mediated or controlled by elected government officials.

Furthermore, such contributions would have the advantage of being committed to a very specific purpose with which the individual agreed. Said in another way, such contributions would not be ear-marked for uses about which the individual had no knowledge and with which the individual might or might not be in agreement.

Thirdly, the location of the referenda events could be held at public places such as schools; libraries, churches, temples, mosques and post offices. Therefore, there would not have to be any costs for renting sites at which the referenda are held.

Fourthly, presumably, one of the conditions of being granted a broadcast license -- whether radio or television -- should be the willingness to make public service announcements. Therefore, such stations should donate a certain amount of air time to promote and publicize, in a non-partisan way, the occasion and issues of a referendum.

All of the above possibilities would reduce, if not entirely cut, the expense of running a referendum. However, if additional funds are needed, then, they would be paid out of public funds. People have a right to expect that their taxes will be used to pay for services that are in their direct interests and that permit the people to have some degree of control over the political process.

Another argument leveled against the idea of holding referenda is that such a process is unwieldy. In addition, the referenda process is said to have the potential for involving a complexity that is confusing to those who are voting in the referenda.

As far as the charge of being unwieldy is concerned, the charge seems, at best, very weak. The referendum process need be no more unwieldy than are elections. And, since elections have, by and large, proven to be quite manageable, one sees no reason why referenda wouldn't be run equally well.

Of course, someone might object at this point that elections might be less frequent than are referendums and, consequently, are inherently more manageable than referenda would be. One also might contend that referenda are more likely to be national events, whereas this is not the case for many elections. For the most part, elections tend to be limited to a provincial level of scale or less.

Let us briefly examine the different kinds of referenda proposed in this document [See Appendix, Section I, items (1)(a), (b) and (c)] and see whether the foregoing sort of objections are persuasive. In the ensuing discussion, we will be foreshadowing a few issues that will be explored at more length in the section on *Senate Reform*. Nonetheless, one does not have to have a complete understanding of the forthcoming issues in order to appreciate the points that will be made in the present discussion.

First of all, although referenda concerning, for example, war necessarily occur on a national level, they would tend to be very infrequent. Therefore, this kind of referendum should be less problematic than national elections, since the former probably will happen more infrequently than do elections.

Secondly, almost all recall referenda (with the exception of those involving the Prime Minister) would take place within a single riding. Because of the restricted level of scale of such referenda, they do not appear to pose any inherent problems above and beyond the usual difficulties surrounding the election process.

In addition, one cannot assume that if the electorate has the power to recall people, this power necessarily will be exercised in an indiscriminate fashion. In fact, one could make a strong case for the following possibility. Precisely because the electorate has such power and, once a year has passed since the date of election, can exercise the power at their discretion, they might be willing to give the elected official some latitude with respect to making mistakes. When one couples the above tendency toward forbearance under such circumstances with the conservative tendency in many electorates to maintain the status quo, the recall procedure does not appear to be likely to be excessive in its occurrence.

One also would have to factor in the perspective of the elected official in estimating the frequency of referenda relative to recall issues. If she or he realizes that the recall procedure is a real option of the electorate, then, presumably, the official will take steps to prevent the recall procedure being initiated. In short, the official will try to do a good job.

Finally, one must consider the problem posed by certain constitutional issues and ask if referenda in such circumstances would be inherently unwieldy. While all these sorts of referenda would be national in scope, one could argue, once again, that there might be a variety of pressures that would work to inhibit the proliferation of these events. In general, the possibility of referenda concerning constitutional issues takes place (as is discussed later in the document) when the Senate subcommittee on constitutional issues either: (a) initiates an amendment process with respect to the written form of the Constitution; or, (b) alters a decision of one of the constitutional forums; or, (c) refers conflicting decisions of different constitutional forums to the full Senate body for discussion and debate.

As far as (a) -- the initiation of the amendment process -- is concerned, there is considerable reluctance on the part of any nation to amend its constitutional process. The Constitution might get amended, but this will occur relatively infrequently.

Furthermore, with respect to (b) above, because the Senate subcommittee on constitutional issues knows that by altering a decision of a constitutional forum it will be setting in motion a process that will lead to a referendum, it will exercise considerable constraint therein. The subcommittee's tendency will be to let the judgments of the constitutional forums stand unless some fundamental principle or value has been undermined by those judgments.

Even in the case of (c) above -- namely, different constitutional forums generating conflicting judgments -- a great deal will depend on the character of that conflict. Ironically, some, but not all, conflicts serve the interests of society as a whole by permitting different people to pursue their interests in different ways.

This positive facet of conflict will be discussed, in slightly more detail, in the section on *Diversity of Equality: A Principle*. For the present, however, one can say that the Senate subcommittee on constitutional issues often will be inclined to permit a certain degree of flexibility in the judgments of different constitutional forums.

The subcommittee will be moved to act only when the problem of conflicting judgments goes beyond some boundary of permissibility. The character of this boundary point will vary with circumstances and the issues involved. Consequently, here too, there will be pressure to prevent the proliferation of cases that are to be decided by referendum.

To be sure, there will be cases that will lead to referenda being held. Yet, at this point, there is nothing to suggest that such a process necessarily should be excessively frequent or should be inherently more unwieldy than the election process. In addition, whatever extra effort will be required by the electorate and the government in order to look after the responsibilities of referenda will be more than compensated for by the opportunity such a process gives the people to participate in the political process and, thereby, to gain a measure of autonomy over their lives.

The previously mentioned criticism that referenda run the risk of confusing or confounding the electorate seems to be somewhat condescending toward the electorate. First of all, the task of explaining the various issues associated with referenda is one of the tasks of the elected officials.

If these officials can't accomplish this task, then, maybe the problem rests, not with the electorate, but with the officials or with the lack of clarity of the issue being subjected to a referendum. Either the government has a clear idea of what it proposes to do, or it doesn't. If the government is clear-sighted in its view, then, it should be able to communicate the essence of this to the people.

Secondly, the wording of the referendum should not be a major concern. One does not have to put forth all the ins and outs of the issue on the referendum sheet.

In fact, these issues should be spelled out ahead of time. The purpose of a referendum is to seek a yes or a no vote that is in support of, or in rejection of, a given proposition, piece of legislation or government policy considered as a whole.

A referendum is intended to provide a means of voting for or against the operative principle that is at the heart of a given issue, irrespective of the riders that might qualify that issue in various, nuanced ways. If one votes in support of an issue, then, one is giving the government authority to pursue that issue, as well as permitting it some degree of flexibility as to the specific wording of the text that gives operative expression to that issue. On the other hand, if one votes against an issue, then one is telling the government that no matter how it tinkers with the wording of the issue, one is opposed in principle to the basic philosophy inherent in the issue.

The final argument that is raised, on occasion, against the idea of a referendum process centers on the charge that referenda subvert the parliamentary process. This is exactly right, and that is what it is intended to do.

What referenda do not do is subvert the democratic process and, unfortunately, this cannot always be said of the parliamentary process. Those who would equate, in rigid fashion, the parliamentary process with democracy have an extremely narrow understanding of the latter.

Moreover, such individuals entirely fail to grasp that people have a need for access to real power that falls beyond the capacity of politicians to subvert or usurp for the latter's own purposes and irrespective of whether, or not, those purposes are legitimate.

To try to argue that giving power to the people is wrong since it permits them, within certain prescribed limits, to serve their own interests directly and, thereby, gain autonomy, of a sort, over their lives, seems a rather ludicrous argument. Indeed, to try to prevent people from having access to, as well as exercising, such power seems to fly in the face of what democracies supposedly entail. One has to wonder about the motivation of anyone who would wish to close off this sort of possibility entirely.

<u>Question of: When?</u>

There is at least one outstanding issue that still needs to be addressed. This issue concerns both the processes of recall as well as that of a referendum. More specifically, one might like to know how to determine when a recall or a referendum is in order.

One obvious suggestion is to make use of the opinion poll expertise that exists in the community. While opinion polls are vulnerable to various kinds of difficulties that can skew the statistics in different directions, nevertheless, polling is rooted in a whole arsenal of statistical techniques and sampling procedures that have been studied thoroughly for a number of years by a large number of professional mathematicians, statisticians, political scientists, sociologists, and psychologists.

These years of effort have sensitized investigators and practitioners to the kinds of biases, methods and tools that have the potential for contaminating or distorting the results of an opinion poll. Consequently, when the appropriate protective measures are taken, polls are capable of generating results that, when properly analyzed and presented, are fairly accurate in the way they reflect the character of people's opinions about specific issues.

Thus, if one wishes to probe the mood of the electorate in a riding, municipality, province, region or the country as a whole with respect to, say, the issue of recalling a particular elected official, a poll could be conducted that would provide insight into the electorate's thinking on the matter. The same process could be invoked in relation to the question of holding a referendum.

If one were to assume, for the moment, that the issue of the desirability of using polls as the means of choice of taking the political pulse of the community has been settled, two problems remain. The first problem revolves around the question of who is to do the polling, analysis and so on. The second problem concerns the costs of such an undertaking.

This latter facet is not a small consideration if one keeps in mind that recall and referenda issues could be raised at every level of government, from home ridings to the federal context. Moreover, there might be an ongoing need to probe the mood of the electorate on a fairly regular basis. Therefore, the expense of running a number of polls over the course of a year would be fairly substantial.

One possible way of defraying such costs is to entice the universities and colleges in the community to be good corporate neighbors and help provide the necessary expertise in polling as a public service. By offering this sort of service, the educational institutions could return something of value directly to the community -- especially to those people who might have little or no contact with these institutions and, yet, who are helping to support the universities and colleges through their tax dollars. On the other hand, those professionals who donate their time to providing such a service could use the activity to help fulfill some of their own needs within the university or college as a kind of employment credit that would be weighed along with the research, teaching and administrative duties that are used in determining promotions, tenure and pay increases.

Election Reform

Another possible avenue for helping the electorate to gain more direct control over the political process that affects their lives concerns the way in which election campaigns are run and financed. More specifically, if one asks people what factors should weigh most heavily in determining the outcome of a truly democratic election process, more often than not, one will receive answers like: the issues; or the quality of the candidates.

By "issues", people usually are referring to the policy or program options being advocated by the various candidates. These options have different projected ramifications for the community (whether municipal, provincial, regional or national) and are construed as serving, or not serving, the interests of specific groups or some collection of such groups.

The answer of "the quality of the candidates" is fairly straightforward. It encompasses characteristics such as integrity, commitment, leadership abilities, intelligence, work ethic, humanity, and so on.

Neither of the aforementioned answers (i.e., issues, quality of the candidates) is about the ability to finance a campaign. Unfortunately, money, as it does in most things, has a way of confusing matters. Nonetheless, anyone who is truly interested in democracy, principles, or political fairness does not take kindly to the idea that elections can be won on the basis of the size of campaign expenditures rather than on the basis of the quality of issues or candidates.

Furthermore, there is a growing cynicism among many voters about the way campaign money plays an increasingly corrupting role in the electoral process. More and more, seemingly, campaigns are about who has the most money to spend on advertising campaigns. More and more, campaigns are about which candidate can be packaged most alluringly.

More and more, campaigns seem to be based on the tactics of illusion, deception, evasion and manipulation. Campaigns seem less and less to be directed to the needs, interests, concerns and problems of citizens.

More and more, campaigns seem to be reduced to 30-second spots, photo opportunities and repetition of names or slogans. Less and less, are campaigns about an in-depth debate concerning, and discussion of, essential and relevant issues.

More and more, campaigns are about individuals and parties winning elections. Less and less, are campaigns about ensuring that the community wins through the election of people and the promotion of issues that are most responsive to the needs and concerns of citizens.

Of course, some politicians will argue that, with all due modesty, they are the best people to serve the interests of the electorate. Their arguments might or might not be true. In addition, such politicians will claim their approach to the issues is the one that is most conducive to the enhanced welfare of the community. Again, these claims might or might not be true.

Under the best circumstances, determining the worth of these arguments and claims is fraught with difficulties. The presence and expenditure of money in the campaign process muddies the political waters considerably. In fact, one cannot establish any substantial, meaningful, positive correlation between the size of campaign expenditure and the worth of candidates or the positions they support.

Consequently, one way of helping to eliminate such problems, and, thereby, assist the electorate to gain some control over the electoral process, rather than be its manipulated victims, is to require that all political contributions be directed to a general election fund that serves the interests of the community as a whole. This fund would be used to underwrite the cost of such things as: debates, non-promotional campaign expenses, as well as publicizing the philosophical positions of all the candidates on various topics, issues and problems.

In order to work toward eliminating the deleterious or distorting effect that the slickness of campaign advertising or packaging strategy might have on the electorate's perception of the quality of candidates or issues, all campaigns should be tied together. In other words, any campaign literature would have to include material on all the candidates, say, in a given riding.

Or, all candidates would have to be given equal exposure on radio and/or television, and they all would have to be given equal access to the peak listening/viewing times. No independent advertising would be permitted.

Moreover, no negative advertising would be allowed. Therefore, candidates' advertising could only be about promoting their own political/philosophical ideas, values, beliefs, hopes and policies.

Campaign advertising could not denigrate or criticize other candidates' qualifications, directly or through innuendo.

In addition, remarks about another candidate's political position would have to be restricted to stating, in matter-of-fact terms, differences of perspective, emphasis and priorities. In doing this, one could not resort to scare tactics, vilification, ridicule or distortion. Furthermore, such remarks would have to be offered in a context (e.g., debates) that permitted one's political opponent(s) an opportunity to respond.

Canada, in general, has less difficulty with the problem of negative campaign advertising than does, say, the United States. However, this practice does arise in Canada from time to time, and it should be avoided. Let every candidate put his or her best foot forward, and let the people decide the matter solely on the basis of the talents and abilities of candidates, together with the political positions of the candidates on various topical issues.

There will be those who will maintain that placing the foregoing sorts of constraints on the campaign process is undemocratic because, for example, such constraints interfere with a person's right to contribute to whichever candidate that individual wishes. Moreover, such constraints interfere with an individual's capacity to give financial support to those issues in which one believes and to which one is committed.

However, democracy is best served when one can ensure that the wielding of power does not: sway, corrupt, bias, distort or skew the electoral process. And, most assuredly, money tends to be used as a tool of power that serves the interests of those who have it by undermining the electoral process through skewing it in their favor while disadvantaging those who do not have the money necessary to make their own values and concerns known to the electorate.

If people are truly interested in serving the ends of a democratic process, then, let the political playing field be level so that everyone has an opportunity of putting forth his/her case to the people under equitable conditions in which the only things that matter are the quality of issues and candidates. Permit the electorate to have control over the election process rather than permitting them to be controlled by power groups, vested interests, or bankrolls and marketing strategies.

Quite frankly, if people feel they have to buy an election in order to win, they have very little faith in their own political position. In effect, they are saying that their ideas and/or candidates would not win in a fair, equitably run election.

In order to win, they are saying we must subvert or skew the election process. This might be politics in action, but it is not democracy in action.

There is another side to the proposal that would require campaign contributions to be given to a common election fund. When a poor person or an individual from a minority sees that one's contribution to the political process will not be lost, that one's contribution will not be swamped by a rich and powerful majority, and that one's dollars will help purchase a fair, equitable and just electoral process, then, such people will not only feel that they have more control over their political life, but, in actuality, they will have more power over their own lives.

One of the central principles of participatory, as opposed to representational, democracy is to provide people with more access to a real political power with which to control their own political destiny. A common campaign fund from which all candidates could draw and that could be used to promote a variety of political philosophies would provide access to real participatory power.

Consistent with the foregoing ideas would be a waiver on all nomination or filing fees. Frequently, these fees run into the thousands of dollars, and constitute a serious impediment to the poor and disadvantaged with respect to meaningful participation in the political process.

One can come up with other, fairer ways of placing manageable limits on the number of candidates, as well as protecting against frivolous campaigns, than by charging filing fees. For example, one could specify that in order to qualify as a candidate (i.e., one who is entitled to draw upon the general campaign fund for all 'official' candidates), one must receive the nomination, in one's constituency, of one of the five or six major parties in Canada, or one must be supported, through petition, by, say, 10% of the eligible voters in the riding in which one wishes to stand for election.

Sovereignty: A First Encounter

Let us examine yet another area involving the issue of personal autonomy as a basic expression of participatory democracy. Recently, the British Columbia Supreme Court handed down a decision that denied the land claims of a group of Native people.

The essence of the court's decision is that the Native land claims had no merit since such claims had all been extinguished during colonial times. This act of extinguishing was accomplished by those who were acting on behalf of the authority of the sovereign power of the King or Queen of England.

The apparent ethnocentric prejudices that are ingrained in certain aspects of Canadian society and that are reflected, unfortunately, in the judgment of the learned justices of the B.C. Supreme Court run so deeply that many people do not seem to have properly appreciated just how revealing the court's judgment is about the assumption underlying the world view of many Canadians concerning Native peoples.

Moreover, the court's judgment is not an isolated phenomenon. Other judges and governmental officials in other localities and times have made statements or rendered judgments that are similar to that of the British Columbia Supreme Court.

More specifically, the justices are saying, in effect, that one source of sovereignty has a perfect right to extinguish the sovereignty of another people, and, thereby, make any claim for autonomy, on the part of the latter people, null and void. Stated in another way, the justices seem to be saying that robbery, enslavement, displacement and cultural genocide are quite acceptable as long as these sorts of activities proceed in accordance with the dotting of legal is and the crossing of judicial is as stipulated by the justices' own self-serving sense of sovereignty. Thus is everything tied up in a nice, neat, solipsistic, legal tautology that never touches on anything except the imperialistic desires and whims of a people who would appropriate that which does not belong to them, as well as who would attempt to extinguish the sovereignty of a people that is not capable of being extinguished merely because some law is passed or edict is given.

The sovereignty of a people is not a function of law. It is an a priori given that has been recognized, appealed to, alluded to and invoked across thousands of years and in virtually every society about which there exists recorded knowledge.

In fact, the roots of this a priori principle are so fundamental and so pervasive to the human condition that no one has been able to mount a plausible, let alone convincing, argument that would justify the denial of such sovereignty in a way that would be acknowledged as a tenable philosophical position by most people. The central importance of this issue of sovereignty also is reflected in every kind of human rights document that has issued forth from the United Nations and its predecessor, the League of Nations.

Law is predicated on, and presupposes the existence of, such sovereignty. Law is derivative from sovereignty. Indeed, although one can conceive of sovereignty without law, one cannot conceive of law without presupposing the existence of a source of sovereignty to generate such law. Law does not generate itself.

One might use law to obscure and obfuscate the issue of sovereignty. One also might use law to generate delusions, illusions and distortions concerning the nature of sovereignty. Nevertheless, no one can use law to unilaterally extinguish such sovereignty. Such an act can never be justified, although people do attempt to rationalize it.

For example, when Britain was reveling in its imperialistic and colonialist glory, it used might as an argument for its "right" to impose its will on other peoples. British officials, then, proceeded to dress up this act in an ethnocentric, self-serving clothing of a Divine destiny that shines Its favor on the civilized (i.e., British) world. Many other countries, including France, Spain, Portugal, Germany, Russia and the United States, have rationalized similar actions in similar fashion.

Legitimate constraints and limits can be placed on the exercise of sovereignty only through mutual agreement. This sort of reciprocity is exhibited in the case of a social contract between an individual and the larger community in which both parties agree to restrain themselves in certain ways in order to preserve the autonomy and integrity of the other party to the agreement.

Each party has rights in such an agreement. Each party has duties of care with respect to the other party under the reciprocal character of the agreement.

However, the willingness of a person or people to accept constraints upon one's sovereignty should not be confused with the idea of extinguishing a people's sovereignty. The latter idea is a figment of the fevered imagination of those who would shamelessly, and with an inflated sense of self-importance, try to rationalize their attempts to deny, if not usurp, the sovereignty of another people.

Neither the Supreme Court of British Columbia, nor the court system of any province, nor the Supreme Court of Canada has any jurisdiction in the matter of the sovereignty of Native peoples. In and of itself, the sovereignty of the Native people is entirely extra-legal in character.

However, as indicated earlier, the trappings of legitimate legality arise in conjunction with the sovereignty of Native peoples only to the extent that, of their own free will and volition, Native peoples agree to enter into a social contract with the peoples of Canada. This contract gives expression to the sort of constraints on sovereignty that are deemed necessary in order to protect and, where possible, enhance the integrity, autonomy and access to real power of the respective parties.

Unfortunately, historically, the non-native peoples of Canada tend to have misconstrued and misunderstood the nature of their relationship with Native peoples. The former have been inclined to consider themselves: the superior, "civilized", divinely favored party that has the right to impose their values, policies, programs and will on the Native peoples.

In short, most non-Native peoples of Canada believed they alone had sovereignty. For the most part, there has been a dearth of any semblance of mutuality and reciprocity that has characterized the intentions and attitudes of non-Native peoples in their dealings and interactions with Native peoples on the issue of sovereignty.

Canada took some 50 years to apologize to the Japanese Canadians for subjecting these citizens to all manner of indignities during and after the Second World War. Canada still has not apologized for the indignities that it heaped, over a much longer period of time than occurred with the Japanese, upon the Chinese immigrants to this country.

The plight of the Native people is further historical evidence of the disturbing penchant of all too many "mainstream", majoritarian Canadians, or their political representatives, to fail to come to grips with the whole issue of sovereignty. Unfortunately, the suffering of Native peoples has been far more long-standing than the cases of either the Japanese or the Chinese peoples.

All of these cases demonstrate that all too many "white" Canadians believe only their own sovereignty is of any value. All too many Canadians seem to believe that such sovereignty underwrites their right to deny, usurp or intrude upon the sovereignty of other peoples.

The resolution of the sovereignty problem of Native peoples is complicated immeasurably by the fact that money, natural resources and land have become inextricably caught up with the issue of sovereignty. On the one hand, vested interests-both public and private-stand to lose a considerable amount of power, property and money, both in the present as well as the future, if the full significance and ramifications of the sovereignty of Native peoples is finally acknowledged and acted upon. On the other hand, Native peoples cannot give full expression to their sovereignty as autonomous peoples unless they can exercise control over the land and resources that were taken from them.

In fact, for Native peoples, the land plays a central role in their spiritual traditions, since it is a sacred responsibility that has been entrusted to them. They are the trustees of the land over which they have authority and on which they live their lives. If they are denied the capacity to nurture their relationship with the land and to fulfill their spiritual responsibilities as trustees, then, they are being denied the opportunity to pursue a fundamental aspect of their religious tradition.

Giving all of Canada back to the Native peoples might be far too problematic and impractical at this late stage-not to mention being unfair to a lot of present day non-Native peoples. Nonetheless, non-Native Canadians are going to have to face up to the fact that there is, in principle, only one way to right the wrongs that have been perpetrated against the Native people. Some sort of package of land, autonomy and compensation is going to have to be extended to the Native peoples, and this is going to require substantial sacrifices on the part of both the Federal as well as the Provincial governments.

Presumably, Native peoples will be prepared, as they always have been, to enter into a form of social contract with the non-Native peoples of Canada in which reciprocity, mutuality and co-operation become the central shaping forces of that contractual process. This means that the Native peoples will have to assume certain kinds of restraints upon their sovereignty and, therefore, they will not get everything they would like or to which they, morally, might be quite entitled. However, there must be a dimension of reciprocity to this constraining process. The foregoing considerations also indicate that all non-Native Canadians are going to have constraints placed on their sovereignty as well with respect to the Native peoples, if we are to resolve the problem in as equitable a fashion as possible under a very complicated and messy set of circumstances.

This is likely not going to be a pain-free process on either side. Nevertheless, as long as the problems surrounding the sovereignty of Native peoples continues to fester, then, Canada will have lost its moral authority to speak out against intrusions upon the sovereignty of people that occurred in the past, are occurring now and, very likely, will continue to occur in the future. For Canadians to denounce the usurping or suppression of sovereignty in other places while standing neck deep in its own cesspool of usurpation and suppression, would be hypocritical in the extreme.

A Possible Solution

Before outlining our proposal, one or two points need to be stated clearly. First of all, I do not consider what follows to be necessarily either the best way, or the only way, of resolving the problems that plague the Native peoples issue. This issue is complex, and any solution will have ramifications for all Canadians. Indeed, many of the ramifications that ensue from any given attempt to resolve the problem likely will have unpalatable aspects for a variety of groups, communities, levels of government and individuals.

Consequently, proposed solutions for dealing with the attendant problems of Native peoples' issues face the imposing challenge of having to be both maximally fruitful as well as minimally injurious with respect to a variety of interests and parties. As a result, any solution that is offered up likely will be criticized as being: either not sufficiently fruitful with respect to one group or another; or, not sufficiently free from injurious implications for one group or another.

There might be those, perhaps many, from within the Native peoples community who will find our proposed solution problematic, maybe even completely unacceptable. Undoubtedly, there will be people, perhaps many, from among the non-Native peoples of Canada who will consider our proposed solution as being 'unhelpful'. People from both sides of this issue will have these opinions because they will feel that our solution is asking them to give up something that is, to their understanding, rightfully theirs.

Generally speaking, tug-of-wars can have only one winner. One side or the other usually ends up being dragged in a direction in which it does not want to go. On the other hand, sometimes the rope on which the competing sides are tugging breaks under the strain, and nobody wins. Yet, everybody suffers from the ordeal.

The rope, of course, is a metaphor for Canada. More and more strain is being imposed on the fabric of that rope as people, especially in both the federal and provincial governments, become dug in with respect to their conceptual positions in relation to Native peoples' issues.

Under such circumstances, I wanted to introduce the idea of a different kind of conflict resolution activity. In this approach, many people might be required to give up something, but, hopefully, everyone would gain something substantial in return that would more than compensate for that which had to be surrendered.

In any event, I believe the problems surrounding Native peoples issues are of fundamental importance to the moral, political, economic and spiritual health of Canada. Consequently, our proposed solution should be seen as an attempt to stimulate discussion in the direction of creative, win-win situations and away from the enervating tug-of-war that now seems to be taking place.

One possibility for resolving the sovereignty issue of Native and aboriginal peoples might revolve around the Yukon and Northwest Territories, together with some added incentives. More specifically, the government of Canada and the provinces could cede substantial portions of these territories to the Native and aboriginal peoples of Canada, along with, say, certain areas of the northern portions of a number of provinces extending from British Columbia to Ontario. Such ceding would be done in partial exchange for all outstanding land claims in the various provinces.

In addition, some sort of monetary compensation package should be added that will help the Native and aboriginal peoples to establish themselves in whatever way is most congruent with their conception of sovereignty. This compensation package could be used to construct, if desired, a communications network, television stations, an economic infrastructure, and educational systems-including higher education-all of which would be done according to the designs, values, policies, needs and aims of the Native and aboriginal peoples.

If the ceded land were given the status of provinces, then, one might consider foregoing the idea of monetary compensation arrangements. This possibility warrants careful thought since, by having provincial status, one would be entitled to certain lands of transfer payments on a continuous basis rather than a limited number of one-shot compensation packages.

The ceded areas should be selected with the ecology of Native and aboriginal peoples in mind. In other words, the lands should be rich with game, fish and resources that would enable Native peoples to sustain themselves in accordance with their spiritual values and close affinity with the environment. The ceded lands should not be marginal, nor should the designated areas be polluted.

Furthermore, the ceded lands should hold the potential for Native peoples to develop in whatever way suited them-as individuals and collectively. Moreover, the ceded land must have the potential for permitting Native and aboriginal peoples to be able to bequeath to later generations the prospects of an enhanced, and progressively developing, quality of sovereignty.

The two territories, plus certain portions of the northern areas of a number of the provinces, seem to be well suited to satisfying a number of the stated needs of Native and aboriginal peoples. In addition-and, unfortunately, this is not a small consideration-the overall inconvenience to both Native peoples and non-Native peoples might be less if pursued in the foregoing fashion.

For example, if the above proposal were pursued, there will be Native peoples who will be faced with the prospect of having to move to a new land and having to start a new life. The fact that they would be going to their own land and not a reservation, and the fact that life in the new land would be rooted in principles of Native sovereignty, cannot hide the possibility the migrant Natives could encounter significant psychological, sociological and spiritual difficulties.

Some, but not necessarily all, of these difficulties might be alleviated, if not eliminated, by funds from the monetary compensation package that accompanied the land ceding aspect of the deal. Consequently, although there is the imposition of having to move, along with the inconvenience and difficulties this potentially entails, the value of what an individual receives in return with respect to sovereignty (and, thereby, the opportunity, finally, to gain autonomy over one's life in an environment that is conducive to one's values) might far outweigh the aforementioned inconveniences and difficulties.

There might be a further advantage for Native and aboriginal peoples if they were to accept the idea of one, large tract of land as part of a negotiated settlement, rather than pursuing a multiplicity of land claim disputes. More specifically, even if one were to suppose that Native peoples were successful with every one of their land claims (which is a highly questionable supposition), the result would leave Native peoples isolated from one another in a sort of archipelago of Native and aboriginal islands in a massive non-Native sea of land.

The geographical, economic, political and social constraints that would tend to impinge on Native and aboriginal peoples under such circumstances might not be in the long-term best interests of Native and aboriginal peoples. Such constraining influences would exert an extremely potent force that, in time, could undermine the sovereignty of Native and aboriginal peoples.

One also must give some reflection to the fact that not all Native peoples have outstanding land claims. Many Native peoples, especially in northern Ontario and Manitoba, live on reservations that will not be expanded. Even if the courts were suddenly to decide in favor of Native peoples with respect to all outstanding land claims, many Native peoples would, so to speak, be left out in the cold as far as having an adequate land base through which to sustain themselves.

Furthermore, pursuant to Bill C-31, that changed certain aspects of the Indian Act, reservations have become increasingly burdened by the needs of those individuals who are returning to the reservation after being reinstated as so-called 'Status Indians'. Reservations simply cannot resolve the problems of housing, crowding, employment, and lack of community facilities that currently are facing many Native people.

Indeed, quite frankly, reservations were always intended as a tool to manage Native people in accordance with the needs of white political, economic and religious interests. Reservations were never intended as a means of sincerely addressing the essential needs of Native peoples as human beings.

Consequently, those Native peoples who stand to benefit if their land claims, eventually, are honored by the courts or government, have a duty of care with respect to those Native people who will not benefit from such land claim decisions. Sharing their reservations is not the answer, since everyone's standard of living gets lowered in the process.

On the other hand, one solution that might make long-term sense for all Native peoples is the one suggested earlier-namely, in exchange for all outstanding land claims, Native and aboriginal peoples would be given one tract of land with provincial status. This land area would cover portions of the Yukon, the Northwest Territories and certain aspects of the northern parts of a number of provinces extending from British Columbia to Ontario.

Whether the ceded land is to be one province or several provinces could be determined through negotiations between Native peoples and the rest of Canada. I have suggested at least two provinces in an attempt to reflect, in a very small way, that Native peoples really encompass a diverse group of peoples. Therefore, some attempt should be made to provide for different venues of provincial opportunity in order to accommodate some of these differences among Native peoples.

The foregoing proposed solution offers the possibility of simultaneously satisfying the needs of self-autonomy and self-sufficiency for all Native and aboriginal peoples. Without this dual dynamic of self-autonomy and self-sufficiency, many, many Native people are doomed to a fate of endless poverty, degradation and dependency on others for their sustenance.

On the other hand, from the perspective of the provincial and federal governments, ceding the aforementioned land areas might be less conducive to the possibility of becoming entangled in the sort of complex legal/social problems where a spectrum of vested interests are at cross-purposes with one another. Said in another way, the above arrangement might least intrude upon, or interfere with, issues of sovereignty involving non-Native and non-aboriginal people.

To be sure, there will be some non-Natives who will be inconvenienced as a result of the proposed solution. Moreover, there undoubtedly will be economic interests that either will have to be terminated or run in accordance with the wishes of Native and aboriginal peoples. However, as is the case with some of the Native peoples who will be inconvenienced, some sort of monetary compensation might help assuage the inconvenience and difficulties suffered by non-Natives during the process of transition in which lands of sovereignty are generated for Native and aboriginal peoples.

The bottom line, for both Native and non-Native peoples, is the same if the solution outlined previously be followed. In other words, there will be difficulties and inconveniences on both sides of the ledger, but the resolution of the long-standing problems would bring benefits to all people concerned. Native and aboriginal peoples, finally, would have their sovereignty which has been usurped unjustly by the European immigrants to this country-an unseemly condition that has been perpetuated by subsequent generations of non-Native peoples. In addition, non-Native peoples could enjoy the fact that principles of real democracy, outlined previously, finally had won out over a set of values, prejudices and practices that, for far too long, have been corrupting and polluting the fabric of democratic institutions in Canada.

If Native and aboriginal peoples were given their own provincial sphere of responsibility through the land ceding proposal outlined earlier, they would need to be given certain guarantees that the land ceding arrangement was not just one more ploy by non-Native people to marginalize the needs and concerns of Native peoples. In other words, Native and aboriginal peoples need to know that they are not being moved to just one more reservation, albeit a much bigger one.

History clearly has shown that the promise of inviolability of the reservation-a promise that was to be honored and protected by non-Native peoples-has been broken many, many times. This goes on even today when, for example, public utility companies, logging and mining concerns, as well as paper mills run roughshod over the concerns and needs of Native and aboriginal peoples.

Whenever corporate and political interests have found it expedient and profitable to do so, Native peoples were pushed aside. Repeatedly, the lands of the latter have been stripped of resources, as well as polluted, through the insatiable appetite of a human greed that has respect for nothing except its own hunger and lust.

Moreover, Native peoples often have not been free even to run their own lives or practice their spiritual traditions. This is the case because they have been interfered with constantly by the Native Affairs Ministry and other levels of government. All of this violation of the sovereignty of Native and aboriginal peoples must stop.

In order to achieve this, I would offer several suggestions. First, the Ministry of Native Affairs, together with the concomitant Indian Act, must be dismantled.

This Ministry is a remnant of a colonialist mentality that is a completely inappropriate way of interacting with Native and aboriginal peoples. Furthermore, this Ministry is saturated with a paternalistic ethnocentrism, that is injurious to the integrity and sovereignty of Native peoples.

Secondly, the political arrangements instituted in the New Provinces (that are to be created through the land-ceding proposal) must always permit Native peoples to retain a majority position in those provinces. While some people might view such a restriction as being undemocratic when considered from the myopic perspective of majority rules, this proposal is perfectly in keeping with the principle of diversity of equality being given expression in this present document. In addition, this instance of asymmetry in the treatment of the political institutions of the Native peoples' Provinces will be counterbalanced by the kinds of Senate reforms that are being introduced in the section on *Expanding the Scope of Participation*.

Before leaving the issue of the sovereignty of Native and aboriginal peoples, a difficult question must be raised. Many, if not most, Native peoples speak in terms of having a custodial relationship with the land. This custodial status is not one of ownership. It is, rather, one of fulfilling the responsibilities of a sacred trust.

The sacred trust has, at the very least, two fundamental themes. One theme concerns the duty of care that the present generation of Native and aboriginal peoples owes to future generations.

A second theme indigenous to the sacred trust concerns the duty of care that is owed to the land itself, along with the forms of life, both animal and plant, that inhabit that land. From the perspective of Native and aboriginal peoples, all creation, whether 'living' or not, manifests spiritual properties. As such, all aspects of creation must be respected for the qualities of spirituality to which they give expression.

Given the foregoing, the question that must be asked is this: Do Native and aboriginal peoples suppose that they, and they alone, have been charged with such a sacred trust?

If the answer is yes, then, certain facets of the Native peoples' claims might be on very shaky spiritual and philosophical ground, so to speak, because of the exclusionary character of their sense of sacred trust. It would be exclusionary because it seems to deny the possibility that other people also might have been invested with the same sacred responsibility and concomitant duties of care, vis-a-vis the whole of creation, including the land.

If, on the other hand, the answer to the foregoing question is no, then, the nature of the problem becomes somewhat different. Under these circumstances, the emphasis must be on issues of sovereignty.

For, only through a properly secured sovereignty, will Native peoples truly be in a position to discharge their sacred trust in its fullest, most broadly applicable sense. In addition, through a properly secured sovereignty, Native peoples will have like-hearted and like-minded non-Native companions with them to work toward the realization of an overlapping set of objectives and values.

To speak in terms of land claims is problematic in a variety of ways. First of all, it risks succumbing to the mentality of ownership that is at the root of so many problems in our country, if not the world. The philosophy of ownership is, by and large, antagonistic to the qualities of sharing and generosity that are, now more than ever, very much needed in our country. The philosophy of ownership tends to lead to a smallness and meanness of spirit.

Indeed, the Prime Minister's recent announcement to establish a fast-track program to settle, over the next four or five years, all land claims that are for less than a certain amount of money, appears to be a clever gambit. It seems to be built around the seductiveness of the philosophy of ownership. By offering the few an inducement of what amounts to land ownership, resolution of the real problem of sovereignty that plagues the _many_ will remain elusive.

Secondly, the language of land claims has a tendency to narrow the focus of the underlying sacred trust. Instead of being extended to all of creation, it might become reduced to a particular, small parcel of land.

Of course, the moral and spiritual decay in the world has reached such proportions that fulfilling the sacred trust for even a small piece of land becomes a courageous struggle. However, the more essential, more fundamental struggle might be to work toward extending the duty of care to as wide an area as possible.

By proposing that Native and aboriginal peoples be given custody of certain lands in the north and that these lands have provincial status, I believe the Native peoples would be in a much stronger, more tenable position through which to fulfill the spiritual responsibilities that have been entrusted to them. Furthermore, with such provincial status, I believe Native and aboriginal peoples would be in a much better position to assist the rest of us to work towards redeeming the

Canadian environment as a whole and, thereby, fulfill the sacred trust that many non-Natives also believe they have with respect to the land.

<u>Canadian Identity</u>

This principle of sovereignty, and its attendant problems, actually goes to the heart of who we are as Canadians. Being a Canadian is not about CBC, Via Rail, the National Film Board, the RCMP, the Maple Leaf Flag or any other symbol one cares to choose as that which helps bind us to one another and helps define our collective identity as Canadians rather than as something else.

All of these institutions and symbols have roles to play. Moreover, they have a value to Canadians that goes beyond the merely functional since they each, in their own way, introduce certain nuances, color and orientation into our collective identity. However, they are all peripheral factors as far as understanding who we are as Canadians.

From the very beginning of our history as a place and a people that eventually would become known, respectively, as Canada and Canadians, the issue that has brought us together and forged our identity has been the problem of sovereignty and our attempts to deal with the issues surrounding that problem. Whether we have been successful or we have failed, whether we have agreed or disagreed, whether we have co-operated with one another or thwarted one another, Canada and Canadians both have been built upon a unique history of engaging the issue of sovereignty through the many ways in which that issue has manifested itself over the years and from place to place. No one else in the universe has our history.

Whether we are talking about regions, provinces, municipalities, ministries, institutions or the federal government, we are talking about family, and we interact with the members of that family in a way that we don't interact with governments and people beyond our borders. The affection, pride or exasperation we feel toward one another has a political/cultural chemistry of its own that is not the same as the sort of chemistry that is generated by the affection, pride or exasperation one might feel toward other peoples.

The straw that stirs the political/cultural chemistry of Canada and Canadians is the problem of sovereignty. The history of: French

Canada or the Maritimes; the West or the Northern Territories; the provinces or the federal government; Native peoples or immigrants -- all revolve around the search for asserting or claiming or fighting for their sovereignty.

The story of Canada is a story of the attempts, failures and successes of a variety of peoples as they sought to enter into a social contract with others. Such a social contract emphasized a reciprocity or mutuality of understanding and, therefore, a concomitant willingness to place constraints on their respective sovereignties in order to work out a system of rights, duties, freedoms and responsibilities that would enhance the quality of sovereignty of the parties involved in that social context.

The sense of betrayal that all peoples in Canada have experienced, at one time or another, can be traced directly to the perception, whether accurate or not, that there is an inequity with respect to the sort of reciprocity and mutuality that defines the social contract that links the sovereignty of one people with other people. Essentially, this means that when a people feel betrayed, they feel they have placed constraints on their own sovereignty as a people that either: (a) are not being reciprocated by others; or, (b) are not leading to a sufficient level of enhancement in the quality of that aspect of their sovereignty that is not under constraint.

Sovereignty and Democracy

The issue of sovereignty involves the desire to have substantial control over, or play a fundamental role in, shaping one's destiny. Sovereignty involves the desire to have access to, and the opportunity to exercise, real power.

Such power enables one to structure, orient and color the character one's living will assume. To have access to real power in an unmediated fashion, goes to the heart of the difference between representational and participatory democracy.

Representational democracy is about people giving up power to other people, i.e., the elected officials and those whom these elected officials appoint or hire. Representational democracy is mediated by, and filtered through, the understanding, likes and dislikes, weaknesses and strengths, ambitions and visions (if not delusions) of the people who are seeking power through elected office. Representational democracy does for the few - namely, the elected officials and their appointed helpers - what participatory democracy intends for the many: namely, to provide access to the power that is necessary to work toward controlling one's own sovereignty.

Representational democracy is indirect, unresponsive, and focuses on channeling power through the few. Participatory democracy is direct, responsive and focuses on sharing power with the many through a variety of channels that are specifically designed with such sharing in mind.

Participatory democracy is not a utopia, nor does it mean that everyone gets whatever one wants. However, it does come closer to the central principle underlying the historical reasons for moving toward democracy than representational democracy does.

More specifically, participatory democracy emphasizes the structural character of the process through which we arrange and regulate the social contracts that we forge with one another. The operative principle in these contracts revolves around the issue of reciprocal sovereignty-for individuals, for communities, for regions and for governments.

Often times, when people are asked about the meaning of democracy, the buzz words that are used are: "majority rules", "rights", "equality" and "freedom". Without wishing to downplay the importance of the concepts that stand behind these words, these ideas may be somewhat misleading.

For example, if by "majority" one means the people in general, then, with the possible exception of elections, very rarely does the majority rule in representational democracy. Even in the case of elections, if there are more than two parties contesting a given seat, the winner usually garners less than 50% of the vote. The majority of the people voted for the losing parties, but they do not rule.

In the case of a two-party election, the majority often still does not rule since: (a) not all eligible voters vote; and, (b) there are many people in the country who are not eligible to vote. As a result, the winning side may capture as much as 55% or 60% of the vote (which would be a huge landslide win) and still constitute the will of far less than a majority of the people.

Once elected, governments, especially in a parliamentary system, often are not run along democratic lines but autocratic ones in which power hoarding and manipulations of power tend to become paramount. The world of 'real-politik' is about the seeking, gaining, wielding and hanging onto power. In this realm, the principles of democracy merely become watch words that are used to clothe the naked power game in order to create an illusion of democratic modesty when, in reality, nothing of substantive value actually exists as far as democracy is concerned.

When the members of the Supreme Court make judgments, or when Parliamentary committees cast votes, or when governmental boards and commissions arrive at decisions, although the rule of the majority holds within the restricted confines of the court, committee, board or commission, there is no guarantee that the respective judgments, votes and decisions reflect the wishes of the majority of the population. Consequently, all of these narrowly construed powers of majority rules constitute potential sources of encroachment upon the sovereignty of the people of a nation, province, region or municipality.

The individual often has little or no power to shape, constrain, modify or resist the aforementioned sorts of judgments, votes and decisions. Moreover, unless provisions are established that permit individuals, within certain limits, to have direct, unmediated access to the kind of power that will give them the opportunity to shape, constrain, modify or resist the process of 'real-politik', then, democracy becomes a vacuous exercise for the majority of people.

At this point, an argument may be put forth that says, in effect, that if people want to have an impact on events, then, they should get involved in the political process: join riding associations, run for office, and so on. However, as indicated previously, indigenous to the idea of representational democracy is the fact that there tend to be strong forces that come into play and place severe constraints on the extent of participation that will be permitted.

While one may or may not agree with Lord Acton who spoke about the corrupting effect of power, the fact is that political/economic power carries with it a strong tendency toward being exclusionary of others. It is a tendency that can only be controlled with great strength of personal integrity and humility, and very few people who have walked the corridors of power have exhibited such strength.

The operative principle in a democracy is not that the majority rule. Instead, what actually rules is a set of principles to which the overwhelming majority of the people agree or to which they are committed as a means of defining, establishing and regulating the social contract that underwrites a democracy. This set of principles both determines boundaries of constraints as well as provides for a spectrum of degrees of freedom within which, or through which, individuals and the collective pursue their respective sovereignties.

Representational democracy tends to spin one kind of set of constraints and degrees of freedom, while participatory democracy generates another kind of set of constraints and degrees of freedom. Naturally, there is likely to be a certain amount of overlap in the structural character of these two different approaches to implementing democracy, but in many ways, these two perceptions have quite different sorts of priorities, emphases, interests, orientations and styles.

In effect, what rules in a democracy, whether of a representational or participatory variety,' is a process or procedural framework that is accepted by the majority of people. This process or framework must offer a countervailing influence against arbitrary, prejudicial or autocratic assaults upon, intrusions into, and usurpations of sovereignty.

Moreover, what permits such a process or framework to rule is the degree of confidence that people have in the capacity of that process/framework to provide a means of both protecting as well as helping to actualize the sovereignty of individuals and the collective alike. Presently, the Canadian public, on both an individual and a collective basis, is indicating that it has lost confidence in the capacity of the current approach to democracy in Canada to be able to resolve the problems that presently exist with respect to various aspects of the social contract-a contract that is supposed to bind us together within a common democratic framework.

Rights and Duties of Care

Another one of the buzz words of the mythology of democracy is that of the idea of rights. Everyone likes to talk about and assert their rights. Rights are expressions of our sovereignty as individuals and, therefore, we are jealous about any intrusion onto that sovereignty by the denial or undermining of our rights. On the other hand, an unrestrained and mindless assertion of rights on the part of everyone is tantamount to chaos and anarchy.

The reality of our situation is that not everyone's "rights" can be honored simultaneously. The claimed rights of one person often clash with the claimed rights of another person.

At a more fundamental level, democracy is not primarily about rights, per se. Democracy is about the search for a balanced, principled way of, on the one hand, protecting rights whenever possible and, on the other hand, of providing various means of resolving competing or conflicting claims of rights.

Unfortunately, people often conflate and confuse rights with their interests, desires and likes. Many people seem to assume that if they are interested in something, or desire it or like it, then, somehow, there must be a right that entitles them to pursue that interest, desire or like in an unhindered manner. Rights, however, are not a function of just any sort of interests, desires or likes.

Rights are about the constraints and degrees of freedom that are to structure our interactions with one another within the framework of the social contract to which we agree as a means of making government and society possible. Rights are about the sovereignty of the individual, but rights also are about the sovereignty of the collective. Rights are about the search for win-win situations such that the quality of sovereignty of both individual and the collective can be advanced and enhanced simultaneously.

Of course, a win-win situation may not always be possible or feasible. Sometimes the individual's rights will gain ascendancy over the rights of the collective. Sometimes the collective's rights will be promoted to the detriment of the individual's rights.

Nonetheless, in general, the emphasis should be on finding solutions to competing or conflicting rights that will protect and enhance the quality of the sovereignty of the different parties to a dispute. In order to work toward such win-win situations, the idea of rights, in and of itself, will not point the way to how to go about resolving disputes concerning conflicting and competing rights.

Another concept is necessary. This additional concept might be referred to as having a 'duty of care'. In order for the sovereignty of both individuals as well, as the collective to be protected and enhanced, there must be a balance established between rights and duties of care.

The social contract is not just about demanding rights. It is also about reciprocity. Reciprocity requires one to undertake the responsibilities of various duties of care toward other individuals and society in general.

Duties of care are not restricted to active respect for, and implementation of, the rights of other individuals or the rights of the collective. Duties of care are rooted in an understanding that acknowledges the need for sacrificing, within certain parameters, one's own interests. Duties of care involve a willingness, under various conditions, to place constraints on one's sovereignty in order to both enhance the quality of the collective sovereignty as well as to increase the likelihood that the quality of one's own long-term sovereignty will be enhanced.

A duty of care is the finger in the social dike that keeps out the relentless ocean of competing and clashing claims of rights. Duties of care reflect a sensitivity and responsiveness to the kinds of economic, social, cultural, physical, political, moral and intellectual destruction that can be wreaked on others by a self-centered insistence on one's rights irrespective of the costs. Duties of care are an index of the preparedness of both the individual as well as the collective to take on the responsibilities inherent in not just making the social contract work, but in helping it to flourish.

Diversity of Equality: A Principle

Along with "majority rules" and "rights", "equality" is a further entry in the lexicon of democracy. Usually, people understand equality to mean that everybody must be treated in exactly the same way.

Another way of giving expression to the idea of equality is that no one should be given an unfair advantage or opportunity that permits him/her to enhance his/her position or circumstances at the expense of other people. Alternatively, equality also refers to protecting people against being unfairly disadvantaged with respect to opportunity, status, treatment, and so on.

A key feature of the idea of equality is a function of what is meant by, say, being given an unfair advantage or being disadvantaged unfairly. Moreover, implied in this judgment of unfairness is the idea that standards or criteria of fairness exist by means of which one can distinguish between, on the one hand, fair and unfair advantages, or, on the other hand, fair and unfair disadvantages.

For example, suppose one student works hard to pass an exam, while another student spends his or her time having a good time doing whatever pleases the individual except studying for the exam. The fact that the former person passes the test while the latter individual flunks the test does not confer an unfair advantage on the first individual, nor does it unfairly disadvantage the second person.

The element of unfairness only enters the picture if there are forces at work that corrupt the situation and skew it prejudicially. Thus, if, in the case of the two students, the person who studied hard is marked down because of color, race, ethnic origin, gender or philosophical beliefs, while the person who didn't study is given a passing mark largely, if not exclusively, on the basis of being liked by the teacher or because the person is a valuable athlete, then, one student (the one marked up) is unfairly advantaged, while the other student (the one marked down) is unfairly disadvantaged.

Let's pursue the student example a little further, but this time a few changes will be introduced. Assume that the two students have studied equally hard and that they are equally intelligent. Further, suppose that there are no untoward forces present -- such as racism, sexism or bigotry -- that would prejudicially differentiate between the two.

However, let us assume that person A does very well on essay type questions but does not do very well on multiple choice questions, whereas student B is just the opposite -- doing poorly on essay questions but very well on multiple choice questions. If the teacher gives a test that involves only essay questions, then, student A is, in a sense, unfairly advantaged, while student B is, in a sense, unfairly disadvantaged. The teacher may not have intended this, but, nonetheless, a situation has been created in which unfairness of a sort has been permitted that treats the students in an unequal fashion.

The moral, so to speak, of the above example is that even if there should be no prejudice of any sort present, and even though people may be subjected to the same sort of condition and treatment, still, one may not have satisfied the conditions of equality. Equality is not necessarily about subjecting people to a monolithic process. In fact, real equality may only be possible in some, perhaps many, cases if one offers to people an opportunity to choose, from among a set of alternatives, the one that best suits their circumstances or abilities.

For instance, let's return, for a moment, to the previous student example. Assume the teacher giving the test realizes students have different strengths and weaknesses. Suppose, further, the teacher really only is interested in finding out what the students know or do not know in order to be able to plan how, and what, to teach in future classes.

Under such circumstances, the teacher could provide the students with a choice: namely, they could select either several essay questions, or they could do the multiple choice section. In this way, the teacher allows the various students to put forth their best academic effort and obtains valuable information that will shape the content of subsequent classes.

The students are treated equally, but they have been allowed to go about things in different fashions. Consequently, the principle of equality does not necessarily mean that everyone must be treated in the same monolithic, rigid, unvarying, static fashion. There is room within the principle of equality for a spectrum of possibilities.

In the United States, there had been, in the past, an attempt to maintain segregationist practices by implementing a policy of "separate but equal". There are a number of fundamental differences between this idea of "separate but equal" and the principle of diversity of equality being discussed above.

In the case of the "separate but equal" policy, blacks were not given any choice in the matter. The policy was thrust upon them, and they had no opportunity to participate in shaping, affecting or regulating that ruling.

Moreover, the resources and finances made available to the black community were, in fact, not the equal of the resources and finances made available to the white community. Finally, the value of the end result of the two educational systems was entirely different, since white students would be given a multiplicity of opportunities to either get further education or to enter the work force. The same set of opportunities was not open to the black students.

In short, the policy of "separate but equal" was intended to give the appearance of freedom, while putting into play the reality of racist practices. The effect of this was to take away freedom from the black community.

The principle of diversity of equality alluded to above, on the other hand, is, in contrast to the idea of 'separate but equal', an exercise in participatory democracy. In this approach to equality, people are given access to real freedom of choice.

This sort of freedom permits people to exercise control, within limits, over how they interact with a given set of circumstances. It permits people to choose, from among a set of alternatives, those possibilities that are most conducive to -- and congruent with -- their needs, interests, capabilities and resources. Furthermore, the set of alternatives is not imposed on people, but can be developed in conjunction with the individual's participation in the structuring of those alternatives.

The principle of diversity of equality is a means of providing people with alternative routes to equality of treatment. No one is unfairly advantaged or unfairly disadvantaged.

All individuals must be permitted to pursue their alternative of choice in a way that does not unfairly advantage them with respect to enhancing the quality of their sovereignty, nor does it unfairly disadvantage others in relation to the protection and/or enhancement of the sovereignty of the latter people. This is so because the alternatives from which people are permitted to choose, and that, ideally, they could have had a hand in developing, are to be pursued within the framework or boundaries established by the dynamic tension between rights and duties of care with respect to both individuals and the larger collective.

For example, by permitting Native peoples to have autonomy in the manner in which they conduct their affairs among themselves and with the rest of Canada, one is providing them with an alternative means of seeking an equality of treatment with respect to the protection, development and enhancement of their sovereignty as a people that is congruent with their needs, interests and inclinations as a people. Similarly, by permitting the people of Quebec to have autonomy in the manner in which they conduct their affairs among themselves and with the rest of Canada, one is providing them with an alternative means of seeking an equality of treatment with respect to the maintaining and realization of their sovereignty as a people that is conducive to who they are as a people. In this sense, Quebec is a special and distinct society. At the same time, the societies of the Native peoples are also distinctive and unique in character.

Indeed, the very idea of multiculturalism is inextricably caught up with the acknowledgment that there is a multiplicity of special and distinct societies within Canada. Our task as a multi-cultural nation is to construct a set of alternatives from amongst which the different peoples of Canada can choose those that are most conducive to, and congruent with, the needs, interests and characteristics of different peoples and that will permit all of them the opportunity to preserve and enhance the quality of their respective sovereignties as a distinct and special people.

If one wishes to give meaning to the notion of sovereignty association, then, it would seem to involve the principle of diversity of equality. In activating this principle, we must provide the peoples of Canada with the opportunity to participate in the decision process. The activation of such a principle will generate the alternative pathways that will provide each people with equality of treatment in the context of a diversity of choices. Through these choices, people seek, secure and realize their sovereignty as communities that are different one from another.

Furthermore, all of this must be done within a balanced, though dynamic, framework woven by the dialectics of rights and duties of care. It is the balancing of the dynamic dialectic that establishes the conditions of association that mark the character of the social contract governing our relations one with another. Moreover, realization of the principle of diversity of equality is what underwrites our respective quests for sovereignty.

Senate Reform

The ways in which things are institutionally arranged in our present representational approach to democracy are inherently antithetical to the sort of steps that are going to have to be taken if the many problems facing us as a nation are going to be resolved in a direction that is more reflective of the needs of the different peoples of Canada. For example, the Senate is often neither representational nor participatory in character.

In terms of cost efficiency and providing tax payers with a fair return on their money, the Senate is probably one of the least productive and least effective Canadian institutions in existence. By and large, it is an old-boys patronage club that on occasion, in spite of itself, accomplishes something of marginal value for the people of Canada.

On the one hand, the Senate is highly exclusionary in character and, on the other hand, it represents the people of Canada only sporadically and, more often than not, only as the spirit of political caprice happens to motivate some of them. It is a body over which the people of Canada have virtually no control and upon which people can exert little or no pressure.

Moreover, even if one could find a way to bring pressure to bear on the members of the Senate, such pressure, generally speaking, contributes little more than a tilting at windmills since the Senate is extremely limited in real power. Its greatest claim to fame is that, at some considerable cost, it produces Royal Commission reports to which almost everyone alludes, few read, and to which almost no one within government pays any attention.

The idea of changing the structure of the Senate is not a new one. Furthermore, the winds of change in the current atmosphere of discontent with the institutions of democracy are blowing at gale, if not hurricane, force. Almost all of the proposals for change indicate that the Senate should be an elected body, but after this point of agreement, consensus gets blown to the four corners of political opinion. Consequently, while the suggestions that follow do not reflect any sense of unanimity among Canadians, the possibilities discussed below may constitute a way of helping to establish the process of participatory democracy that is necessary both to complement, as well as to act as a countervailing force against, some of the tendencies of representational democracy.

The Senate should consist of elected members made up of four individuals drawn from each of the provinces, as well as the Northwest Territories and the Yukon. Three of the individuals elected from a given province or territory should represent the largest traditional parties, namely, the Liberals, Conservatives and NDP.

The fourth person could represent a non-traditional party that commands the respect of, say, at least 10% of the population of the province or territory in question. Or, the fourth person might be drawn from a group, party or community that commands less than the indicated level of 10% support.

One should even entertain the possibility of permitting the fourth position to be a sort of independent category that could be contested by people who have no party affiliation but who do have a desire to participate in the shaping process of political activity. There is a fairly large percentage of people in Canada as a whole, as well as within individual provinces and territories, who do not share the values, commitments and orientations of any of the presently existing parties, but who, nonetheless, are deeply concerned with what goes on in Canada.

The latter possibility might serve to induce people to seek alternatives to traditional party politics by providing an opportunity for entry into the political process that is not otherwise available because of the numbers game of mainstream politics. This might especially be the case in provinces that tend toward a sort of monolithic power structure revolving around an entrenched, incumbent party.

There should be a certain amount of flexibility in the character of the political affiliations of these elected officials in order to reflect the current political realities of a given province or territory. For example, if the politics of a certain province or territory exhibited a party profile that was different from the traditional one of other provinces, then, obviously, the people elected to the Senate would have to reflect these differences.

In addition, regardless of from which party a person is elected, the individual would not be required to follow the party line while malting decisions concerning any given issue before the Senate. The reason for doing things in this fashion has two aspects.

The first aspect revolves around being able to introduce into the Senate a spectrum of philosophical perspectives with respect to issues, policies, programs and political style. These perspectives should be somewhat reflective of primary political/ philosophical currents running through the electorate. The second aspect underlying the reason for doing things in the way outlined earlier is to give the elected Senate officials some discretion concerning how and when they enter into dialogue, negotiation and co-operation with other members of the Senate.

From the point of view being advocated in the present document, the Senate should consist of six subcommittees (one subcommittee for each of the areas of responsibility to be discussed shortly) that are under the auspices of the Senate body taken as a whole. These subcommittees each should consist of eight members (assuming that four Senators have been elected from each of the 10 provinces and two territories) drawn by lot (more on this later).

Furthermore, although each subcommittee would operate on the basis of the principle of simple majority in any votes it takes, the decisions of the subcommittees would be subject to the full vote of the Senate in which a two-thirds majority would be required to pass measures in order for them to be implemented. Measures that are passed through subcommittees, but voted down by the full Senate, are returned to the appropriate subcommittee for further disposition.

Senators should be elected for a period of six years. This differs from the four-year period that is suggested later in this document for members of the House of Commons. There are several reasons for suggesting that things be done in this manner.

For instance, because the functioning of the two parliamentary bodies would be quite different from one another, if modified along the lines suggested in the present document, and because their respective spheres of responsibility and interest also would be different from one another under the proposals being put forth, the interests of Canadians might be better served if the Senatorial elections be kept as separate as possible from the election for the members of the House of Commons. This would give Canadians an opportunity to concentrate on the issues germane to each body and become more focused in their study of the problems surrounding the respective elections.

However, if the tenure period of office for each body is made too long, then, one loses the opportunity to infuse new energy, ideas and commitment into the political process. If, on the other hand, one sets the tenure period of office for each parliamentary body for too brief a time, then, one may prevent elected officials from having time to learn their jobs or do them with any degree of efficiency or proficiency.

Six years was decided upon for Senators, as opposed to four for House of Commons members, because there seems to be a need for a longer period of continuity for Senatorial duties than for the duties of the House members. At the same time, the needs of continuity have to be weighed and balanced against the need to revitalize the political process. In this respect, as well, a tenure period for Senators of six years seemed to be an appropriate choice for harmonizing the needs of continuity and revitalization.

The method of selection for these six Senate subcommittees would be as follows. The names of the 48 Senators (four from each province plus four each from the two territories) would be put into the technological equivalent of a hat. Names would be drawn from that process, one at a time, in a random manner.

Only one elected member per province could be on any subcommittee. Moreover, a maximum of two members from any party could be selected for a given subcommittee.

If a province was already represented on a given Senate subcommittee, or if a given party already had two representatives on a subcommittee, then, further names would be generated through the random selection process until an elected member from a new province and/or party had been produced. In this way, a maximum number of provinces would gain representation on the various subcommittees, while, at the same time, ensuring a balanced diversity of political philosophies.

The subcommittee for which random selections are to be made lastly would be the Appointments subcommittee (discussed shortly). Due to the character of a random selection process, one could end up with an unbalanced Appointments subcommittee both in terms of provincial representation as well as in terms of political philosophy. If this should occur, then, on a random basis, switches should be made with other subcommittees in order to achieve provincial and philosophical parity in each of the committees.

Although not every province would be represented on any given subcommittee, eight provinces would be represented on a specific subcommittee. Furthermore, every province would be represented on a number of different subcommittees. Consequently, there would be considerable diversity and breadth of provincial representation on any given subcommittee.

If the Northwest Territories subsequently were to be divided into two provinces, as has been proposed by some people, then, there would be an extra four Senate members to distribute among various subcommittees. This would mean that, for example, there would be four subcommittees with nine members each (instead of eight) and two subcommittees still with eight members each.

I suggest that the four subcommittees that are to have, under such circumstances, an extra member each, should be: (1) Education; (2) Environment; (3) Basic Research and Technological Development; and (4) Constitutional Issues. The other two subcommittees namely, Budget/Finance and Appointments-still would have eight members each. The arrangement is somewhat arbitrary, but I feel the first four areas deserve a greater number of provincial representatives than do the latter two subcommittee areas.

The compositional structure of the Senate, as outlined above, is predicated on the premise that the best government often, though not always, is a result of minority government. In minority government, elected officials are forced to find ways of entering into alliances with one another in order to make the process work. Similarly, establishing a context in the Senate in which the political process would be run along the lines of shifting coalitions from issue to issue, may well provide the opportunity for a process that is: (a) more likely to be reflective of the needs of a wider proportion of the electorate; (b) more given to compromise and negotiation rather than to ideologically rigid confrontations; and, (c) more likely to be focused on the strengths and weaknesses of issues per se rather than getting entangled in partisan politics.

Spheres of Senate Responsibility

The following pages outline the six areas of Senate responsibilities. Some of these areas are discussed in much more detail than others, especially in relation to the aspect of philosophical issues surrounding some of the proposed subcommittees. The discussion is intended to be suggestive rather than definitive.

The recommended spheres of responsibility of the Senate would be as follows. They fall into six basic areas.

First, the Senate should be responsible for all government appointments. This includes the members of the Supreme Court.

In addition, half of all such government appointments should be women, and these appointments should be equitably distributed across the board rather than restricted to certain areas of government activity.

The reasons for arranging things in this manner are fairly straightforward. It provides a countervailing force against the tendency of governments in power to, on the one hand, succumb to the practice of patronage, and, on the other hand, to choose people who will reflect their thinking or political inclinations. The interests of neither democracy nor the electorate are served well when governments in power are permitted to indulge themselves in either of these political pastimes.

By letting the Senate make such decisions, people are likely to be selected who are the best individuals available for the job. This is so because no one party or philosophy has a monopoly on power in the Senate. Therefore, appointment decisions will be based on consensus, co-operation, compromise and negotiation.

Secondly, the Senate should have the responsibility of approving the budget that is prepared by the government that rules the House of Commons. Included in this responsibility would be the power to: (a) suggest cuts, program deletions and modifications in the proposed provincial budget; (b) send the budget back to the House for further deliberations; and (c) ensure that the government in power stays within the parameters of its budget.

The House of Commons is free to take heed of, or ignore, suggestions from the Senate, but the course of action pursued by the House must be done with the understanding that until the Senate approves the budget, the budget cannot be implemented. In effect, by placing the power of budget approval in the hands of the Senate rather than at the sole discretion of the ruling government, one is forcing the government to be more sensitive and responsive to a diversity of opinions that reflect a wider proportion of the electorate than does the party in power.

One also might wish to equip this Senate subcommittee with other kinds of watchdog powers with respect to the financial affairs of the federal government. For example, the activities of the Bank of Canada might be one of the institutions that could be subject to a review process, as well as some degree of regulatory control, by this subcommittee.

The third, fourth and fifth areas of responsibility of the Senate concern: particular portfolios that are of fundamental importance to the welfare of Canada as a vibrant nation. These areas involve the environment, education, together with basic research and technological development. All of these areas possess the potential to have substantial impact on the quality of life of all Canadians, both now and in the future.

The above statement should not be interpreted to mean that other ministries of government have no importance or that they do not have the potential for having substantial impact on the quality of life of all Canadians. Obviously, neither of these interpretations is the case.

However, problems of environment and education, together with issues of basic research and development, touch on the lives of all Canadians in a way that might be far more fundamental and of essential importance than is the case with many, if not most, other ministries. Moreover, the aforementioned three areas tend to lend themselves more naturally to the potential for individual participation across all strata of society by non-politicians and non-government officials than do many of the other ministries that are either fairly exclusionary (e.g., Defense, Attorney General) or fairly narrowly conceived (e.g., Mining, Agriculture, Fisheries).

In addition, the three indicated areas of concern require not only a special sensitivity and responsiveness to the needs of the people of Canada -- that often are not provided by a ruling party -- but these areas need to be removed from the shifting priorities and commitments that mark transitions in going from one ruling party to another ruling party. All three areas require constant attention and nurturing in a non-partisan fashion. Therefore, a revised Senate having the characteristics outlined earlier seemingly would be in a better position to provide the sort of care, concern, sensitivity, responsiveness and constancy than would the House of Commons or even provincial governments.

Each of the foregoing five areas of responsibility should emphasize the principle of participatory democracy. Indeed, the Senate, as here conceived, is intended to be a body that stresses, encourages and provides opportunities for participation by, and involvement from, the general public in a way that the government, in general, and the House of Commons, in particular, does not. The House of Commons operates on principles of representational democracy with little or no opportunity for participation by non-politicians, and, generally speaking, is not interested in sharing power. The emphasis is on controlling power in order to pursue whichever of the two species of representational government strikes the fancy of the members of the House. Naturally, this is especially true of the party in ascendancy in the House.

In any event, each area of Senate responsibility should operate on the premise of drawing into their sphere of activity and concern as many people as is possible, feasible and practical. For example, the subcommittee on appointments should actively go into the community and consult with professional groups, institutions, businesses, organizations, religious circles, unions, editorial boards and individuals that could provide the subcommittee with a list of candidates who might be well suited to the appointments to be made.

The subcommittee could, at the same time, gain insight into the needs, problems and concerns of the community. This understanding would help them arrive at decisions that might better reflect the issues that are affecting the communities they visit.

Consider another example that gives expression to the theme of participatory democracy that is to be stressed in a reconstituted Senate. Education is an area of fundamental importance to individuals and communities alike. Education plays an essential role in the establishing, maintaining and realizing of sovereignty.

The Senate subcommittee on education should manage a dynamic program of training, consultation, outreach, cross-fertilization, research, symposia and publication that would bring together, from diverse backgrounds, educators, theorists, as well as people who might have no professional experience but who are deeply concerned about educational issues. The idea would be to establish a national think-tank focusing on educational issues both theoretical and practical.

This think-tank could be centered in a variety of localities across the nation, but it also would be capable of moving around and setting up shop on a temporary basis in a variety of other localities and communities. The purpose of such efforts is to provide a venue through which the people of Canada could be united in a common cause: to improve the quality of education in Canada as a whole and at every level of educational opportunity. At the same time, a great deal of costly duplication might be eliminated.

The intent of all this would not be to take control away from the community or to impose, from above, a monolithic curriculum on all schools. Instead, the intent is to provide a powerful, multi-faceted, flexible set of resources that could be utilized at the discretion of the community. In addition, the intent would be to establish channels of communication that are conducive to a dialectical process of sharing: successes, failures, problems, needs, methods, expertise, theory, practice and goals.

One could continue the foregoing process of spelling out how each area of responsibility of a Senate could be developed in ways that emphasize the principle of participatory democracy. The foregoing discussion has been intended to be suggestive of the sort of things that are possible. However, there is no limit to the ways one could go about implementing social participation on a greater scale in each of the six areas of Senate responsibilities.

In all of these cases, the subcommittees become like so many boards of directors that oversee the operations and management of these exercises in participatory democracy. Ideally, not only would the Senate be a body that invites participation and extends power sharing to a diverse group of non-politicians, but it also could be a body that promotes national unity in the very process of making available opportunities of participatory democracy to people in every province or territory of Canada and on every level of scale of society.

Concomitant with the creation of Senate subcommittees for Environment, Education, as well as Basic Research and Technology, I propose that the provincial ministerial counterparts to these three areas should become regional expressions of a Senate presence. In effect, this proposal means that the provincial ministries that are counterparts to the three Senate subcommittee areas would no longer be provincial ministries, per se. Instead, they would become mediators and arbitrators between various Federal and Provincial themes and currents within the respective areas.

Each of these areas is of sufficiently fundamental importance to, and with essential ramifications for, all of Canada that they should not be left to the partisan politics of either federal or provincial governments. Therefore, there should be a strong centralist/ federalist component to the decisions made in these areas, but the nature of the centralist/ federalist component should not be left to the vagaries, inconsistencies and politics of representational democracy.

On the other hand, precisely because each of the three aforementioned areas are of interest and of value to all of Canada, there should be an attempt to permit as many Canadians as possible to contribute to, and thereby help, organize, shape, color and direct the decisions made in such areas. This suggests that the politics of participatory democracy assume significance here.

In both facets of decision making (that is, the centralizing and decentralizing tendencies in the areas of environment, education, as well as basic research and technology), a Senate reconstituted along the lines suggested in the present document would appear to be better placed to meet the challenges of the indicated areas than does representational government on either the federal or provincial level. This is so because what is needed is co-operation, compromise, consultation, and planning on a national basis.

However, this must be done in such a way that the process lays heavy emphasis on local/regional participation in, and shaping of, national policies and programs in the indicated areas. Representational government often has difficulty accomplishing these sorts of things, whereas participatory government rooted in a federalist/centralist framework would seem to be well equipped to accomplish what is required.

The Judicial Problem

The final area of responsibility for a reconstituted Senate would be as guardians of the Constitution. This suggestion has a number of facets that have tremendous ramifications for how to conceive of, as well as conduct, the process of arranging the social contract that both preserves and enforces our sovereignty as individuals and as a collectivity of peoples in a multi-cultural society.

To begin with, the Constitution must be removed entirely from the judicial system. There are a number of basic reasons for doing this.

For instance, at the level of the Supreme Court, there is much in the judgments of the courts that is, strictly speaking, extra-legal in character. The systems of interpretation, the philosophical assumptions, the theories of law, and the styles of logical mapping that judges employ in reaching legal decisions are part of the practices and conventions that surround statutes, legal rules and the Constitution. Nonetheless, they are not themselves either statutory in character (a legal rule that has been clearly articulated as such and that is legally incumbent upon justices to follow), or constitutional in character.

Justices are, of course, empowered to make judgments on legal issues and are permitted judicial discretion in reaching such decisions. However, the boundaries of this discretionary power are so extremely vague, arbitrary and problematic that, in fact, if the justices had to rule on a statute, for example, that exhibited the same qualities of vagueness, arbitrariness and contentiousness as did judicial discretion, the justices very likely would be unanimous in their opinion that such a statute is unconstitutional.

Although judicial discretion is integral to the process of generating legal decisions, this discretionary exercise is functionally dependent, as previously indicated, on a whole set of considerations that are extra-legal in character. Consequently, the time has arrived for us to come to grips with the mythology that permeates Supreme Court decisions.

The mythology tends to claim that there is some self-contained body of law that can be discerned objectively through judicial methods that are entirely legal in character in the sense that those methods are universally agreed upon by all justices and, therefore, are incumbent upon one and all justices to follow. None of this is necessarily true. What justices say is the law is what the law is, but the impression is often given that there is some body of law independent of the judges, and that judges are merely stating what the law is.

Justices of the Supreme Court are answerable to no one except themselves. They give their interpretations of the law. These interpretations have: implications for the quality of sovereignty of individuals as well as many ramifications for the sovereignty of various levels of government and institutions.

Now, the question that must be asked is this: Why should anyone believe that such interpretations will best serve the interests of protecting and ensuring the quality of sovereignty that is at the heart of the social contract that binds individuals together? This question becomes especially critical when one realizes that judicial interpretations hold us hostage to the past in a variety of ways.

More specifically, justices purport to be able to determine what the structural character of legality is in a given issue or set of issues that are before the court. They meticulously map out the web of logic that supposedly links an issue in contention with, say, the "meaning" of the Constitution.

But whose "meaning" is this? Is the meaning that of the people who wrote the Constitution? Or, is the meaning that of those who voted the Constitution into existence? Can we be sure that everybody who voted for the Constitution understood the document in the same way that the authors intended it to be understood? Or, is the meaning of the Constitution that of those government officials who subsequently interpreted the Constitution and, thereby, generated a wealth of documented conventions, practices and methods for doing politics?

Even more importantly, what relevance does the intentions of either: (a) the framers of the Constitution; or, (b) those who voted for the Constitution, or, (c) those who subsequently interpreted it, have for us today if those intentions don't: address our problems, meet our needs, or provide a direction that makes sense in the context of our current circumstances? Why should we be held hostage to what other people in another time believed or felt <u>unless</u> what they believed or felt resolves difficulties to the satisfaction of a majority of the people in the present?

Judicial decisions are, by necessity, narrowly focused in the sense that they are inextricably tied to the past. The precedents justices seek, the logic they attempt to uncover, the meanings they try to unravel have to be justified in terms of legal documents as intended, understood and meant by the people who generated those documents.

However, we can ask whether these historical actors were omniscient. Did they ever make mistakes? Did they subscribe to positions of political/economic philosophy that are unassailable with respect to the wisdom, insight and comprehensiveness to which such positions gave expression?

Were they really clear in their own minds and hearts about what they meant or intended by these documents? Was there unanimity of opinion, or even a general consensus amongst those actors as to what was meant, understood or intended? Can we be sure that justices have captured what those meanings, understandings and intentions were?

Even if, through a miraculous stroke of serendipity, we could get definitive, unambiguous answers to all of the foregoing questions, none of this really addresses the issue at hand: Is the law as determined by justices at all relevant to what is going on today? What requires that we adhere to what people thought, believed or were committed to in the past? Are we under a moral obligation to do so? Is it a legal obligation and, if so, what exactly does this mean? What force is it that requires people today to be bound to the past in the same way and sense in which the justices of the Supreme Court are tied to the past?

To say that we must follow the law because it is the law is both circular and evasive. Besides, law, per se, is not what binds us together. Law itself emerges from, presupposes and derives its authority from the underlying social contracts to which people have committed themselves. Law is absolutely empty without the existence of the underlying covenant that encompasses people's willingness to both place certain constraints on their own sovereignty as well as to extend certain degrees of freedom within which the sovereignty of other individuals might be developed and realized.

That law that is not rooted in the willing compliance of people to adhere to it and observe its requirements will fail. Similarly, that society that is not rooted in the willing compliance of people to establish a social contract that supports the sort of sacrifices, constraints and freedoms that laws require also will fail.

The courts are, in many respects, inherently incapable of addressing the issue of the social contract. The courts are incapable of addressing this issue because they are looking to the past for their answers, whereas the people of today are becoming increasingly disinclined to continue to accept the terms of the sort of antiquated social contract that underwrites the legal issues that defines the parameters of the jurists' world.

The jurists are stuck in another world and time. As a result, they cannot address the political, cultural, sociological, philosophical, economic, religious and psychological issues of today from anything but a narrowly conceived legal focus that is rooted in the past.

In effect, what the justices are saying is this: If you wish to continue to operate according to the conditions of the social contract of a given time and place, then, you must do, X, Y or Z. However, the structural character of the social contract should not necessarily be tied to how things were done in the past. The desirability of doing so depends entirely on the character of how and why things were done in the past and whether or not those ways of doing things have a capacity to arrange and regulate people's lives today in a manner that guards and enhances the quality of the individual and collective sovereignty of people today.

The social contract is a living, breathing, on-going, dynamic entity. It should be capable of being revised, altered, and modified under a variety of circumstances that are not a function of legal considerations.

Moreover, this transformational process should be done according to the discretion and judgment of the people who have to live with, and are responsible for honoring the condition of, that contract in the present. Because the courts are lost in the past, they are not the proper venue for issues involving that contract. At best, they could serve as consultants who would provide expert opinion about what the social contract meant to people at a particular time and place.

Consequently, the mandate of the courts should not be extended to empower them to dictate to people of the present time that the latter must subscribe to the requirements of the social contract as understood by the people of the past. Moreover, the mandate of the courts should not be extended to permit them to generate interpretations of how the social contract was understood and intended by people of the past and, then, proceed to impose those interpretations onto the people of today.

The mandate of the courts should be restricted to ensuring that proper procedures are observed with respect to evidence, testimony, examination and general conduct of all participants, both before and during the trial process, as well as during the sentencing and award phases of legal proceedings. Anything within the context of legal proceedings that raises constitutional issues should be referred to either the Senate subcommittee or its appointed body (more on this in a moment) for dealing with such issues.

The Constitution and Social Contract

The immediate response of some, perhaps many, people to the foregoing position is that constitutional issues will become inconsistent at best and chaotic at worst. Such people might argue that the woof and warp of the Constitution are made of legal materials, methods and processes, or that the design of the Constitution necessarily is a legal one. Such people might argue that only the judiciary is capable of consistently and methodically identifying the nature of the problems inherent in the Constitution, or that only the judiciary is competent to deal with such issues.

Without in any way wishing to impugn the integrity of the members of the judiciary, in point of fact, the judiciary is really not competent to deal with constitutional issues. The judiciary is narrowly focused. They engage, analyze, evaluate and understand constitutional issues only from a legal perspective.

Yet, the Constitution is far more than a document with legal implications. It is a document that is permeated by, and rooted in, a wide variety of political, social, philosophical, emotional, religious, economic psychological and historical influences.

Justices are experts in the law. They cannot claim to be, nor can they be expected to be, experts in all these other spheres of influence that shape, color and orient constitutional issues.

Furthermore, one would be making a potentially disastrous mistake to suppose that, with respect to all of these influences and forces that are entangled in constitutional issues, the only dimension that matters is that which gives expression to the legal perspective. For a long time, this legalistic assumption or bias has veiled and skewed thinking about constitutional matters. In effect, this assumption requires one to suppose that the legal approach or perspective is the only way of trying to resolve constitutional issues.

Moreover, this assumption tends to force one to conflate the idea of a constitution with the idea of law. As such, the assumption is inappropriately reductionistic since it makes the Constitution a function of law when, in reality, law is a function of the Constitution.

The Constitution is the fundamental written expression of the social contract that establishes how people are to arrange their affairs in order to be able to protect, maintain, preserve, develop and realize their sovereignty as individuals, as peoples, as communities and as collectives of people and communities. Law comes into existence as an attempt to reflect certain dimensions of the structural character of this underlying agreement. Without the underlying agreement, law becomes empty, meaningless and a mere exercise in imposed, non-reciprocal, non-participatory power arrangements that have absolutely nothing to do with democracy of any species.

Because the Constitution is an <u>on-going</u>, dynamic, social, cultural, political, psychological dialectic of individuals, peoples and communities, law cannot possibly keep pace with the changing currents of constitutional issues. The law, relative to the Constitution, is static and backward looking, whereas the Constitution, relative to the law, is dynamic and oriented primarily to the present and the future.

The Constitution is linked to the past only in as far as the past contains the sort of values, practices and insights that might help us to resolve our problems today. Nonetheless, the people of the past have no right to place obligations upon the people of the present with respect to which, if any, values, practices or insights are chosen to assist the people of today in their search for sovereignty.

In effect, the courts are arguing that not only do the people of the past have such a right, but the people of today, as well as the people of tomorrow, are obligated to identify with, honor and actualize such a right. This argument does a great disservice to both the constitutional process as well as to democracy; for, not only does such an argument deny the people of today and tomorrow representation, it also denies them participation except on the terms and conditions stipulated by the people of the past.

As far as the issue of consistency is concerned (in which the claim is made that law is the thread of consistency that alone permits a coherent constitutional fabric to be sewn), there are certain realities that one ought to keep in mind. Justices, lawyers and law professors do not understand constitutional issues with anything remotely approaching consensus. There are areas of agreement, but the history of judicial interpretation is fraught with disagreement, reversals and fractiousness.

The idea of legal consistency in constitutional matters is more akin to acts of prestidigitation than it is to an expression of some incontrovertible truth. As is the case with the weather in Canada, so too in legal treatments of constitutional issues, all one has to do is wait long enough and such treatments will change.

What links the people of today with the people of the past is not law or consistency of law. The link of consistency is that we both have been confronted with the problem of the social contract as that affects issues of sovereignty.

That which links us with the people of the past is not a matter of judicial pronouncements but, rather, is a function of the common desire to have the power and opportunity to help shape our constitutional destinies. The people of the past made their own choices about how they would go about undertaking this shaping process.

The people of today also must make their own choices, irrespective of whether these choices reflect, to some extent, the values of the people of the past or divert, to some extent, from those values. Whatever the character of their choices might be, the people of today are better placed than the people of the past, with more up-to-date, intimate knowledge and understanding of what constitutional choices will be most reflective of, consistent with, and consonant in relation to, the needs, problems, pressures and issues that exist in the modern world.

The *Constitution Act of 1982* was a disaster because the people involved in constructing that Act were caught in the past and holding the rest of the country hostage to the past. As a result, the main actors in the formation of the Act attempted to resolve modern problems and issues with antiquated methods, ideologies and processes.

The *Constitution Act of 1982* was, and is, a failure because the people responsible for that Act were using representational democratic procedures in a Machiavellian manner when what was called for was a participatory style of democracy that was rooted in reciprocity, duties of care, and a sharing of the responsibilities for shaping our Constitutional destiny. *The Constitution Act of 1982* was a failure because the people who bequeathed the Act upon posterity failed to address the fact that sovereignty is not just a matter of intergovernmental relations and the distribution of power between federal and provincial governments. Sovereignty is, first and foremost, a matter of people.

Governments exist due to the largesse of the people. Governments exist in order to assist individuals, peoples and communities to manage their social contract, one with another, in terms of how the interactions of people affect their respective sphere of sovereignty.

Unfortunately, the principle actors of the *Constitution Act of 1982* somehow became confused and thought that sovereignty was the preserve of governments only. Indeed, even the one area of the *Constitution Act of 1982* that purportedly dealt with the issues surrounding sovereignty of people as people-namely, the Charter of Rights-was undermined by the insistence of the political players that sovereignty was, by virtue of the 'notwithstanding clause', really a matter of governments, not people.

The reason for reconstituting the Senate along the lines suggested earlier is to re-establish the issue of sovereignty as primarily about individuals and peoples and only secondarily and derivatively about governments. The reason for reconstituting the Senate in the fashion previously indicated is to emphasize the fundamental necessity of providing opportunities and processes of participatory democracy to complement processes of representational democracy.

Constitutional Forums

In keeping with the spirit of the proposed Senate reform and its emphasis upon the participatory aspects of democracy, the Senate sub-committee on constitutional issues would establish a number of constitutional forums across the country. This would include, perhaps, one forum for each of the provinces and territories, for a total of 12. However, in heavily populated areas, more than one forum might be necessary.

The forums would be made up of, say, thirteen people. Half of the people appointed to the forums would be women (Since 13 is an odd number, this provision would refer to the country as a whole, with each province coming as near to this distribution as possible over a given period of time).

These people would be selected from a variety of areas of expertise-both professional as well as qualified "amateurs". These areas of expertise could involve business, labor, law, religion, science, psychology, mathematics, sociology, education, political sciences, philosophy, literature/arts and the media.

Those selected would serve tenures of three years in which, as with jury duty, their places of employment would have to hold open their jobs. In this sense, the places of employment as well as the individuals selected would be providing a community service.

The function of these forums is to hear cases involving disputes concerning the social contract as that contract is given expression in the Constitution of Canada after the Constitution has been rewritten to suitably reflect the themes of: sovereignty, rights, duties of care, participatory democracy, the principle of diversity of equality, a reconstituted Senate, a modified House of Commons structure (more on this shortly), the acknowledgment of the sovereignty of Native peoples, the principle of multiculturalism, and the transformed character of the election process. Almost all of these themes have been touched upon previously in this document.

The task of the forums would be to resolve disputes, complaints, problems and questions that arise in the course of day-to-day living In a sense, these forums offer a process of binding arbitration concerning constitutional issues Yet, they do so in an extra-legal context since the process, methods of investigation, styles of evaluation, theories of interpretation and so on that are employed will be rooted almost entirely in non-legal perspectives.

Evidence will be sought. Witnesses will be examined. Statements and depositions will be introduced. Arguments and cases will be made and questioned. But, all of this will be done from a variety of different perspectives that reflect the non-legal areas of expertise of the members of the forum.

The members of the constitutional forum have the responsibility of helping to work out the details and particulars of constitutional principles in the context of the present. Nevertheless, these decisions must be arrived at with an eye to the future as well. While later generations are under no obligation to accept the judgments of such forums, nonetheless, the members will be providing a great heuristic service to the community and nation if they can generate decisions that possess a lasting wisdom.

The Senate subcommittee for constitutional issues will have the task of managing and reviewing the conduct, performance and decisions of these forums, but the subcommittee will not be responsible for selecting the members of these forums. That aspect will be handled by the Senate subcommittee on government appointments. In addition, although the Senate subcommittee on constitutional issues is responsible for reviewing the conduct and decisions of the various forums, nevertheless, it has the discretion to bring under further scrutiny only those decisions that seem to leave certain problems unresolved or questions unanswered or that raise problems of consistency across forum decisions.

In the case of the issue of consistency, however, the measure of consistency will not be that of a self-sameness of rules in which one attempts to force a monolithic rule onto all situations irrespective of differences in those situations. Instead, the criterion of consistency will be a matter of the self-similarity of a principle as it is given expression in different circumstances.

As will be discussed in more detail in the section *The Quality of Tolerance and the Need for Guidelines*, there must be a certain flexibility permitted in the way various constitutional forums arbitrate similar constitutional cases. At the same time, one of the tasks of the Senate subcommittee on constitutional issues will be to protect against the occurrence of too much flexibility.

This will be accomplished by placing certain constraints on the degrees of freedom that are to be permitted to various constitutional forums that are arbitrating cases involving similar constitutional issues. Thus, while the judgments of these forums do not have to be self-same, one with another, they do have to exhibit a certain self-similarity within a set of boundaries or parameters that are to be determined by the Senate whenever the need to do so arises.

In disputes between specific provinces and the federal government, or in disagreements among provinces, or among municipalities and the provincial/Federal governments, or among different regions of the country, these sorts of problems would be handled initially by one or more of the constitutional forums. If, for example, an action were begun within a particular province against, say, the Federal government, one of the provincial constitutional forums would listen to arguments on the matter. A decision would be rendered by that forum, together with the reasoning on which that decision is based.

If any of the parties to the dispute were dissatisfied with the decision process and concomitant reasoning, such parties could launch an appeal to the Senate subcommittee on constitutional issues. The subcommittee would have several choices: (a) let the decision of the constitutional forum stand; (b) review that decision to determine if there were any procedural or evidential irregularities or omissions that could have altered the character of the decision; if substantial irregularities or omissions emerge during the review process, the matter is to be returned to the level of the constitutional forum, together with the subcommittee's recommendations for further deliberations; or, (c) initiate a new set of hearings under the auspices of a special intergovernmental constitutional forum that is designed to mediate and, if necessary, arbitrate disputes between provinces and the federal government, or between province and province, or between municipalities and the federal and/or provincial governments.

If choice (c) is made, then, the Senate subcommittee has several more options once a decision is rendered by the special intergovernmental constitutional forum. First, the subcommittee can let that decision stand. Secondly, the subcommittee can review the special forum's decision in order to check for procedural irregularities and relevant evidential omissions. If such problems are uncovered, the matter would be sent back to the intergovernmental constitutional forum, together with recommendations for reconsidering certain aspects of the issue. Thirdly, once the second option has been selected and the intergovernmental forum has given a second decision (which might be the same as, or different from, the initial decision), the Senate subcommittee has the right to accept that decision or put the matter before the entire Senate.

If an issue should be debated within the entire Senate and voted on, then, the House of Commons has the right to (a) let the Senate vote stand; or, (b) discuss and vote on the issue. If option (b) is exercised, then, the people of Canada have a right to seek a referendum on the matter.

In a referendum held under such circumstances, the people have the option of selecting from among four possibilities (a) the position of the House; (b) the Senate's position; (c) the intergovernmental forum's decision; or, (d) the initial constitutional forum's decision. The choice would be: yes or no, with respect to each of these possibilities.

If the people did not show a two-thirds majority preference for any of the four alternatives, the issue would revert to the full Senate body for further discussion and a new vote. However, both this discussion and subsequent vote should make every effort to incorporate and reflect as much of the voting pattern displayed in the referendum as is possible.

The advantages of such constitutional forums are considerable For example they will be far more accessible to the community than is the Supreme Court. This is especially true in view of the fact that only lawyers are permitted to argue cases before the Supreme Court. In constitutional forums, on the other hand, people will be permitted, if not encouraged, to advance their cases by themselves or, if they wish, in conjunction with one or more consultants (who would be present on a volunteer only basis).

Moreover, the proposed forum approach likely also would be less intimidating and less inhibiting than courts since none of the formality of courts is to be used or encouraged. The emphasis would be on a serious informality.

Constitutional forums also could take a burden off already overburdened courts. At the same time, constitutional forums will not require complainants or participants to bear exorbitant legal costs since the forums would be conducted free of charge.

With respect to this latter point concerning costs, although the forums are to be run free of financial charges, all participants would be expected to pay some sort of a negotiated "fee". This fee would be paid by the individual through giving time to community service.

Money could not be given in lieu of time. The only acceptable currency would be temporal. In addition, the temporal fee would have to be paid directly. It could not be delegated to a third party.

Hardship cases would affect the character of what fees are negotiated. However, such cases would not affect the fact and manner of how that fee must be paid-namely, by direct, non-delegated, temporal service to the community.

None of the decisions of the forum would carry criminal penalties. On the one hand, forum decisions would result in the placing of enforceable constraints on the activities of certain people, or in providing added degrees of freedom for those whose sovereignty had been breached in some unacceptable fashion.

On the other hand, sanctions could be levied in the form of compensatory fines or by requiring the individual to provide some sort of community service (e.g., providing volunteer help for the constitutional forum or during elections, referenda and recall activity) for a period of time. Such community service would be above and beyond the community service "fee" exacted from all forum participants on a negotiated basis.

In all of these cases, the emphasis and intent would be on finding ways of healing and restoring the social contract to a condition of balance where rights play off against duties of care in a more harmonious fashion than was the case prior to the arbitration hearing. However, if people fail to conform to the mediated/arbitrated decision of the constitutional forum, then, pending a review of the case by the forum, they could be faced with criminal contempt charges.

Principle of Civil Disobedience

Part and parcel of the responsibility of both the Senate subcommittee on constitutional issues -- as well as the forums to which the former delegates authority -- would be cases involving appeals to a principle of civil disobedience. Such appeals might be launched by people in the community as a defense with respect to certain criminal actions directed against them. In order to launch such an appeal, however, certain conditions must be met.

To qualify as a potentially defensible act of civil disobedience, the act cannot involve violence, physical injury or terrorism of any kind. In addition, the act cannot involve damage to private or public property, nor could it involve theft, extortion, fraud, prohibited sexual displays or illicit drug activity. Acts of civil disobedience concern acts that, on the basis of philosophical/religious principles, focus on: intentional non-compliance with some provision of the rules and regulations that exist in society.

Generally speaking, the very nature of civil disobedience involves the violation of a law. When tried in court, the case often reduces down to whether or not the person did commit the offense. The reasons for doing so tend to be considered irrelevant or not germane to the evidential issues on which guilt or innocence is established, although such reasons might have some bearing on the kind of sentence given for the offense.

By appealing to the principle of civil disobedience before a constitutional forum, the individual has an opportunity to bring in the relevancy of the reasons or intentions underlying the action in question. Moreover, when such cases are heard by the forum, values, methods and perspectives would become activated that are more flexible and diverse than are allowed by the legal perspective. Nonetheless, if the constitutional forum should reject the individual's appeal to the principle of civil disobedience, then, the individual stands trial for whatever infraction of the law that might have been committed by the individual.

The principle of civil disobedience is intended to provide a venue for permitting individuals, organizations, institutions, associations and governments direct opportunity to help shape and contribute to the structural character of the Constitution. By permitting individuals an opportunity, under certain circumstances, to be able to challenge the law, a recognized procedural means is established for breaking, where warranted, the circularity of legal thinking.

Such thinking tends to be interested only in whether or not a law is broken, and not with whether or not justice is being done or with whether the law is a good one in the sense that the law enhances the quality of the social contract among people. The principle of civil disobedience provides individuals with direct access to the constitutional process, unmediated by judicial biases and preoccupations.

The Quality of Tolerance and the Need for Guidelines

One last point about the Senate subcommittee on constitutional issues and its appointed forums needs to be addressed. There must be a certain amount of willingness to tolerate, and make allowances for, a diversity of judgment from forum to forum with respect to similar constitutional issues. Just as municipal and provincial ordinances differ, respectively, from municipality to municipality and from province to province without everyone supposing that the Constitution, somehow, has been compromised in the process, so, too, lead-way must be given to accommodate the likelihood that not every forum necessarily is going to reach the same arbitrated judgment about one and the same constitutional issues.

Democracy, at its best, is a study in experimental living. Individuals, organizations, peoples, institutions and governments all try things out in order to see: what works and what doesn't work; what brings piece of mind and what brings misery; what is of benefit and what is problematic; what is feasible and what is not practical.

Part of the responsibility of assuming duties of care, as a sort of fee that is exacted for enjoying the fruits of the social contract, is the willingness of all of us to accept, within limits, a certain amount of experimentation in our lives. Nonetheless, there is a big difference in our attitudes toward, and commitment to, duties of care when: (a) such experimentation is imposed on one as the result of some sort of authoritarian power play; and, (b) such experimentation becomes a matter of reciprocity and willing participation by virtue of the degree of control one has over the situation through a properly constructed Constitution.

In order to try to strike a happy balance among: democratic flexibility of experimentation; issues of sovereignty (both individual and collective); as well as the need for a certain degree of constitutional rigor, there should be a provision entitling the Senate subcommittee on constitutional issues to reserve the right to review various cases after a stipulated period of time. This period should be neither too long nor too short-perhaps a year. The cases that would be particularly appropriate for this sort of review process would be those in which an arbitrated judgment was given by one forum that conflicted, in some fundamental fashion, with the arbitrated judgment given by other forums when dealing with the same or a very similar constitutional issue.

If the nature of the constitutional issues involved were too critical, injurious or problematic to make waiting a year feasible, the Senate subcommittee could proceed to render a further arbitrated judgment. This review process could either: (a) endorse a given forum's judgment; or, (b) combine aspects from several forum judgments as a sort of constitutional compromise; or, (c) deliver an entirely different kind of arbitrated judgment.

When finally approved, this sort of arbitrated judgments would become guidelines or parameters within which the different constitutional forums would have to operate during the tenure of the Senate subcommittee. As such, these guidelines and parameters would serve to help delineate the arrangement of constraints and degrees of freedom that generate the constitutional framework out of which, and through which, the forums conduct their business.

At the same time, the constitutional forums should be entitled to make appeals to the principle of civil disobedience if they find themselves in fundamental opposition to the constitutional guidelines set down by the Senate.

Under these circumstances, a hearing would be held before both bodies of Parliament, followed by a combined, free vote of conscience. A two-thirds majority would be required to carry a vote either in favor of the Senate's position or in favor of the forum's position.

If the people of the nation should be unhappy with the combined vote of both bodies of Parliament, then, the people would have the option of calling for a referendum on the matter. 'Depending on circumstances, the referendum could call for: (a) a yes or no vote on the result of the combined Parliamentary vote; and/or (b) a yes or no vote on the Senate's position; and/or (c) a yes or no vote on the position of that constitutional forum that made the initial appeal under the principle of civil disobedience. In this way, the referendum could make clear how the people felt about a given constitutional issue.

However, as indicated previously, if the referendum does not establish a clear-cut, two-thirds majority preference of the electorate, the matter reverts to the full Senate body for additional deliberation and disposition. In addition, the discussion and vote of the Senate must reflect as much of the character of the referendum vote as possible. In order to do this properly, the Senate body might have to employ a variety of post-referendum polls as a means of probing the significance and meaning of the referendum vote.

The results of such a referendum, or of the full Senate's post-referendum vote, would be the final arbiter in all constitutional matters until the next referendum held on that issue. Moreover, such referenda would serve to help spell out some of the constraints and degrees of freedom within which the House of Commons, the Senate and the constitutional forums would have to operate.

Diversity, Equality and the Social Contract

The willingness to tolerate a certain degree of diversity in the constitutional process is not a new practice or concept. In point of fact, Canadians have displayed such a willingness with respect to the manner in which they have tolerated, over the years, various courts giving differential rulings on similar, or the same, constitutional issues, as the compositional character of the philosophies of law characterizing the members of these courts have shifted.

Moreover, not all criminal courts are carbon copies of one another, as far as, what might be termed, their "styles of conduct" are concerned. The same is also true of civil courts.

More specifically, that different judges run their courts differently is a fact of life. Each judge has his or her own set of expectations about how lawyers will comport themselves in the judge's court. Each judge has his or her own set of 'do's and don'ts' within the court. Each judge has his or her own set of criteria for determining what they will and will not permit in his or her court.

Some judges run on a short fuse; others are more forbearing. Some judges are willing to provide more leniency and flexibility in the lands of motions they are willing to entertain and under what circumstances; other judges are less flexible. Some judges are more biased than are other judges. Some judges are more stringent in the sentences they give for particular crimes; other judges are less stringent in this regard for the same sorts of crimes.

These differences lead to self-similar, rather than self-same, activity from court to court. In other words, these differences reflect the exercise of discretion that is extended to the judges. As long as the exercise of such discretion does not transgress beyond certain procedural lines, the diversity of conduct is tolerated.

Lawyers also introduce an element of diversity into legal proceedings. Gathering pre-trial evidence, processes of discovery, introduction of evidence, questioning of witnesses, cross-examination, presentation of their client's cases, making objections, seeking motions, and summation are all skills that a lawyer needs.

Not all lawyers have these skills, or, at least, do not have them to equal degrees. However, as long as lawyers do not exceed certain minimum boundaries of conduct, practice and skill that mark the realm of malpractice, then, such diversity of capacity and ability are tolerated by the legal community.

When one combines the diversity of judges with the diversity of lawyers, together with a soupçon of diversity in juries, one gets a diversity of treatment for those who are brought before the courts in civil and criminal matters. To claim that everyone gets the same treatment within the judicial system is a myth that is not true now, was not true in the past, and will not be true in the future.

Furthermore, these differences in treatment are not trivial, peripheral issues. They lead to real consequences in the lives of people ranging from: whether the individual will win or be convicted in his/her case, to whether or not the individual will be sentenced, and, if so, how long the sentence will be. However, such differences of consequences and treatment often are pushed into the background in the attempt to argue that the judicial system constitutes a uniform way of dispensing justice and a uniform way of providing for equality of treatment before the law.

As envisioned from the constitutional perspective advocated in the present document, diversity of judgment need not be a liability as long as certain conditions are satisfied. First of all, people must have a real opportunity to participate in the judgment process. This means that the process must be: accessible, inclined to participatory modes of interchange, inexpensive, and responsive to the needs and concerns of individuals.

Secondly, there must be considerable flexibility in the way the judgment process unfolds. For rules of diversity to be an asset, then, the individual must be provided with a spectrum of alternatives from which to choose the one(s) that are most resonant to the individual's circumstances.

Fairness does not necessarily mean that everything is done the same way, but it does mean that everything that is done will satisfy criteria that help bring rights into line with duties of care. Circumstances vary from place to place, and the balance necessary in one place might not be the sort of balance necessary in some other locality.

Thirdly, the very fact of the existence of diversity in the judgment process must be brought, to front and center stage as a focal issue, rather than as a background issue from which we try to hide or that we try to deny altogether. By being aware of diversity as an issue, we stand a better chance of finding ways to countervail its potentially adverse affects.

Fourthly, there is nothing necessarily intrinsically wrong with the idea of competing systems of justice, as long as people are happy with the sorts of choices and consequences that those competing systems might offer. One of the truly ironic and intriguing aspects of Canadian history is that a Parliamentary and judicial system that has been as concerned, over the years, about promoting and protecting the principle of open and fair economic competition should be so resistant to the idea of competitive fairness in the realm of justice.

The traditional defense for the aforementioned resistance is that our approach to issues of justice and law must be monolithic in character or else we will not be able to provide equality of treatment in different cases, and, surely, so the argument goes, equality of treatment is one of the cornerstones of dispensing true justice. Whether or not equality of treatment is a necessary condition for justice, the fact is, as indicated previously, that if one means by the idea of "equality of treatment", sameness of treatment, then, such equality does not exist in Canada, nor has it existed in the past. Indeed, given human variability, one well might question whether equality of treatment -- when construed as sameness of treatment -- is either feasible or even possible.

On the other hand, if people are provided with a number of competing perspectives concerning the idea of justice, and if they are aware of the constraints and degrees of freedom associated with each of these alternatives, and if they are aware of the upsides and downsides of these alternatives, as well as the strengths and weaknesses of such alternatives, then, let the people make their own choices. The important considerations are: (a) that each of the alternatives is a fair process; (b) that a person is prepared to accept the judgment of such a process, irrespective of whether the judgment will turn out in their favor or against it; and, (c) that a person feels their judicial system of choice is reflective of, or congruent, with his or her sense of what justice involves.

Just as is the case with other areas of competition, competition in the area of the judicial system could lead to a heuristically valuable process of cross-fertilization that generates improvements in the respective systems of justice. However, even if there were no process of cross-fertilization, the quality of sovereignty of both individuals and the collective would be enhanced through the diversity of judicial styles that permit selecting the one that was nearest to one's sense of justice.

Thus, if Native peoples have a totally different sense of justice than do, say, English or French Canada, how could anyone feel that one would be justified in imposing on the Native peoples a system of justice that is alien to, and in conflict with, values, beliefs and practices in which the understanding of Native peoples' understanding of justice are rooted? Only the worst, most virulent sort of ethnocentrism could be sufficiently deluded to suppose that such gross intrusions into, and abuses of, another people's sovereignty could be acceptable.

Similarly, if the people of a given province believe that, under certain circumstances, the death penalty is warranted-that the death penalty gives expression to one of the facets of justice, then, what arguments are to be invoked that can be shown, to the satisfaction of one and all, that such a conception of justice is mistaken? One of the truly remarkable aspects of the House of Commons' free vote of conscience on the death penalty is that the result was in opposition to virtually every Canadian poll that had been taken leading up to that vote. The vast majority of people in Canada wanted the death penalty, but the people's conception of justice conflicted with the sense of justice of those members of the House of Commons who voted against retaining the death penalty.

The deciding factor was not necessarily who was right or who had the better concept of justice. The deciding factor was who had power, and, in the case of the death penalty vote, the people were powerless. A small group of people were able to impose their sense of justice on millions of people who had a different conception of justice.

The concept of a social contract does not necessarily mean that each individual signs the same standard contract with some mythical, abstract entity called society. The social contract encompasses the entire realm of dialectical, dynamic negotiations between, and among, individuals.

These constitutional negotiations establish the spectrum of constraints and degrees of freedom that are to regulate to our handling of the issue of sovereignty. There is nothing in the dialectic that demands everyone's contract be the same. As long as the structural character of the social contract is such that it permits alternatives and that people have a right to select from among these alternatives, then, the social contract is fully capable of handling, among other things, diverse approaches to the manner in which justice is implemented.

Quebec and Sovereignty Association

A sufficiently sophisticated social contract also is fully capable of dealing with the idea of sovereignty association that is being sought by many people in the Province of Quebec. In the experimental spirit that should form an integral part of the democratic process, there is enough fluidity and flexibility to entertain provisions for a variety of political/social arrangements. The kinds of arrangements that are possible are limited only by our failure to come to grips with the structural character of the principles involved in sovereignty and participatory democracy.

In effect, there is a strong current within Quebec that wishes to run an experiment in democracy. There are all kinds of opinions about what the short-term and long-term effects of such an experiment would be for both the people of Quebec as well as for the people in the rest of Canada.

The truth of the matter is, however, that no one really knows. People have formulated their null hypotheses, but only real, live data has a chance of providing possible answers to this debate.

If Quebec establishes some sort of sovereignty association with the rest of Canada, and if that process should work well or moderately well for the people of Quebec, then, the rest of Canada should be happy that things have worked out for Quebec. Moreover, if the experiment works out well, there might be valuable lessons in the results of that experiment for the rest of Canada, in terms of how things might be done differently in other parts of Canada.

If, on the other hand, the experiment does not work out well, then, steps should be taken to assist the people of Quebec to enhance the quality of their sovereignty in the post-experimental context. Yet, such assistance does not mean that some arrangement should be arrogantly and contemptuously imposed on Quebec.

Instead, a new experimental program must be established that will display compassion, empathy or willingness to accommodate Quebecers, within negotiated limits, according to their needs in conjunction with the needs of non-Quebecers. The active principle should be a spirit of generosity in which there is a reciprocal eagerness to see one another enhance our respective sovereignties.

One must understand that Quebec might be on the verge of stepping into the unknown. They are taking a risk, but it is a risk that carries potential benefits for people beyond the boundary of Quebec. This is so because, whether the experiment works or it doesn't work, Canadians as a whole will have gained useful knowledge and understanding about the process of democracy.

All Canadians have a duty of care to one another. This means that, as far as the people outside of Quebec are concerned, they should be prepared to lend constructive assistance to the people of Quebec in ways that will permit the latter people to gain autonomy over their lives in a manner that reflects, both as individuals and as a people, the orientation of the Quebecois to the idea of sovereignty.

If the people of Quebec are willing to run a risk, then, the rest of Canada should attempt to find ways of helping the people of Quebec to minimize those risks. At the same time, the people of Quebec need to give some serious consideration to establishing various precautionary measures that will serve to minimize their own risks in their possible venture, as well as help minimize the risks that the rest of Canada might be willing to run in order to help Quebec in our collective experiment in democracy.

One way of minimizing those risks for both Quebecers and non-Quebecers is to start with some intermediate position between the present situation and full-fledged sovereignty association. For example, instead of seeking provincial control over some twenty-two areas that are presently under federal jurisdiction (as has been suggested in several reports), why not start out with seven or eight such areas? Because so many unknown variables are entangled in the proposed experiment, Quebec's long-term and short-term interests might be best served by running a small-scale experiment before contemplating a more massive project.

Another way of helping to minimize the risks is to build a review process into the proposed undertaking. In other words, if the people of Quebec decide to pursue the experiment of sovereignty association, let the people of Quebec sit down with the rest of the people of Canada after, say, four years in order to review the situation.

The review process should be geared toward looking at both the successful aspects as well as the not-so-successful aspects of the process of sovereignty association. It would be an opportunity for both sides of the experimental set-up to make adjustments of a reciprocal nature that would be mutually beneficial. Such a review process could continue on a regular basis.

The duty of care principle, however, is a two-way responsibility. Just as the rest of Canada has a duty of care to help the people of Quebec enhance the quality of their sovereignty, the people of Quebec have a duty of care toward other peoples of Canada. Therefore, Quebecers have a responsibility to lend constructive assistance to other peoples in order to help those peoples enhance the quality of their respective sovereignties. In this regard, there are three issues that immediately come to mind.

First, if the people of Quebec enter into some form of sovereignty association, they are not free to do whatever they like with respect to Native peoples. As indicated elsewhere in this document, Native peoples are now, and always have been, a sovereign people or group of peoples.

No one has had the right to extinguish that sovereignty, irrespective of whether that act is done in the name of some monarch or it is done in the name of the government of the Province of Quebec. Sovereignty-association is not the private preserve of the people of Quebec, nor are the people of Quebec the only ones who qualify as a special and distinct society.

Extending a duty of care toward the sovereignty of Native peoples in Quebec means that the people of Quebec are going to have to make some decisions that will be as painful for them ... as will be the decision: to let the people of Quebec explore the world of sovereignty association that must be made by the rest of Canada. If the people of Quebec want powers of immigration, unemployment insurance, energy, regional development and environment transferred from the federal government to the jurisdiction of the Province of Quebec, then, the people of Quebec are going to have to be prepared to transfer the same power to the Native peoples in their province.

As someone has once said, what is good for the goose is good for the gander. Thus, this means, among other things, that the entire James Bay project is going to have to be reassessed since it intrudes on the sovereignty of the Native peoples in, among other things, areas of energy, regional development and environment.

A second issue that arises with respect to the people of Quebec extending a duty of care to other peoples of Canada concerns the non-Francophone peoples of Quebec. Those peoples are entitled to an arrangement in the social contract that will provide them with guarantees that protect and enhance the quality of their sovereignty.

While such non-Francophone peoples might not want control over all of the sorts of powers that the Francophone people of Quebec might want transferred to the province, and while such non-Francophone peoples might be quite content to let the Francophone majority go about arranging provincial sovereignty in a way that is most consonant with the special and distinct characteristics of Quebecois society, nevertheless, such non-Francophone peoples are owed a duty of care by the Francophone majority. This duty of care requires the Francophone majority to be sincerely committed to constructively helping the non-Francophone minorities to establish a form of sovereignty that is most consonant with the cultural characteristics of those non-Francophone minorities.

The third issue that emerges in the context of working out the Quebec side of the duty of care relationship with the rest of Canada concerns the Francophone people residing elsewhere in Canada. Is the province of Quebec going to abandon those people, or is the province prepared to offer a variety of services in an outreach program that is directed toward helping those people retain their distinct and special orientation toward their own sovereignty as Francophone people? Although the rest of Canada also has a duty of care to extend to the Francophone people living outside of Quebec, do the Francophone people of Quebec feel that a duty of care is owed to the Francophone people residing outside of Quebec only by the non-Francophone people of Canada?

One possibility does suggest itself with respect to the duty of care Quebecers owe to the Francophones outside of Quebec. An outreach program might be established that would bring Francophone communities outside of Quebec under the provincial jurisdiction of Quebec.

Such an outreach program would be administered, staffed and operated entirely in accordance with the specifications of the people of Quebec. However, the program would be funded by Federal money, together with money from the provinces in which such Francophone communities existed. By underwriting the costs of this sort of outreach program, the Federal and provincial governments would be fulfilling, in part, their own duty of care to the Francophone communities outside Quebec.

Some people might wish to argue that by transferring certain federalist powers to Quebec, one is destroying Canadian identity and unity, thereby reducing Canada to, in the words of one observer, little more than a post office. The defining essence of Canadian identity and unity is not federalism, nor is it provincialism, nor is it a combination of federalism and provincialism.

The essence of Canadian identity and unity is the dialectic between the democratic process and the issues surrounding sovereignty. By permitting the people of Quebec to change the character of the dialectic in a variety of ways, through something called sovereignty association, Canadian identity and unity will not be affected in the least. Such a move would simply be another chapter in the history of how we, as Canadians, have attempted to handle the many problems that are generated when the democratic process engages the phenomenon of sovereignty and vice versa.

As suggested previously in this document, neither: monarchy, federalism, Via Rail, the National Film Board, the Maple Leaf Flag, CBC, the National Anthem, nor any other symbol or institution is what lies at the heart of Canadian identity and unity. What lies at the heart of these two cornerstones of our nationhood is our willingness to assist one another to seek our respective sovereign destinies through a democratic process. Everything else might pass away or fall into disrepair, but as long as we democratically permit one another to struggle toward those arrangements of sovereignty that are reciprocal and mutually beneficial, then, Canada remains intact, and we will continue to know who we are as a collection of peoples.

A further item concerning the issue of Quebec sovereignty association remains to be touched upon. This item actually reinforces the nature of balance that needs to be sought between the centralist/federalist tendencies in the country and the decentralizing tendencies in Canada.

More specifically, if the people of Quebec were to take the route of sovereignty association, this would be counterbalanced by a Senate reconstituted along the lines suggested previously in this document. Nowhere would this countervailing function be more in evidence than in relation to the Senate subcommittee on constitutional issues and the concomitant constitutional forums that are to be implemented in the provinces.

Constitutional forums constitute an intriguing, complex and flexible mixture of centralizing and decentralizing currents. The centralizing aspects of these forums will link the people of Quebec in an intimate, if not inextricable, manner with the rest of Canada. At the same time, the decentralizing facets of the constitutional forums will introduce themes into Quebec society that will both place constraints on, as well as give degrees of freedom to, the people of that province in ways that the provincial government will not be able to control. As a result, the forums have the potential for enhancing the quality of sovereignty of all the peoples of Quebec, as well as the rest of Canada.

Before leaving the topic of sovereignty association in relation to Quebec, one further observation seems warranted. Many people in Quebec have become so preoccupied, if not consumed, by the issues of sovereignty association, separation and independence, that many individuals have permitted these issues to overshadow a fundamental reality.

There will be only one difference between a pre-independence (or pre-sovereignty association) Quebec and a post-independence (or post-sovereignty association) Quebec. This one difference concerns the names of the people who will have control of the province.

In neither case (i.e., before or after) will the people have effective, meaningful access to unmediated power. In neither case will the people of Quebec have gained real sovereignty and autonomy over their lives. In neither case will the people be permitted, except through elections, to participate in the decision process.

In neither case will the people of Quebec have a fundamental hand in directly shaping the constitutional process that will govern the life of the province. In neither case will the destiny of the people's sovereignty be in their own hands; rather, in both cases, that destiny will be shaped by politicians who have their own agenda-an agenda that will be beset by problems if people are permitted real participatory power.

In short, independence, or sovereignty association, of whatever political character one cares to choose, does not address the critical problems of sovereignty <u>unless</u> that mode of association provides the people with a variety of alternative paths through which to pursue, protect and enhance that sovereignty -- alternatives that are rooted in a rigorous, participatory methodology and not just a representational process. By defining oneself solely in terms of the presuppositions and properties of the separatist/independence/ sovereignty association dialectic among different levels of government, one lets democracy of a more substantive sort slip through one's hands. This latter democracy is a function of people, not governments, in which the latter serve the former and not vice versa.

Religious Freedom: Some Problems

Previously, various aspects of the constitutional crisis concerning the Native peoples and the people of Quebec have been addressed. These sorts of issues are well known to Canadians.

Indeed, much of the talk that is devoted to the current crisis usually focuses on these two peoples. However, there are others in Canada whose needs and problems must be taken into consideration if a revamped Constitution is to serve all Canadians.

To begin with, there is the question of religious freedom. While Canada prides itself as a nation in which, theoretically, individuals are free to commit themselves, if they wish, to a religion of their choice without any interference from the government, in practice this is not always the case.

Religion is not just a matter of having places of worship or having particular beliefs or values. Religion is also a matter of putting into practice what one believes, as well as acting in accordance with the values one holds in esteem.

Moreover, these beliefs and values are not meant to be activated only when one enters a place of worship and switched off when one leaves that place of worship. Religious beliefs and values are meant to be put into practice in day-to-day life.

In Canada, there is said to be a separation between church and state, or temple and state, or mosque and state. This separation is intended to curtail the possibility that people in power might try to impose a certain kind of religious perspective-namely, their own-onto the citizens of the country, irrespective of the wishes of those citizens.

What, in fact, happens, however, is that government officials either: (a) use a variety of strategies, diversionary tactics and Machiavellian manipulations to camouflage their religious prejudices; or, (b) wield a set of non-religious biases in order to place obstacles in the way of, as well as impose constraints upon, the way one can pursue one's religion of choice. Although, in the latter case, the people in power claim that they are being neutral with respect to religious beliefs and practices, in reality there is a huge difference between being neutral and being oriented in an anti-religious manner.

Being neutral in matters of a religious nature means, to be sure, that one does not favor one religion over another. On the other hand, being neutral also means that one does not favor a non-religious perspective over a religious perspective, or vice versa.

Neutral governmental decisions should establish constraints and degrees of freedom within the community that are based on a consistent principle (or set of principles). Such a principle should be geared toward helping people in general-irrespective of whether these people have a religious or non-religious orientation-to work toward enhancing the quality of their respective sovereignties while balancing considerations of rights and duties of care for individuals as well as the community as a whole.

Unfortunately, what happens in practice is that many governmental authorities, elected officials and justices often tend to interpret the idea of separation of state and religion to mean that a non-religious, rather than a neutral, perspective should be adopted in interpreting law, policies, programs, directives and the Constitution. This is the case, despite the fact that the *Constitution Act of 1982* clearly states Canada is founded "upon principles that recognize the supremacy of God". In reality, if any governmental official or jurist actually made a decision based on an articulated principle that recognized the supremacy of God, that individual would wreak upon himself or herself the collective wrath of the gods and idols of secularism who would be exceedingly jealous of such supremacy.

No jurist or government has ventured forth with sufficient courage to delineate, in a legal opinion or in government policy, just precisely what is meant or entailed or encompassed by the notion that Canada is founded "upon principles that recognize the supremacy of God". They have not said what such principles are; nor have they said what it means for such principles to "<u>recognize</u>" the supremacy of God; nor have they said what the ramifications of such recognition and supremacy are; nor have they said what they mean by God. In fact, almost every decision the courts and governments have made virtually ignore such questions, problems and issues.

In effect, the opening words of the Canadian Constitution, the single most important document in Canadian society, are devoid of official meaning and have no explicit, official role or function in determining government policy or judicial decisions. To the extent that such constitutional words have any role at all, they do so in the dark recesses of unstated assumptions, biases and predilections that shape, color and orient the decisions made by officials-decisions that frequently have prejudicial consequences for the members of minority religions or for the members of majority religions with whom the officials disagree or for whom such officials hold antipathy.

The realm of education gives expression to just one facet of the aforementioned biases. Education should not be just a means to a job. Furthermore, education should not be a tool of assimilation as long as the meaning of "assimilation" requires individuals to submit themselves to someone else's imposed conception of sovereignty, identity, commitment and truth.

Becoming a loyal subject of Canada has nothing to do with being assimilated into some sort of pre-fabricated, monolithic, standard set of assumptions, values, beliefs, commitments and practices that public education is, among other things, intended to promote. Supposedly, such a monolithic process constitutes an allegedly unifying social and political medium. Yet, one can be taught values such as freedom, rights, democracy, social responsibility, justice and multiculturalism without going to public school and without presupposing that everyone must engage these topics in precisely the same way.

On the other hand, public education cannot teach, say, a Jewish, Muslim, Hindu, Buddhist, or Native child about how to be a good Jew, Muslim, Hindu, Buddhist, or Native child. In addition, public education cannot actively assist such children to establish a spiritual identity or to adopt a spiritual way of life.

Public schools cannot do this because they have virtually no expertise in, or understanding of, what spirituality involves. Nor do public schools have the capacity to help an individual learn how to put all of this into practice on a day-to-day basis.

Religious communities are told, however, that such educational topics are not the responsibility of the public education system. Such issues are the responsibility of parents and must be done at night or on weekends or during the summer. Consequently, a supposedly neutral state has made it a matter of law, practice and convention that the public education system, despite being funded by tax money from religious communities, cannot accommodate a spiritual education.

Religious communities are free, of course, to begin their own educational system, but they are not permitted to have access to the taxes that they contribute to the government in order to be able to use that money for the purposes of religious education. Thus, Muslims, Jewish, Hindu, Buddhist, Sikh, Native Peoples and Protestant Christians must bear a special burden of paying twice if they want an education that reflects the values and practices of their religious tradition. The Catholic community, on the other hand, is permitted -- more so in some places than in other places -- to have access to public money to promote an educational process that does reflect that community's religious values and practices.

That Catholics should be entitled to educate their children according to the values and religious beliefs of their tradition is not in dispute. What does need to be critically examined is the decision process that singles them out as being, when compared with all other religious traditions in Canada, the only ones entitled to such public support.

Apparently, to paraphrase an insight made by George Orwell in another context nearly 50 years ago, in the barnyard of Canadian democracy, all animals are equal, but some are more equal than others. Those that are more equal than others enjoy the opportunity to pursue their religion of choice and learn about their religion of choice in ways that those who are 'sort of equal' do not enjoy the opportunity to do.

Such inconsistency is indefensible: morally, philosophically and logically. It is not neutral. It is discriminatory. It does not reflect the spirit of multiculturalism.

The aforementioned sort of inconsistency clearly points out that the religious freedom of a great many people in Canada has been seriously circumscribed and inhibited. This is the case since the powers that be have taken something of fundamental importance to the pursuit and practice of religion-namely, education-and placed obstacle after obstacle in the path of certain peoples and communities of Canada with respect to their ability to pursue their religion of choice freely. These obstacles prevent many, if not most, religious minorities in Canada from having access to anything but a curriculum of subjugation to a preconceived master plan of assimilation. As a result, these people and communities are required either to: (a) submit to the values and practices of public education that are often antithetical to religious values and practices; or, (b) pay twice for the kind of education they want.

Education is an area that is very amenable to the implementation of the previously discussed principle of diversity of equality. Catholics, Protestants, Jews, Muslims, Sikhs, Buddhists, Native peoples, atheists, agnostics, humanists, and so on, all have their own ideas about what constitutes an appropriate educational process. The equitable way to handle this multiplicity of beliefs, values, interests, practices, and goals is not to impose a monolithic educational system on everyone and, thereby, treat everyone the same way by marginalizing, ignoring and denying, to an equal degree, the reality of everyone's perspective. The equitable solution is to provide people with educational alternatives from which they can select the one that is best suited to their needs, circumstances, and values.

In short, equality is best served by means of offering a diversity of alternatives. Educational programs do not have to be the same to be equal. The conditions of quality are satisfied when different educational systems meet the needs and reflect the values of the communities being served, respectively, by these different educational systems.

One might never be able to achieve a perfect fit between the diversity of educational alternatives that are offered and the diversity of values that exist in the community. Nevertheless, one needs to struggle in the direction of providing more flexibility and alternatives than presently exist.

<u>Repairing the House</u>

In addition to the radical program of reconstruction that has been recommended for the Senate, there are also a few structural changes that are to be proposed with respect to the House of Commons. The most fundamental of these changes stipulates that every House member be given at least one, and perhaps two, free votes of conscience per sitting of the House. How and when, or if, these free votes would be used would be left to the discretion of the individual members of the House. The intent of this proposed change is to allow for more than one kind of representational democracy to be exercised during the legislative process.

As things presently stand, the members of the various parties are required to follow party discipline and policy with respect to how the respective parties are oriented toward any particular legislative issue. Yet, the stance of a party does not necessarily reflect the will of the people who voted for that party or who voted for the members of that party who were elected to the House.

By giving members of the House one or two opportunities per sitting to vote against party policy, one would open up the possibility of allowing elected members to serve their constituents according to the actual desires of those constituents, rather than according to a "visionary" party policy that is imposed on people, irrespective of whether the latter like that policy or not. At the same time, by limiting the free votes to one or two per House session, one still permits parties-especially the one in power-to try to fulfill their legislative program or policy agenda for the country.

The presence of this discretionary power also could encourage a range of negotiations, compromises and co-operation that is difficult to achieve under the present Parliamentary set up in which aggressive, if not hostile, partisanship is the bedrock of legislative etiquette. Such antagonism naturally follows from the political need of the opposition to challenge, if not embarrass, the ruling power. This sort of conflict naturally follows, as well, from the attempts of the ruling power to skirt around the problems, questions and issues being raised by the opposition.

In addition to the foregoing suggestion for change in the House of Commons, there are several other possible modifications that are proffered here. First of all, the rule should be abolished that stipulates that a government loses its authority if it is defeated on matters of finance, such as the budget. In conjunction with the jettisoning of this rule, however, will be the fixing of a specific date, occurring once every four years, for elections to be held with respect to the members of the House of Commons, including, of course, the position of the Prime Minister.

By fixing a specific date as the time when House elections are held, one frees the election process from the caprice of choices based upon the ups and downs of a ruling party's popularity. Parties in power should not have the luxury of choosing times for elections that are most advantageous to them and/or least advantageous for their political opponents or for the people of Canada. Elections should be focused on specific topics, and on the capabilities of candidates rather than on opportunistic strategies.

Another suggested structural change concerns the question of who has the right to commit the Canadian people to war. In the recent Persian Gulf War, there were those who argued that the Prime Minister had the authority to commit Canada to war. Others claimed that the Prime Minister was not empowered to act on his own, but needed the vote of the House of Commons and the Senate.

I suggest that, with the exception of those cases in which Canada is physically attacked by hostile forces and, as a result, the Prime Minister orders that immediate defensive measures to be taken, the ones who really ought to make this sort of decision, by means of referendum, are the people of the country. Moreover, there should be a clear choice offered between four kinds of options-namely: (a) offensive war (carrying the attack to an opponent in a way that is designed to lead to the opponent's defeat); (b) defensive war (i.e., Canadian forces will defend themselves if attacked, but will not initiate hostilities or carry out offensive strategies designed to defeat an enemy); (c) peacekeeping operations; and, finally, (d) none of the above.

A final suggestion in connection with changes concerning the House of Commons is more a matter of convention than of legal requirements. More specifically, the person selected for Prime Minister should be chosen on the basis of the quality and integrity of the person, and entirely independent of linguistic abilities.

Leadership should not be distorted by linguistic issues. There have been capable people, both within the French community as well as the

English community, who have been passed over for consideration only because they did not speak English or French.

There will be those people, of course, who wish to argue that a person cannot be an effective Prime Minister unless such a person can communicate with the people of both linguistic communities. This sort of argument seems weak from a number of perspectives.

To begin with, there are an increasing number of people in Canada who have, at least, only marginal fluency in either English or French. These people are more at home in, and understand issues better when approached with, some language other than English or French. As long as there are people within government who can communicate with these people so that all parties concerned can address issues of substance, then, the linguistic capabilities of the Prime Minister are not of paramount importance.

Secondly, someone once described the English as a people divided by a common language. One possible moral, so to speak, of the foregoing observation is that communication is not a matter of what is conveyed by the tongue, but what is spoken by the hearts and actions of people. A person might be a brilliant speaker but a lousy person. Or, a person might say things that are inspiring to hear, but the person might belie those words with his or her actions.

Considered from another perspective, the same words do not always have the same meaning for different people. Interpretation often varies from person to person. As a result, misunderstanding occurs quite frequently because people communicate as if they are speaking the same language, when, in reality, the underlying semantics is altogether different, despite the sameness of the surface meaning of the words being spoken and heard.

Indeed, in this latter regard, one might even argue there are some advantages to not knowing the language of the Prime Minister, since, in translation, one can concentrate on issues and not get caught up in rhetorical style. Under such circumstances, more care and consideration might be directed to the problem of how translation can change meaning and, consequently, more attention might be devoted to making sure that the speaker and recipient understood the words in the same way. Some features might be lost during translation, but not as much as one might suppose to be the case.

In any event, as indicated earlier, actions speak a lot more loudly and clearly than do words. Indeed, actions often times are a much truer reflection of someone's state of heart or sincerity than are that individual's words.

The Centralist/Decentralist Dynamic

All of the suggestions made in the previous pages of this document provide for a strong central/federalist presence in Canada. At the same time, the structural character of that presence has been transformed substantially, from what is currently the case in Canada, by the various proposals in this document.

On the other hand, the centralist/federalist presence is counterbalanced with an extremely strong theme of decentralization that is manifested in the form of various kinds of power sharing arrangements and opportunities for participation by a far larger number of the people than is presently the case. Especially noteworthy in this push toward decentralization is the manner in which the constitutional process is made accessible to the people in a variety of ways that permit the average individual a greater array of choices through which to protect and enhance the quality of the individual's sovereignty.

Another way of stating the centralizing/decentralizing character of the proposals being advanced in the present document is in the form of a simile. From the perspective being advocated here, Canada is like an ellipse in mathematics.

The structural character of an ellipse is defined by the mathematical character of its two foci. These foci are the two points of mathematical moment, as it were, about which the perimeter of the ellipse rotates. Alternatively, each point of the ellipse's perimeter can be said to be under the dual influence of the mathematical function being given expression through the two foci.

Translated into concrete terms, the simile means that: each social/political aspect of the structural character or form of Canada is governed by the influences of the dialectic of Canada's internal foci -- namely, representative and participatory government. Said still less abstractly, from the perspective of the present document, the constraints and degrees of freedom that outline the perimeter of Canada as a social/political entity are a function of the dialectic between the Senate and the House of Commons.

Both bodies of Parliament should give complete expression to a combination of centralizing and decentralizing influences. In the altered character of the House of Commons that has been discussed in these pages, the ratio of centralizing to decentralizing tendencies is weighted in the direction of the former.

On the other hand, in the proposed reconstituted Senate, the ratio of centralizing to decentralizing tendencies is weighted in the direction of the latter sort of influences. In both cases, however, clear centralist/federalist themes are present.

Vested Interests and the Constitution

The proposals in these pages are fundamental in scope, import and ramifications. They call upon Canadians to look at the process of democracy in a way that is quite different from what Canadians historically are used to. In addition, the proposals introduced in this document will alter considerably the way power is acquired, exercised, delegated, distributed and implemented.

There might be many people who, for a variety of reasons, will resist these suggested changes. For example, presently, there are three facets of the *Constitution Act of 1982* that cannot be changed without unanimous consent of the provinces, together with the federal government. These three features involve: (a) the continued presence of the monarchy; (b) the composition of the Supreme Court; and, (c) the amending formula.

Each of the foregoing themes is supported by vested interests that will resist any attempt to change the character of these constitutional precepts. How else is one to explain the fact that out of all the, quite possibly, far more worthy themes that could have been considered untouchable with respect to constitutional tinkering, just these three were selected?

All three of these constitutional themes, along with a number of other themes, will be jettisoned if the transformation of the Constitution suggested in the present document were to be adopted.

Therefore, one can be sure that the previous proposals will generate considerable resistance. Such resistance, however, is not necessarily based on sound, democratic thinking.

As an illustration of what is meant by the claim at the end of the previous paragraph, consider the following. The idea of the monarchy has absolutely no place in a Canadian Constitution. It is a symbol of colonialism, not Canadian identity or unity. It is an intrusion upon Canadian sovereignty since our loyalties and our duties of care are to other Canadians, not to the Queen or King of England. Monarchy is a relic of history that belongs in the archives of Canada and not in the Constitution.

For those people in Canada who have a deep respect and love for monarchy, let them be free to observe that in their own fashion. Such people should be free to honor the occasions and events that give expression to the tradition of monarchy.

However, there is absolutely no tenable justification that can be given as to why paying homage to the English monarchy is incumbent upon, and must be imposed on, the sovereign citizens of Canada. Canada is a distinct and special society that is functionally, morally, politically, legally and socially independent of the English monarchy.

Similar sorts of arguments can be advanced against other entrenched themes of the *Constitution Act of 1982*. For instance, on the surface, the amending formula theme that is entrenched in the Constitution would appear to be a safeguard of democracy. In reality, the amending formula protects existing power structures of both federal species as well as provincial varieties.

The *Constitution Act of 1982* is a Constitution of the governments, for the governments and by the governments. The vast majority of the people of Canada have no place in the present Constitution. The one area of the Constitution -- namely, the Charter of Rights -- that pays even token attention to people -- as people -- is elsewhere in the Constitution made subservient to the whims of governments.

In effect, the amending formula renders the generality of Canadian people powerless, for they are at the mercy of politicians to "represent" them. Unfortunately, in the political dictionary, the entry under "represents" all too often has a primary meaning of: the act of imposing one's ideas on others.

The current amending formula ensures that the vast majority of Canadians have no direct access to the constitutional process. Everything in that process is mediated through those over whom one has no control.

Contrary to the hype of politicians, elections do not constitute effective control, since, far too frequently, elections are merely the point of contact between a rock and a hard place. In other words, either one can vote people out of office once irreparable damage has been done, or one can vote people into office and watch helplessly as they proceed to do irreparable damage. If Canada is to become a truly democratic society in which more than politicians can participate in a meaningful, fundamental and empowered manner in relation to the constitutional process, then, the amending formula, as presently conceived, cannot be retained.

The final entrenched, untouchable theme of the *Constitution Act of 1982* concerns the composition of the Supreme Court. Much already has been said in the previous pages about the problematic nature of using the judiciary as the point of leverage through which the constitutional fulcrum moves Canadian society. Nonetheless, one might repeat the following point.

Let us suppose (and this is a highly contentious supposition) that the Supreme Court jurists could definitely capture the structural character of what was believed, thought, intended and felt by those who created, voted for and implemented laws, statutes and constitutional directives. Let us further suppose (and, again, this is a highly contentious supposition) that the jurists could demonstrate the logical links between present cases and what the "creators" of the past intended. Despite these "givens", the fact of the matter is, all of this is largely, if not entirely, too narrow in scope to be of much value in helping the people of today resolve the issues of sovereignty, social contracts and participatory democracy.

Moreover, in many ways, such legalistic pronouncements are irrelevant since, in effect, they enslave the people of today to what was thought, believed and intended at another time and place. Why should the people of today legally be held responsible for a contract that they had no part in shaping, arranging, ordering or making?

To be sure, there must be some framework that permits continuity of sorts from one period to the next. Otherwise, there would be complete anarchy and chaos.

Nonetheless, the constitutional process we bequeath our children should be one that is flexible, fruitful and fair, rather than one that is stagnant, stale, and star-crossed. Consequently, while one might wish to keep the composition of the Supreme Court intact, the role of the Supreme Court, vis-a-vis the Constitution, must be terminated and replaced with something like the Senate subcommittee on constitutional issues and its associated constitutional forums.

How many people will seek out those alternative constitutional rooms (such as have been proposed in the present document) that have the potential for freeing the former from the shocks and pain caused by the present constitutional set-up remains to be seen. The uncertainty surrounding the willingness and capacity of Canadians to find a 'safe', or safer, less shocking, constitutional context is uncertain. This is the case because the degree to which Canadians have succumbed to a spiritual/conceptual condition akin to learned helplessness is still an open, unanswered question.

On the other hand, the amazing events in Eastern Europe that have taken place relatively recently have proven radical change is possible to achieve peacefully. One might suppose that if the people of those countries have been brave enough to seek to take control of their own lives, can Canadians afford to show any less courage as we step into the future?

Some people might wish to argue that the people of the Eastern bloc countries were in a desperate situation due to the brutal authoritarian, dictatorial manner in which they had been treated by their respective governments. In other words, sometimes desperation drives one to take chances that one wouldn't take under more congenial circumstances such as exist in Canada.

Furthermore, this line of argument might wish to maintain that we already have democracy in Canada, and, consequently, our situation cannot be compared, even remotely, with the situation that confronted the people in the Eastern bloc countries. We are free; they were not. We have democracy; they did not. Therefore, there is no need for Canadians to have courage with respect to our constitutional crisis.

The most difficult shackles of bondage to lose are those that are built from self-deception. In a sense, the people of Canada are faced with a more insidious form of totalitarianism than were the people of Eastern Europe.

In those countries, the enemy was external, concrete and palpable. In Canada, the enemy is internal and invisible. Here, the enemy is a mythology that has shaped and colored how Canadians see themselves and the world.

More specifically, despite the existence of a great deal of evidence that shows each of us to be: (a) powerless in many fundamental ways; (b) marginalized from the real essence of the constitutional process; as well as, (c) lacking in any effective autonomy with respect to the structural character of our own sovereignty, we still believe we are free participants in a democratic society. Consequently, because our political vision is blinkered, colored and distorted by the mythology of democracy that we are fed from infancy, we need even more courage than did the people of Eastern Europe.

We must not only come to grips with our own, internal demons of self-deception, we also must throw off the habits of a false mythology of democracy. Like some incredibly potent narcotic, this mythology binds us to constitutional ways that are not serving the interests of our sovereignty, either as individuals or as a collective.

Constitutional issues are far too important to be left to politicians. The non-elected people of Canada, who comprise over 99.9% of the population, cannot afford any more presumptuous, prematurely self-congratulatory Meech Lake travesties. The idea that politicians should negotiate our future -- whether behind closed doors or in open session -- is no longer (if it ever was) acceptable.

Canadians have an opportunity to do something very special with respect to constitutional issues. Canadians have an opportunity to be a shining example for the whole world. We have an opportunity to undertake a grand experiment in participatory democracy in a way that few, if any, other countries in the world have ever tried, let alone achieved.

The Constitutional Challenge

There has been considerable discussion recently concerning the idea of holding a constituent assembly to deal with the constitutional crisis. This idea has considerable merit, but it also entails a variety of potential problem areas.

For instance, two questions that readily come to mind are the following: Who is to be picked for such an assembly, and who is to do the picking?

The first question raises the issue of representation. Should just first ministers be invited to such an assembly? Should the participants only be elected officials of one sort or another? Should just provinces be represented? What about municipalities or regional governments? Should the invitees only be drawn from recognized political parties? Should partisan politics have any role in the deliberations of the proposed assembly? Are minorities to be included? Will half the delegates be women? Will the people attending the assembly be restricted to experts or professionals? Or, will so-called "common" people be admitted to the proceedings? How many people will be selected for the assembly?

The second question stated above-namely, Who is to do the picking of the delegates to a constituent assembly?-is a process issue. Is selection to be done by election? If so, how are candidates to be identified? Are participants to be appointed? If so, how will the appointment procedure be implemented? Who will make the decisions concerning such appointees? Will appointments be done on a random basis, or will certain kinds of criteria be applied in determining suitable constituent assembly participants?

In addition to the foregoing sorts of questions, there are numerous other problem areas. Each of these further areas involves critical issues. For example: Who is to set the agenda. for the assembly? What is to be the mandate of the assembly? How long will the assembly proceedings last? What procedural process will regulate the assembly meetings? Who will ratify the finished product of the assembly? What if the assembly's efforts are not ratified? Can the assembly's effort be modified in any way? If so, then, by whom and to what extent can it be modified? Who will ratify such a modified document? Who will pay for the expenses of a constituent assembly?

Whatever answers one gives to the foregoing questions, there will be the additional problem of having to justify the judgments one makes with respect to each issue. Attendant to the justification issue will be disputes about the degree of persuasiveness of the various justifications that are given.

Finally, as if the foregoing questions, problems and issues are not enough of a burden with which to have to deal, there is one further difficulty. More specifically, none of the foregoing questions addresses the issue of what criteria are to be used to determine the substantive shape and character of a new or modified constitutional package.

In other words, there needs to be an articulation of the principles of democracy that are to be given concrete expression in any proposed constitutional package. Quebec, Native and aboriginal peoples, the status of women, senate reform, the amending process, electoral reform, regional disparities all have been the focus of an underlying desire for change with respect to how the present Constitution Act handles, or fails to handle, these issues. However, there is a need to discuss, in specific detail, the democratic principles and values that will link these issues together in a consistent, comprehensive, equitable and flexible fashion.

As I understand the situation, there seem to be at least four conventional ways of attempting to resolve the current constitutional crisis. Each of these has several variations associated with it.

1. The government in power decides on its own what constitutional course to pursue. This could be done with or without debate in the House of Commons. Moreover, if there were a vote in the House, this could be according to party discipline or a free vote of conscience.

2. The government in power puts forth a constitutional package and seeks ratification either through provincial legislative assemblies or by means of a public referendum. If provincial legislatures are

involved, this might or might not involve one or more first Ministers conferences.

3. A constituent assembly is selected or appointed to draft a constitutional package. This package, then, would be subject to ratification through: (a) the House of Commons; and/or, (b) the provincial governments; and/or, (c) a public referendum.

4. The status quo is maintained although some minor, cosmetic tinkering would be undertaken in accordance with the existing amending formula.

Although all of the foregoing possibilities have their upsides and their down-sides, I don't propose to discuss them. Instead, I would like to outline a further possibility. One might refer to the suggestion that follows as: the Constitutional Challenge.

In essence, it would be an essay-like competition (20 pages or less) whose theme would be the construction of a Canadian constitution. Anyone, 17 years of age or older who was either a citizen, a landed immigrant or had refugee status, would be eligible for the competition.

Essays would be judged according to a variety of criteria. Among these criteria would be: originality, fruitfulness, clarity, completeness, fairness, feasibility, potential for resolving outstanding constitutional crises, fiscal responsibility, flexibility, capacity for growth, rigor, and simplicity.

The competition would have a deadline, and the jurors would have six months to evaluate the entries. Furthermore, there would be a $20.00 entry fee to help defray the expenses of running the competition.

The jury judging the competition would consist of 13 people. At least six of the jurors would have to be women. The 13th juror's sex would be determined by some random means.

One juror would be drawn from each of the ten provinces plus two territories. The thirteenth person would be drawn from the federal government.

In addition, a number of different political groups would have to be represented. These groups include: Conservatives, Liberals, NDP,

Social Credit, Reform, Christian Heritage, Parti Quebecois, Libertarian, Communist, Monarchist, Green Peace, Rhinoceros and Independent.

Furthermore, a number of different religious orientations would have to be included among jury members. Suggested possibilities are: Protestant, Catholic, Anglican, Jewish, Muslim, Hindu, Sikh, Buddhist, Native spiritual traditions, Zoroastrian, Taoist, Agnostic and Atheist.

The people appointed to the jury also should be drawn from a variety of different backgrounds. For example, one might select from among the following areas: business, labor, media, arts, law, medicine, science, humanities, technology, politics, religion, volunteer groups, police and retired people.

Finally, the jury members should be selected to ensure as much racial and ethnic equability as possible. Obviously, not all ethnic and racial groups might be capable of being accommodated on a 13-person jury, but every effort should be made to be as inclusive as possible.

In order to satisfy the foregoing criteria, each juror will have to fulfill multiple roles. For example, a selected juror could be a black female Catholic medical doctor from British Columbia who is a member of the Social Credit party.

The positions of juror would be selected on a random basis. Each time a juror was selected, a number of categories of personnel criteria would be eliminated so that subsequent juror choices would involve a narrower set of parameters that had to be satisfied.

The task of the jury would be to select four finalists from among the competition entries. These finalists would be judged according to the kind of criteria outlined earlier. Once the finalists had been selected, these entries would be forwarded to the House of Commons. The members of the House would debate the pros and cons of each of the candidates.

Eventually, after an agreed upon time limit for debate (set before the competition begins),' the House members would be given a series of free votes of conscience through which two candidates are to be selected from among the four finalists. The two finalists, then, would be subject to a public referendum. The winning entry would have to garner 51 % of the vote in the country.

There would be no provincial distribution requirements with respect to the vote since there would be an agreement by all provinces and the federal government to abide by the results of the competition. The fail-safe point for this agreement would be after the four finalists had been selected by the jury, but prior to the House of Commons debate and vote.

There are several guiding principles underlying the essay competition process outlined above. First of all, politicians and lawyers are not the only ones in Canada who are capable of constructing workable constitutional documents. In fact, there is considerable evidence to suggest that many politicians might be incapable of creating a workable, fair constitutional arrangement since they are too preoccupied with maintaining, or extending, their power base at the expense of, and to the exclusion of, the people.

In any event, there are a lot of talented, creative, intelligent, committed individuals in Canada. Politicians are doing Canada and Canadians a huge disservice if they do not call upon the plentiful human resources that exist in Canada to help resolve our constitutional crisis. The essay competition process provides a way of permitting this to happen in an equitable, representative, practical manner that invites, rather than discourages, the participation of Canadians.

For far too long, politicians have cajoled the sort of trust from Canadians that would enable the former to have virtually carte blanche authority to do whatever they pleased. Very rarely has this degree of trust ever been reciprocated by politicians with respect to the non-politicians of Canada.

In fact, even elections cannot be cited by politicians as an example of how politicians place deep trust in the wisdom of the people. Unfortunately, too many politicians tend to look at the election process as a calculated gamble rather than an exercise in trust.

The time has come for politicians to demonstrate a fundamental expression of trust in the people of this country. To paraphrase Prophet Moses (peace be upon him), I say to the politicians of Canada, let the Canadian people go. Give us an opportunity to resolve our own problems in our own way.

Secondly, the essay competition idea would offer women, Quebecers, Native peoples, minorities, Westerners, Maritimers and others who are deeply dissatisfied with the present Constitution an opportunity to come up with a package that addresses not only their own individual interests, but the interests and problems of Canada as a whole. While the essay competition process is certainly unconventional and non-traditional in style and substance, it offers a plausible and feasible methodology to afford many Canadians the sort of opportunity to participate in the constitutional process that very likely will be denied to them if any of the four conventional choices outlined previously become the method of choice for dealing with the present constitutional crisis.

Part 2: <u>A Constitutional Possibility</u>

The Purpose of Canada

Canada is a participatory democracy governed by principles. These principles involve a series of rights, procedural counterbalances, and duties of care that constitute protections and entitlements for, as well as responsibilities of, every resident of Canada.

The aforementioned principles set forth the conditions of social contract that give meaning and scope to the idea of a participatory democracy. These conditions underwrite the sovereignty of Canada as a nation of people who share a common perspective with respect to certain values and who continue to express a collective desire to live in accordance with the values inherent in that perspective.

Chief amongst these values is a commitment to constructively assist one another to develop educationally, economically, emotionally, politically, intellectually, physically and spiritually.

The intent underlying such constructive assistance is to support the development of every individual in Canada.

This assistance should be offered to such an extent that each person becomes capable of gaining substantial autonomy over one's life. In addition, the aforementioned assistance should lead the individual toward being able to constructively contribute to the enhancement of the quality of the various levels of sovereignty of Canada as a collection of peoples and communities.

The sovereignty of the people of Canada is vibrant and viable to the extent that principles of participatory democracy are firmly entrenched in, and rigorously pursued through, the institutional fabric of public life.

The power of government and the authority of law that give expression to that public life are derived from, and are to be critically evaluated in the light of, the principles of participatory democracy in which our sovereignty, both as individuals and as a nation, is rooted.

Consequently, the constraints and degrees of freedom that are established through the exercise of legal authority and government power are themselves circumscribed by the principles governing participatory democracy that are outlined in the ongoing constitutional process that constitutes the social contract of Canadians one with another.

A.The Social Contract

(1) No right is absolute. This means that rights are to be acknowledged within the context of a set of constraints and degrees of freedom. The structural character of the aforementioned set of rights and degrees of freedom will be shaped, colored and oriented by the dynamics of the social contract.

(2) The social contract is not a static, fixed document. It is an ongoing dialectic among individuals, communities and governments.

More specifically, the social contract is an agreed upon process that permits Canadians to pursue, protect and enhance their respective sovereignties. However, in order for such a process to be feasible, everyone who seeks to establish sovereignty must understand that inherent in the social contract process is a principle of reciprocity.

Effectively, reciprocity means that, in exchange for the degrees of freedom that are negotiated through the social contract process, each individual will be required to assume a variety of constraints on one's activities under certain circumstances.

(3) The constraints assumed by individuals, communities and governments are an expression of duties of care that are owed to others in order to allow the latter to pursue, protect and enhance their sovereignty.

(4) Social contracts are an attempt to negotiate a balance between rights and duties of care with respect to the issue of sovereignty. This balance is sought across a multiplicity of levels of scale, ranging from individuals to the nation as a whole.

B. Diversity of Equality

The measure of equality used in assessing the degree of reciprocity and balance present in social contract negotiations is not necessarily a matter of their having to be a sameness of treatment for everyone concerned. The people of Canada should be provided with a constitutional process that is capable of generating an array of alternatives from which to choose.

The set of alternatives generated by the social contract process might not be exhaustive. Moreover, these alternatives will not be capable of satisfying everyone's needs or desires.

Nonetheless, people should be given access to a sufficiently wide array of possibilities in relation to the seeking of sovereignty that the degree of freedom gained will be considered to be worth the constraints assumed in exchange for such freedoms, rights and entitlements.

Such diversity of possibility in the arranging of social contracts increases the likelihood that individuals, communities and governments will believe they have been treated with equality despite differences in those arrangements from individual to individual, community to community, and government to government.

(2) The principle of diversity of equality is capable of being given expression in a wide variety of areas, including: justice, education, religion, economics and politics. Indeed, almost any facet of the social contract is amenable to the principle of diversity of equality.

C. Rights and Duties of Care

In accordance with the principles and spirit of the framework outlined in A. and B. above, there are a series of rights and duties of care that provide primary themes for negotiated settlement within the social contract process that regulates the dynamics of life in Canada. In general, every individual has an entitlement to certain degrees of freedom with respect to:

(a) conscience, personal philosophy, political orientation and religious conviction;

(b) speech, peaceful demonstration, organizational activity, artistic expression, media communication, and acting on one's beliefs and values;

(c) assembly and association;

(d) travel, mobility and immigration;

(e) voting and running for elected office;

(f) seeking employment, attempting to establish a business, engaging in business transactions, and receiving a fair return for one's services;

(g) procuring a place of residence.

The precise nature of the degrees of freedom to be permitted in any given area is to be determined by negotiated settlement among individuals, communities and governments by means of the social contract process outlined in the Constitution of Canada.

While constraints can be placed on the degrees of freedom to which one is entitled under various circumstances, the rights listed under (1) above can never be extinguished, either temporarily or permanently. Furthermore, even when subject to constraints, the degrees of freedom permitted must provide some minimal level of entitlements through which sovereignty can be pursued, protected and enhanced in a substantial, non-marginalized manner.

(2) The foregoing areas, with respect to which individuals, communities and governments are entitled to certain degrees of freedom, also are subject to various duties of care. The constraints associated with these duties of care stipulate that one cannot establish one's own sovereignty while injuring the sovereignty of others due to discrimination, prejudice or bias concerning: sex, religion, political affiliation, economic/social status, age, ethnic background, racial characteristics, nation of origin, and physical or mental disability.

Individuals, organizations, institutions, communities and governments are entitled, under certain circumstances, to appeal to the principle of civil disobedience in order to pursue, protect or enhance their respective sovereignties;

(a) such an appeal is not permitted in any case involving: violence, physical injury, terrorism, property damage, fraud, extortion, theft and illicit drug or illicit sexual activity;

(b) one cannot appeal to the principle of civil disobedience in order to justify overriding the provisions of either C.(1) or C.(2) above;

(c) any action that does not fall under (3)(a) or (3)(b) above, but which involves the violation of municipal, regional, provincial or Federal statute, could be a candidate in relation to which an appeal to the principle of civil disobedience could be made;

(d) all appeals under the principle of civil disobedience are to be arbitrated by the Senate subcommittee on constitutional issues, in conjunction with the appropriate constitutional forum;

(e) if such an appeal is disallowed, the appellant must stand trial for violation of the statute(s) in question;

(f) while the services of the constitutional forums are free of financial charge, a negotiated charge of community service will be exacted from all appellants, win or lose. Payment of this negotiated charge cannot be delegated, nor can a financial arrangement be made in lieu of the service owed;

(g) failure to comply with the requirements of negotiated community service constitutes an act of contempt for the social contract process and is liable to criminal prosecution and/or the forfeiture of future access to the appeal process concerning the principle of civil disobedience;

(h) the arbitrated decisions of a given constitutional forum are considered to be final unless such judgments are revised during a review process by the Senate subcommittee on constitutional issues;

(i) if the arbitrated judgments of a given constitutional forum are revised in any way by the Senate subcommittee on constitutional issues, the matter must be brought before the full Senate for a discussion and vote;

(j) the House of Commons has the right to discuss and vote upon any constitutional issue that has been brought before, discussed by, and voted on by the full Senate body;

i) if the House of Commons chooses not to exercise that right, the decision of the full Senate body will stand;

ii) the vote of the House of Commons on such matters will be a free vote of conscience;

iii) if the House of Commons exercises its right, the electorate is entitled to a referendum on the matter;

iv) if the electorate chooses to exercise its right of referendum, it must choose among four possibilities: 1) the decision of the original constitutional forum; 2) the decision of the Senate subcommittee on constitutional issues; 3) the decision of the full Senate if different from 2); and the decision of the House of Commons if different from 1), 2) or 3). [This issue is explored further in section D.(12), (13) and (14).]

(4) The exercise of all rights, freedoms and entitlements must be done with a concomitant duty of care toward the effect such activity will have on the vitality, stability and preservation of the environment. Ecological issues are intimately connected to issues of sovereignty.

If the air, water, land, as well as the flora and fauna of Canada, are despoiled or economically exploited in an ecologically unsound manner, then, opportunities to pursue, preserve and enhance sovereignty, both individually and collectively, will be severely curtailed and undermined.

Consequently, every individual, organization, business, community and government must be prepared to accept constraints on the degrees of freedom associated with their exercise of rights, freedoms and entitlements with respect to the impact of the latter upon the environment.

(5) Education must be directed toward satisfying a variety of needs on a number of different levels of scale and in relation to a spectrum of social, political, economic, religious and philosophical issues.

More specifically, there must be a concerted effort within the processes of planning and implementing curriculum programs to co-ordinate and balance the needs of individuals, communities and the nation.

This process of educational coordinating and balancing must be capable of giving expression to both diversity of perspectives as well as themes of commonality and shared values.

In this sense, there should be a process of parallel initiation that allows individuals to be integrated with his or her own philosophical/ religious community, as well as to be integrated with the themes of commonality that hold the nation as a whole together.

As is the case with all other constitutional issues, education will reflect a dialectic between constraints and degrees of freedom, or between, on the one hand, rights and entitlements, and, on the other hand, duties of care and responsibilities.

<u>D. The Senate</u>

Each province and territory will elect four representatives to the National Senate:

(a) within every province or territory, one representative will be elected from each of the three parties that are currently most well established (in terms of numbers of constituents) in the given province or territory;

(b) a fourth representative will be drawn from non-traditional and/or independent sources outside of the three established parties within a given province or territory;

i) (b) will hold even in provinces where the total number of independents is low;

ii) this fourth representative will be an inducement to inviting a diversity of perspectives, as well as of participation, from those outside mainstream parties;

(c) every Senatorial representative will be free to vote according to his or her conscience and, therefore, will not be tied to party discipline unless the individual chooses to be.

(2) The term of office is for a period of six years.

(3) No one may serve more than two terms of office in the Senate.

(4) There will be six areas of Senate responsibility:

(a) government appointments on the federal level;

(b) environment;

(c) education;

(d) basic research and development in science and technology;

(e) budget (and, possibly, some additional financial watchdog duties);

(f) constitution.

(5) For each area of Senate responsibility, there will be a subcommittee which oversees that area of responsibility:

(a) each subcommittee will consist of a minimum of eight members;

(b) the elected members of the Senate will be assigned to a subcommittee by random lot;

(c) there can be no more than one representative from any given province or territory on any given subcommittee;

(d) there can be no more than two representatives from any given party or independent political affiliation per subcommittee;

(e) all votes within a given subcommittee will be decided by simple majority;

(f) in the event of a tie vote, one more vote may be taken after an agreed upon period of further discussion; if the second vote is tied, the matter automatically must be forwarded to the full Senate body for discussion and subsequent disposition;

(g) all members of a subcommittee must be present in order for votes to be considered valid; (h) exceptions to (g) must be voted upon by the full Senate;

(i) whatever provinces do not have representatives assigned to the Constitutional, Educational, Environmental and/or Basic Research subcommittees in a given tenure of office, will have one representative assigned, on a random basis, to these subcommittees in the next tenure of office.

(6) The votes of all subcommittees, with one exception, are subject to review by the full Senate body:

(a) the exception to the above concerns those votes of the subcommittee on constitutional issues who endorse and do not modify the arbitrated judgments of constitutional forums;

(b) the review process of the full Senate body can end in one of three possibilities:

i) endorsement of the subcommittee's decision;

ii) rejection of the subcommittee's decision;

iii) endorsement of the subcommittee's decisions with recommended modifications;

(c) if the subcommittee's decision is rejected, the matter cannot be brought before the full Senate again until a year has passed;

(d) if the subcommittee's decision is endorsed with recommendations, the matter is returned to the subcommittee for further deliberation in the light of the suggested changes;

(e) a subcommittee is not bound to accept the recommendations of the full Senate, but it does so at its own peril since the matter in question may be returned, at some point, to the full Senate for further discussion and vote;

(f) votes of the full Senate must be decided by a two-thirds majority in order to be considered valid;

(g) if a vote of the full Senate fails to produce a two-thirds majority result, the matter returns to the appropriate subcommittee for further deliberation;

(h) a quorum of the Senate will be considered to be seven-eighths of the full Senate body;

(i) all votes of the full Senate must be preceded by a debate or discussion;

i) the conditions governing such debates or discussions will be negotiated by the members of the Senate at the beginning of the body's tenure of office;

ii) the conditions governing debates are subject to a mid-term review process (i.e., after three years) in order to determine what, if any, adjustments are necessary to facilitate and improve the quality of Senate activity.

(7) The full Senate body must sit at least once every six months.

(8) Provincial counterparts to the Senate subcommittees on environment, education and basic research will be integrated with, and come under the control of, the relevant subcommittees.

(9) All subcommittees will be committed to, and concentrate primary emphasis on, the exercise of principles of participatory democracy and diversity of equality.

(a) principles of participatory democracy are designed to involve as many people as feasible from across all provinces, territories, regions, communities and municipalities, as well as from all strata of society;

(b) the principle of diversity of equality is designed to encourage the creation of alternative routes to, and choices concerning, the realization, protection and enhancement of sovereignty.

(10) The Senate appointments subcommittee must award half of all positions to women.

(11) The budget/finance subcommittee has the right to suggest additions, modifications and deletions concerning any budget proposal submitted by the House of Commons:

(a) upon completing its review process, the subcommittee will forward the budget to the full Senate body for consideration, discussion, debate and vote;

(b) subsequent to the vote of the full Senate body, the budget will be returned to the House of Commons for debate and voting;

(c) upon voting on the budget, the House of Commons will return the budget to the Senate subcommittee on budget/finances;

(d) no budget can be implemented until it has received the majority approval of both the Senate subcommittee as well as the full Senate;

(e) this subcommittee also has the responsibility of reviewing and, within certain limits, regulating the activities of federal financial bodies, such as the Bank of Canada.

(12) The Senate becomes the primary guardian of the Constitution:

(a) all constitutional issues are to be removed from the jurisdiction of the courts-in effect, this means that any judgment of the court which infringes on constitutional matters is, upon appeal, subject to review by the Senate subcommittee on constitutional issues or one of its designated constitutional forums;

i) court decisions on matter of substantive legal issues that do not infringe on constitutional principles are not open to review by the Senate subcommittee on constitutional issues;

ii) the question of infringement will be addressed, initially, by an appropriate constitutional forum only upon appeal by one of the parties of a legal dispute [see Section M -- Legal Rights, subsections (2) and (3)];

iii) i) above does not preclude the Senate subcommittee on constitutional issues from reviewing and disagreeing with the arbitrated judgment of a constitutional forum concerning the matter of infringement on constitutional issues by legal proceedings;

(b) proposed amendments to, or modifications in, the character of the written Constitution must be initiated through the Senate subcommittee on constitutional issues;

i) constitutional forums do not have the authority to modify or amend the written form of the Constitution;

ii.) the task of the forums is restricted to issues of interpretation and the arbitrated judgments arising out of this process of interpretation;

(c) one or more constitutional forums will be appointed for each province and territory according to need and demand;

(d) constitutional forums will have the authority to accept or reject applications for review of constitutional issues that are delivered to them by individuals, organizations, courts, communities, or governments;

(e) if a constitutional forum accepts an application for review of a case, it will render an arbitrated judgment within four months;

(f) each forum will consist of thirteen members:

i) forum members must be drawn from a diversity of disciplines and back-grounds, including: science, business, religion, psychology, sociology, economics, education, history, law, political science, environmental science and the media:

ii) half of all forum appointments will be women;

iii) the length of term will be for three years;

iv)no one may serve more than two terms;

v) appointments to the constitutional forum will be made by the Senate subcommittee for appointments;

vi) constitutional forums will operate under the authority of the Senate subcommittee on constitutional issues;

vii) no one party, political group, philosophy or religion may dominate a given constitutional forum.

(g) the arbitrated judgments of the constitutional forums are subject to review by the Senate subcommittee on constitutional issues;

(h) sections C.(3)(f) through (j) hold for all constitutional forums;

(i) when the arbitrated judgments of constitutional forums, as well as the correlative votes of the Senate subcommittee, the full Senate, the House of Commons, and referenda, have assumed their final form according to the requirements of the Constitution, these judgments are to be treated as reference points that are to anchor, shape, color and orient subsequent judgments and votes on constitutional issues during the tenure of office of the Senate body;

i) the term "final form" in the above section means those votes that become binding upon the people of Canada;

ii) votes concerning constitutional amendments or constitutional interpretations that take place prior to the last step permitted by the Constitution are not considered to have assumed their final form;

(j) subsequent tenures of office of the Senate body, together with votes of the House of Commons or referenda that occur after the tenure of office of a given Senate body, may be influenced by previous constitutional judgments and votes, but they need not be bound by those judgments and votes;

(k) unless a successful appeal is achieved with respect to constitutional judgments made during previous tenures of the Senate, the constitutional judgments established during the previous Senate tenures of office will remain in effect.

(13) The votes of the constitutional forums, the Senate subcommittee on constitutional issues, the full Senate, the House of Commons, and referenda are all subject to challenge by means of an appeal to the principle of civil disobedience.

(14) In constitutional cases involving disputes between, or among, different levels of government, a special intergovernmental constitutional forum will be convened in order to arrive at an arbitrated judgment with respect to that dispute:

(a) the thirteen members of the intergovernmental constitutional forum will be selected so that each of the provinces and territories will be represented in this forum.

E. The House of Commons

(1) Terms of office will be for four years:

(a) no one may serve more than three terms as a member of the House;

(b) a person who is elected Prime Minister at the beginning of the third term may serve one additional term of office if re-elected as Prime Minister;

(c) elections will be held every four years on a set date;

(d) a government can no longer fall as a result of a non-confidence vote on financial matters in the House of Commons;

(e) no one may serve as Prime Minister for more than two terms.

(2) All elected members of the House will be permitted two free votes of conscience during each sitting of the House. These free votes can be used, or not, at the discretion of the individual members;

(a) any vote concerning a constitutional issue shall not count as one of the allotted two free votes of conscience.

(3) The distribution of powers between the federal government and other levels of government is to be negotiated on a case-by-case basis;

(a) this negotiation will take place during the first three months of the tenure of office of the Federal government;

i) if a new provincial government should be elected after the aforementioned period of negotiation, that government must wait for the next round of negotiations at the beginning of tenure of a newly elected federal government;

ii) the only other avenue for provinces to seek a new power sharing arrangement would be through the medium of constitutional forums or by appeal to the principle of civil disobedience;

(b) the aforementioned negotiations cannot infringe upon any of the areas of responsibility of the Senate;

(c) the negotiations can be asymmetrical in nature. In other words, different arrangements can be made with different provinces, depending on the needs, capabilities, priorities and circumstances of the federal government and the provinces;

(d) the negotiations can involve no more than three areas that are normally under the authority of the federal and provincial governments;

i) the Province of Quebec is one of two exceptions to the provisions of (3)(d). More latitude and flexibility must be given to the negotiations concerning the transfer of powers between Quebec and the federal government. Consequently, up to seven areas of authority may be considered for negotiation;

ii) the Native peoples' provinces are the other exception to the provisions of (3)(d). As is the case with Quebec, up to seven areas of authority, normally under Federal jurisdiction, may be subject to a process of negotiated transfer to provincial jurisdictions;

iii) even in the case of Quebec and the Native peoples' provinces, the structural character of the negotiated arrangement will not be permanent. It will be reassessed at the start of each four-year-tenure of a newly elected federal government. If necessary, adjustments will be made at that time that will be of advantage to both the province and the federal government;

iv) in the case of a breakdown in negotiations, the special intergovernmental constitutional forum will make an arbitrated judgment.

(4) The members of the House must sit at least once in every six-month period.

F. Declarations of War

(1) In cases where the geographical regions of Canada are under direct physical attack, the Prime Minister may take such steps as are necessary to defend the nation;

(a) the decisions made by the Prime Minister cannot undermine, suspend or arbitrarily curtail the rights and entitlements outlined in C.(1) through (3);

(b) any decisions that affect the rights and entitlements of sections C.(I) through (3) must be debated and discussed before a joint session of the Senate and the House of Commons;

i) such a debate/discussion will be followed by a vote of the joint session;

ii) any decision must be supported by a four-fifths majority vote;

iii) the vote will be a free vote of conscience;

iv) this free vote would not count as one of the two free votes allotted to members of the House of Commons;

v) in order for such a vote to be considered valid, a quorum must be present at the time of the vote. A quorum will be considered to be 80% of the members of both the Senate and the House of Commons.

(2) In those cases in which the geographical regions of Canada are not under direct physical attack, any decisions concerning the responsibilities of war-related activities in other parts of the world will be based on a discussion and vote in a joint session of the Senate and the House of Commons. Conditions set forth in sections (b) ii) through (b) v) above will apply in the present case.

(3) If the joint session votes in favor of going to war in another part of the world, the electorate has a right to a referendum on the matter.

(4) If a referendum is held, the electorate will be given the choice between:

(a) offensive actions (carrying the war to an opponent in a way designed to lead to the opponent's defeat);

(b) defensive actions (defending Canadian service personnel and equipment if attacked but not initiating any offensive actions);

(c) peace-keeping operations only;

(d) if a referendum is not held, then, the decision of the joint session will be considered authoritative.

G. Election Reform

(1) Campaign contributions, whether in the form of money, goods or equipment, may not be directed toward individual candidates or parties.

(2) Campaign contributions must be given to a general campaign fund from which:

(a) all candidates may draw in equal shares for non-promotional expenses;

(b) money may be drawn to finance debates or campaign literature in which all candidates are given equal time.

(3) During the election campaign, neither parties nor individuals may engage in mass promotional activities on their own;

(a) mass promotional activities encompass the use of any media -- whether written, spoken or visual -- that is designed to reach a substantial proportion of the electorate within a very short period of time;

(b) all mass promotional activities must be done in concert with other candidates for the same office.

(4) The restrictions on mass promotional activities are not intended to interfere with one-on-one or small group (30 people or less) discussions concerning the campaign;

(5) No one may receive money for advising candidates or providing candidates with consultation services concerning any aspect of a campaign.

(6) All campaign help must be of a volunteer nature.

(7) Candidates may not engage in negative campaigning;

(a) negative campaigning is defined as attacks on another candidate's integrity, character, religion, race, sex, ethnic background, family life or past history;

(b) all criticisms of a candidate must focus on the candidate's political/philosophical position within the context of the issues of the campaign;

i) these criticisms must be carried out in a way that provides the candidate being criticized with an opportunity to respond to the criticisms;

ii) usually, such criticisms must be restricted to public debates, forums, and campaign literature in which all candidates may participate and to which they may contribute.

(8) The mass media must provide time and/or space of equal worth and prominence to all candidates.

(9) Incumbent candidates cannot use their easy access to the media and the public as a means of promoting their own campaign or the campaigns of others. Their campaigning activities must be done in conjunction with other candidates.

(10) There will be no nomination fees required in order to be able to file for seeking office.

(11) To be considered a candidate, a person must either, in the case of traditional parties, win a party's nomination, or, in the case of independent groups, acquire the signatures of 10% of a riding's eligible voters.

(a) there is a distinction to be drawn between eligible and registered voters;

(b) registered voters are those people who have satisfied the conditions necessary to entitle them to vote in a given riding;

(c) eligible voters are those people who satisfy all criteria for being a registered voter in a given riding except that of going through the registration process;

(d) petition initiatives directed toward gaining official recognition as a candidate are subject to verification by an independent party;

(e) the verification process mentioned in (d) above will be done under the supervision of representatives of the Senate subcommittee on appointments.

H. Recall Procedure

(1) Once elected, any official is subject to recall by the electorate;

(a) recall procedures cannot be initiated until one year of an official's tenure of office has passed;

(b) once initiated, recall may assume two forms:

i) a vote is taken by a given constituency that requires an elected official to return immediately to his or her constituency and respond to their questions, criticisms and concerns;

ii) elected officials also are subject to a referendum on recall that could remove the officials from office;

(c) if a move to recall fails to gather enough support, then, further recall action cannot be taken for another year unless substantial evidence of malfeasance of office can be demonstrated during the interim period;

(d) if a move to undertake the first kind of recall outlined above in (b) is successful, the official remains susceptible to further recall action at any time after a period of two months. As such, the official is on probation during the two-month interim period, as well as during the time following that two-month period;

(e) in order for a recall action to be considered warranted, it must be supported by 60% of the electorate of a given constituency This is determined by means of a poll;

(f) in order for a recall vote to be considered valid, 80% of the eligible voters in a given constituency must vote;

i) in addition, two-thirds of the voters who do cast a ballot must be in favor of a recall of either the first or second form [see (b) i) and (b) ii) above] in order for the vote to be considered acceptable and have authority;

ii) voters will have a choice between recalling officials either for the purposes of discussion or for the purpose of removal from office;

iii) if the total number of people voting for removal from office does not achieve the necessary level of majority, but the total number of people voting for one or the other kind of recall does achieve, when taken together, the necessary level of majority, the official will be recalled to be confronted by his or her constituents.

I. Referendum

(1) The electorate is entitled to the referendum process under three circumstances:

(a) decisions of the joint session of the Senate and House of Commons concerning war-related activities;

(b) decisions of the House of Commons concerning Senate and constitutional forum judgments with respect to constitutional issues;

(c) decisions dealing with the question of whether or not a given elected official should be recalled.

(2) Condition outlined in section H.(1)(e) is also applicable to referenda.

(3) Once a referendum has been called for, it must be completed within two months of its time of initiation.

(4) In order for a referendum vote to be considered valid, 80% of the eligible voters in the constituency must vote;

(a) In addition, two-thirds of the voters who do cast a ballot must be for one of the choices in order for the referendum to be considered valid;

i) in the case of recall votes, condition H.(1)(f)iii) holds;

ii) in the case of votes in constitutional issues, if no one choice receives a clear two-thirds majority vote, then, the matter reverts to the full Senate body for further discussion and vote;

iii) this discussion and the subsequent constitutional motion that is to be voted on must reflect, to some substantial degree, the voting pattern expressed in the referendum;

iv) this post-referendum vote of the full Senate body will be considered authoritative.

J. The Use of Polls

(1) Polling techniques are to be used in conjunction with both recall procedures and referendum initiatives.

(2) Such techniques and methods are to be used to determine if there are enough people in a given constituency or the electorate as a whole who favor the taking of a formal vote.

(3) The polling process is to be conducted, as a community service, by universities and/or community colleges.

(4) In order for the results of any given polling process to be accepted as valid, the results must be independently confirmed by two other polls that are run simultaneously.

(5) The assignment of the three polling processes will be done by the Senate subcommittee on government appointments.

(6) The Senate subcommittee on constitutional issues will have the

responsibility of initiating, supervising, verifying and making public the results of the polling process.

K. Native and Aboriginal Peoples

(1) The Indian Act and the Ministry of Native Affairs must be dismantled.

(2) There will be two (possibly three) new provinces created out of portions of: the Yukon, the Northwest Territories and certain areas of the northern portions of a number of provinces extending from British Columbia to Ontario.

(3) Native and aboriginal peoples will retain majority control of their provincial governments under all circumstances.

(4) (3) above does not preclude non-Native minorities from seeking and acquiring public office.

(5) All provisions of a reconstituted Senate will apply to the newly created Native peoples' provinces, subject to the following qualifications:

(a) half of all elected Senators from the Native provinces must be drawn from the Native and aboriginal peoples of those provinces;

(b) half of all elected Senators from the Native provinces must be drawn from the non-Native population of those provinces;

(c) half, plus one, of all constitutional forums in Native provinces must consist of Native and aboriginal peoples.

(6) The Native peoples' provinces will be entitled to send elected representatives to both the National Senate as well as the House of Commons;

(a) half of the elected Senators from the Native peoples' provinces will be non-Natives. This is necessary in order to ensure that the Senate as a whole, as well as individual subcommittees, are not inordinately weighted in favor of Native peoples;

(b) half of the elected Senators must be from the Native and aboriginal peoples. This is to ensure that, should the demographic character of these provinces change so that Native peoples become a minority, their interests, needs and concerns will be protected through a continued presence of Native and aboriginal peoples.

(7) As is the case with Quebec, the provinces of the Native peoples will have, relative to other provinces, an asymmetrical relation with the Federal government. This relationship will encompass a greater degree of flexibility in the number of areas, normally under Federal jurisdiction, which can be subject to a negotiated transfer of powers to the provinces at the beginning of the term of office of the Federal government.

(8) Native and aboriginal peoples will retain control of sacred burial grounds outside of the proposed new provinces.

L. Amending the Consitution

(1) A distinction must be drawn between: (a) the written structural character of the Constitution; and, (b) interpreting the set of degrees of freedom and constraints that give expression to the character of the written Constitution.

(2) Amending the Constitution refers to any addition to, or modification of, the written character of the Constitution.

(3) The amending process can be initiated only by the Senate Subcommittee on Constitutional Issues.

(4) Proposals for amending the Constitution will be put before the full Senate body;

(a) the proposal must be discussed and debated before being voted upon;

(b) a voting quorum is defined according to section D.(6)(g);

(c) changing the written character of the Constitution requires a two-thirds majority vote;

(d) if the proposed changes are rejected, the style of the rejection may take two forms:

i) with recommendations for further changes in the wording of the proposal;

ii) with no recommendation for further changes;

iii) in the case of ii) above, the rejection shall be considered absolute and the proposal in question cannot be reintroduced into the full Senate body for at least one year;

iv) in the case of i) above, the proposal can be rewritten in light of the recommendations and, at the discretion of the subcommittee, can be subsequently reintroduced into the full Senate body for discussion and a vote;

(e) if the necessary two-thirds majority vote is achieved in a quorum vote of the full Senate, the House of Commons has a right to take the matter under advisement.

(5) When a proposed constitutional change is taken under advisement, the House of Commons can accept or reject that proposal;

(a) all votes must be preceded by discussion and debate;

(b) a quorum is defined according to section D.(6)(g);

(c) acceptance of the Senate vote requires a two-thirds majority vote of the House of Commons; anything less than this will constitute a rejection of the proposed amendment;

(d) the members of the House shall be entitled to a free vote of conscience on such issues;

(e) this free vote shall not count as one of the two free votes of conscience per sitting allocated to House members.

(6) Following the vote of the House of Commons, the electorate is entitled to a referendum on the proposed amendment;

(a) the electorate will have three choices:

i) to endorse the proposed change that has been passed by the required majorities of both the full Senate as well as the House of Commons;

ii) to reject the proposed change that has been passed by the required majorities of both bodies of Parliament;

iii) to choose between the votes of the Senate and the House, when the former has passed the amendment and the latter has rejected the amendment;

(b) 80% of the eligible voters must participate in the vote in order for the vote to be considered valid;

(c) two-thirds of voters must indicate endorsement in order for the proposed amendment to be considered to have been accepted;

i) this two-thirds vote must occur in at least eight of the ten provinces and two territories;

ii) one of these eight provinces must be either Ontario or Quebec;

(d) if an endorsement vote greater than 50% does not achieve the necessary two-thirds majority, the amendment is considered to be rejected;

(e) if 80% of the eligible voters do not participate in the referendum, the amendment is considered to be rejected.

(7) A proposed amendment change that has been rejected by referendum cannot be introduced again for consideration during the tenure of office of the current Senate body.

M. Legal Rights

(1) The protections afforded individuals in the *Constitution Act of 1982* concerning legal rights are endorsed herein, but with the following qualifications:

(a) principles of fundamental justice may vary from community to community and people to people;

(b) a people or community has the right to negotiate with the provincial and/or Federal government in order to establish systems of law that reflect, and give expression to, that people's or community's principles of fundamental justice;

i) these systems of law must be administered among only those who are willing participants in such a system:

a) willingness of participation will be indicated through an officially sanctioned registry process;

b) once registered, the individual's willing participation is considered to be in effect until such time as an official application has been filed and approved that revokes one's willing participation;

c) revoking of one's registration in a given system of law will not negate whatever agreements, understandings, contracts, undertakings or obligations were entered into while registered as a willing participant in a given system of law;

d) revoking of registration means that an individual reverts to the jurisdiction of the system of law governing the majority of Canadians;

e) children under the age of majority will be subject to such a system of law only if both parents or the guardian(s) of the children is(are) willing participants in that system;

f) upon reaching the age of majority, a person has the right to register or not register in a given system of law to which one had been bound previously through one's parents or guardian(s);

ii) nothing in these negotiated systems of law may contravene the rights, entitlements, duties of care or principles of the Canadian Constitution;

iii) in order to be established, some substantial proportion of a given people or community must request such a system of law;

a) what constitutes a "substantial proportion" will vary from case to case;

b) in the case of Native peoples and other minorities, this proportion may vary anywhere from: less than 500,000, but more than 20,000 or 30,000 people;

iv) these systems of law need not be all-inclusive bodies of jurisprudence; they may encompass only certain aspects of legal issues;

v) all proceedings of such legal proceedings are subject to review by independent observers in order to ensure that the process is consistent with the provisions of the Canadian Constitution;

vi) as long as the proceedings of these systems of law take place in accordance with the provisions of the Canadian Constitution, they will be considered valid and enforceable;

vii) any appeals to constitutional forums concerning the judgments of the tribunals governing such systems of law may only concern questions of procedural integrity, provided that the provisions of section M, items (1)(b) i), (1)(b) v) and (1)(b) vi), have been observed and maintained;

viii) appeals concerning procedural integrity will be made to an appropriate constitutional forum;

ix) constitutional forums either will verify the procedural integrity of the given tribunal's judgment determination process, or they will uncover evidence of procedural irregularities that warrants a new hearing by a different tribunal within the community in question.

(2) All appellate courts, including the Supreme Court of Canada, are restricted to reviewing only issues involving principles of substantive law (i.e., legal matters that do not contravene or raise constitutional issues);

(a) substantive legal issues encompass events that transpire within a court room, judges' chambers, or the like, during a trial or hearing;

(b) substantive legal issues give legitimate, permissible expression to the constraints and degrees of freedom of constitutional provisions;

(c) the Supreme Court of Canada will have final jurisdiction in all matters of substantive law that do not infringe (i.e., contravene or violate) constitutional principles, values and provisions.

(3) All questions of constitutional rights or constitutional duties of care that arise prior to, or during, a trial/hearing must be referred, upon appeal, to the appropriate constitutional forum;

(a) if a constitutional appeal brings into question the constitutional appropriateness of proceeding to trial in a given case due to, for example, a possible violation of basic legal rights guaranteed under the Constitution, then, the constitutional issue must be settled first;

i) constitutional forums have the authority, upon successful appeal, to stay all legal proceedings, or any portions thereof, that are found to be in contravention of the provisions of the Constitution;

ii) if, subsequent to an appeal, a constitutional forum finds that no provisions of the Constitution would be contravened in a proposed legal proceeding, the trial/hearing may take place;

(b) if a constitutional appeal is made concerning issues that arise while a trial/ hearing is in progress, the legal proceedings normally will be permitted to reach their conclusion;

i) exceptions to (b) above would occur when the constitutional issues raised upon appeal are so substantial that considerable legal/court time, resources, and money could be lost if the appeal were successful, and yet the trial hearing had been allowed to continue;

ii) constitutional issues that are raised through appeal during a trial/

hearing must be settled before the sentencing in a criminal case or the execution of judgment in a civil case can take place;

iii) if a constitutional appeal, initiated while a trial/hearing is in progress, is successful, then, the courts are obligated to reflect the character of the arbitrated judgment of the constitutional forum in their legal deliberations, proceedings and/or judgments;

iv)the findings of constitutional forums with respect to the constitutionality of legal proceedings are considered final unless altered by the Senate subcommittee during its review process of the arbitrated judgments of constitutional forums;

(c) constitutional appeals maybe made in conjunction with a trial/hearing that has been completed; i) successful appeals could lead to a new trial;

ii) if a constitutional appeal is not successful, then, subject to the determination of appellate courts concerning substantive legal issues, the findings/ judgments of the courts will be final;

iii (c) above will not apply to court cases completed prior to 1991;

(d) constitutional appeals concerning legal proceedings may be made only by the parties involved in those legal proceedings.

<u>Suggested Further Readings</u>

Asch, Michael. *Home and Native Land-Aboriginal Rights and the Canadian Constitution*. Toronto: Nelson, 1984.

Banting, Keith and Simeon, Richard (editors). *And No One Cheered: Federalism, Democracy and the Constitution Act*. Toronto: Methuen, 1983.

Borovoy, A. Alan. *When Freedoms Collide: The Case for Our Civil Liberties* (2nd edition). Toronto: Lester & Orpen Dennys, 1988.

Dworkin, Ronald. *A Matter of Principle*. Cambridge: Harvard University Press, 1985.

Ely, John Hart. *Democracy and Distrust*. Cambridge: Harvard University Press, 1980.

Hart, H.L.A. *The Concept of Law*. Oxford: Oxford University Press, 1961.

Rawls, John. *A Theory of Justice.* Cambridge: Harvard University Press, 1971.

Russell, Peter H. *Leading Constitutional Decisions* (3rd edition). Ottawa: Carleton University Press, 1984.

Zuber, T.G. *Report of the Ontario Courts Inquiry*. Toronto: Ontario Ministry of the Ontario General, 1987.

Chapter 2: <u>Leadership – Part 1</u>

The following essay is a critical response to: "New Insights about Leadership," an article that can be found in the *Scientific American*'s magazine: <u>Mind</u>. That piece is authored by: Stephen D. Reicher, S. Alexander Haslam and Michael J. Platow.

Traditional theories of leadership center on issues such as charisma, intelligence, and other personality traits. According to such theories, 'leaders' utilize the inborn qualities that are believed to be at the heart of leadership – whatever one's theory of leadership might be -- in order to apply that quality of 'leadership' to an audience in order to induce the members of target-audience to pursue whatever behavior, ideas, or policies are desired by the leader .

The induction process occurs when a 'leader' instills the individual members of the target audience with a sense of: will power, dedication, motivation, and/or emotional orientation that the members of a given set of people would not have – according to the leader -- in the absence of such assistance. The justification for pursuing such an induction process is to: (a) help a given set of people to accomplish more than it would have without assistance from a leader; and/or (b) to assist a given set of people to realize what is believed to be in the best interests of those people.

Whether, or not, that which is to be accomplished by such a set of people is good thing is another matter. Similarly, whether, or not, that which is to be realized through the assistance of such a leader is truly in the best interests of the people being 'assisted' in such circumstances gives rise to another set of issues and questions other than that of the idea of leadership considered in and of itself.

New theories of leadership postulate that the 'leader' is someone who works to come to understand the beliefs, ideas, values, and interests of the followers in order to lay the groundwork for an effective dialogue through which one will be able to identify how the group should act.

The foregoing idea reminds me of the Communist dictum – 'From each according to his ability, to each according to his need.' I once asked a person who spouted the foregoing maxim about the problem of who would be the one to determine 'ability' or 'need', and in accordance with what criteria would such determinations be made ... and we might just note in passing that the maxim is not gender neutral. The individual to whom my query was directed was unable to answer my question although he was reported to be quite knowledgeable about communism.

Just as questions can be asked about the identity of the members of a classless society who are supposed to give us 'objective' answers to the nature of 'ability' and 'need', so too, one might raise questions about the character of the dialogical means through which one will arrive at solutions to the question of what are to be the ways in which a given group should act. For example, who will be the one to determine what the beliefs, values, and interests of the 'followers' are or should be? What methods will be used? What theories will shape such considerations? How does one know that what the masses believe and value ought to be what is pursued en masse? How does one establish a dialogue between the one and the many, especially when the many are not likely to all believe the same things or value the same things? If the masses already have beliefs and values, then what need is there for leaders to identify those ideas and values in order to get people to act in certain ways? Aren't the people already acting on such beliefs and values independently of 'leaders', and if they are not, then doesn't this suggest that the beliefs and values that might actually be governing behavior are other than what was being professed? And, if so, in which direction should the leaders seek to influence the followers, and what justifies any of this?

The idea of having a real dialog between the one (the leader) and the many strikes me as odd. If a leader has the power or ability to determine which parts of the dialog will be enacted or dismissed, then I am not really sure that we are talking about the notion of dialog in, say, Martin Buber's sense of an 'I-thou' relationship in which the two facets of the dialog both enjoy an equal set of rights (with concomitant duties to respect the rights of the other) and are co-participants in the sacredness of life -- however one wishes to characterize such sacredness (that is, in spiritual terms or in humanistic terms).

It is possible to have leaderless groups who engage in a multi-log in order to reach a consensus about how to proceed in any given matter. Within this sort of leaderless group, there might be "elders" who have earned the respect of the other members of the group because of the insight, skills, intelligence, talents, and/or abilities of those "elders', but the function of these elders is not to direct a discussion toward some predetermined goal, purpose, or outcome, but, rather, their function is the same as everyone else's function within the set of people engaging one another – namely, to enrich the discussion and, thereby, try to ensure that all aspects of a question, problem, or issue have been explored with due diligence.

Many indigenous peoples often operated through such leaderless groups. Westernized people – who tend to insist that any collective or group of people must have a leader or head person – frequently mischaracterized the elders of some indigenous peoples as being leaders in a Western sense and, therefore, as individuals who had characteristics and functions comparable to the leaders in non-indigenous groups or societies when this was not always so.

In such leaderless groups, the set of people as a whole decide actions through consensus. In other words, through an extended multi-log (which might take place in one setting or over a period of time) every member of the group either comes to see the wisdom of collectively moving in a certain way – a way to which all of the members of the group have contributed in and helped shape -- or the group as a whole does not reach a consensus and everyone has the right, without prejudice, to refrain from participating in any collective action that some lesser portion of the whole might take.

A central principle in some modern theories of leadership is, supposedly, to have leaders try to influence followers to do what the latter individuals really want to do rather than trying to impose things on the followers through the application of various forms of carrot-and-stick stratagems. However, one might raise the following question concerning such an alleged central principle: If someone really wants to do something, then why aren't they doing it? What is holding them back? Is that which is restraining them something that is constructive or destructive? Is that which the 'followers' allegedly really want to do something that is constructive or destructive? What are the criteria, methods, and processes of evaluation that are to be used in sorting this all out?

According to some the new theories of leadership, a leader needs to position himself or herself among the people to get the latter to believe that the leader is one of them. If, or when, a "leader" is able to become positioned in such a manner, the belief in such theories is that this will help the leader to gain credibility among the people. That credibility can be used to leverage group behavior.

However, it is an oxymoron to say that a leader is one of the people. After all, there is a reason why two different terms are being used to refer to the two sides of the equation.

The leader is not one of the people, but, rather, is just someone who is trying to induce people to believe that she or he is one of them. If the leader were truly one of the people, then that person would not be in a position to determine what course of action is to be pursued by the set of people being led.

Situations in which sincere multi-logs occur do not have leaders or followers. There are only participants, all of whom are equal with respect to rights and duties concerning such rights\ -- although there might be one, or more, elders within the set of people engaging one another whose ideas might be valued without making the following of such ideas obligatory or mandatory with respect to other participants. The contributions of such elders are valued without necessarily being determinate in relation to the outcome of any given discussion.

Let's return to the perspective of some of the newer theories of leadership in which one of the tasks of a would-be leader is become positioned so as to be viewed as one of the people so that credibility can be established in order to leverage the group in one direction rather than another. How does one know that the values and beliefs of a leader are really the same as those of the followers? What are the criteria, methods, and process of evaluation that are to be used in determining that the ideas and values of a leader and the 'followers' are coextensive?

Isn't it possible that a leader might profess to being committed to certain kinds of beliefs and values in order to garner the support from the people that will generate an apparent mandate to permit the so-called leader to do whatever he or she wishes and, then attempt to argue that whatever such leaders do is an expression of what the people really want? More importantly, how could any given leader credibly claim that she or he shares the same beliefs and values as the followers when every group tends to be highly disparate in many ways when it comes to such beliefs and values?

Not all Blacks think in the same manner, or feel about issues in the same way, or share the same values. This feature of diversity also is true of Catholics, Protestants, Jews, Muslims, Democrats, Republicans, Socialists or any other group or collective one cares to mention.

At any given instance, a leader's values and beliefs might coincide with some of the beliefs and values of the 'followers", but the two sides will never be coextensive. This is why politicians often tend to speak to various groups in different ways in order to induce the latter individuals to believe that the 'leader' is one of them, and, then when the election is won, the leader can't possibly act in ways or advocate values with which everyone who 'followed' that person (by voting for them) might agree.

From the perspective of the most recent theories of leadership, being a leader is not a matter of possessing certain kinds of personality characteristics. Instead, being a leader is a matter of learning the art of how to be a chameleon and, thereby, seem to blend in with any given crowd. The fact of the matter is that a leader could even appear to act in ways that reflect the likes of the followers without any need to actually be the sort of individual that is being projected to the crowd.

Naturally, when, as a result of keeping track of the actual behavior of leaders, people begin to see that there is a distinct difference between, on the one hand, what they -- the general membership -- tend to believe or value and, on the other hand, what the leaders believe and value, then conflicts and tensions tend to proliferate. This is where press secretaries and the other spin-masters enter stage right in order to smooth over such differences and, perhaps, to even re-frame such differences as supposedly being what the people actually needed and wanted.

Drawing a distinction between a collective and a group, at this point, might be of some assistance. A collective is an aggregate of people that is operating within a diffuse or defined framework, and this aggregate of people might not all be operating within such a framework willingly or they might be 'participating' in ways that generate friction, tension, or conflict within the collective as a reflection of such a dimension of unwillingness.

A group, on the other hand, is a segment of a collective that has come together willingly to serve or achieve a particular purpose or set of purposes. Oftentimes, although not necessarily, groups operate through consensus – that is, requiring unanimous agreement for action to take place – and when consensus is present, the group is a said to be coherent or unified in its purposes.

Because of the logistical problems surrounding the process of reaching a consensus, most groups tend to be small. However, the meaning of 'small' might vary with the character of conditions prevailing at a given point in time.

Groups, unlike collectives, often tend to be sensitive to temporal conditions. In other words, groups tend to come together for only a limited time and for limited purposes. When the time and/or the purpose(s) characterizing such a group expire, then, oftentimes, the group might expire as well. As such, groups tend to arise out of, and dissolve back into, a backdrop of collective dynamics involving various historical, social, economic, spiritual, ecological, psychological, philosophical, technical, scientific, legal, and political forces.

To the extent that a set of people is not unified, then that group is not coherent. Incoherent groups tend to be given to friction, conflict, tension, altercation, fragmentation, and dissolution.

Whether a set of people is considered to be a collective or an incoherent group might depend, in part, on the degree to which people are willing or unwilling participants in what is transpiring. Moreover, whether a set of people is considered to be a collective or an incoherent group might also depend on the extent to which such individuals have been induced to cede their moral and intellectual authority to other individuals within the set of people being considered (and there will be more on this issue of ceding moral and intellectual authority shortly).

Coherent groups usually do not need leaders ... although there might be elders within the group whose ideas, values, and talents might be respected and utilized without making such a person a leader. Providing constructive contributions to a group that helps enable a set of people to achieve their goals and purposes is not the same thing as being a leader.

Different circumstances, projects, problems, and so on might come to feature the expertise, wisdom, or abilities of different people within a social setting. It is the quality of contributions that are recognized by other members of the group that come to identify someone as an 'elder', and as various people within a set of people contribute across time, the identity of the elders who play influential roles in any given set of circumstances might change.

Some elders might have the capacity to identify talent and abilities in other people within a group. By advancing the names of other people so that the potential of these individuals can be drawn out to serve the purposes and goals of a group, the 'human resource elder' is not being a leader but is, instead, simply making constructive contributions in accordance with her or his abilities in order to help further a group's purposes.

The wisdom exhibited by any given group often is a direct function of the diversity inherent in that group. However, diversity, in and of itself, is not enough to generate wisdom with respect to any action that a group might take, and, therefore, one also must take into consideration the quality of the diversity that is present in any given set of circumstances.

Not all collectives constitute groups … even incoherent ones. A nation tends to be a collective that consists of a variety of coherent and incoherent groups, as well as any number of non-aligned individuals. A government tends to be a collective that consists of a variety of coherent and incoherent groups, along with any number of non-aligned individuals. A schooling system tends to consist of a variety of coherent and incoherent groups, together with any number of non-aligned individuals. An economy is a collective that consists of an array of coherent and incoherent groups, as well as any number of non-aligned individuals. Many corporations – especially publically traded entities – tend to consist of a variety of coherent and incoherent corporations, along with any number of non-aligned individuals, and, in addition, the bigger a company is, the more likely it is to be a collective rather than a group.

In addition, one should draw a distinction between, on the one hand, a goal or purpose, and, on the other hand, an agenda. A goal or purpose is self-contained and does not extend beyond the essential character of the goal or purpose being pursued, whereas, an agenda is a process that seeks to usurp the goals and purposes of another to serve some end that is independent of such a goal or purpose.

For example, seeking to feed the hungry is a goal or purpose. Using the former activity – that is, feeding the hungry -- to help bring a person to power constitutes an agenda.

Specific goals and purposes are what they are. They are not intended to extend beyond the character of a given purpose or goal – although, on occasion, the pursuing of one goal or purpose might have ramifications for other aspects of a social setting that were not originally intended when such a goal or purpose was originally envisioned.

Agendas, on the other hand, usually extend beyond the context of some given purpose or goal. Furthermore, agendas tend to involve techniques and strategies of undue influence that are intended to illicitly persuade – and, thereby, exploit -- someone with respect to the issue of ceding away an individual's moral and intellectual authority to another human being. As such, agendas are used to re-frame social settings to induce people into believing that they are striving for one thing when, in reality, those people are being manipulated into serving some other purpose or set of purposes. The more narrowly defined purpose is the 'Trojan Horse' through which a hidden agenda gains access to people's original intentions and destroys those people in the process.

The intellectual aspect of one's essential, existential authority gives expression to one's capacity to search for, and within certain limits, either find truth or to peel away that which is not true and, thereby, establish a closer, if rather complex, relationship with the nature of truth in a given set of circumstances. The moral facet of one's essential, existential authority entails an individual's sincere struggle to act in accordance with one's understanding of the nature of truth at any given point in time.

The way in which a person attempts to do due diligence with respect to her or his moral and intellectual authority might not always be correct. Mistakes might be made and errors committed with respect to the exercise of either moral and/or intellectual authority.

However, if such mistakes and errors are the result of sincere efforts, an individual will continue to struggle to shape the exercise of moral and intellectual authority into a process of learning through which that person has the opportunity to develop a rich, experience-based wisdom. Ceding one's moral and intellectual authority to another short-circuits the learning process and prevents one from developing wisdom in relation to improving one exercise of one's moral and intellectual authority as one engages, and is engaged, by life's experiences.

Techniques and strategies of undue influence are designed to obstruct, undermine, or co-opt an individual's efforts to struggle toward realizing either one's intellectual authority and/or one's moral authority. In addition, techniques and strategies of undue influence seek to induce people to be willing to cede their moral and intellectual authority to another individual, group, organization, party, or government thereby enabling the latter 'entity' to draw upon the ceded authority to 'legitimize' or 'rationalize' some given action, policy or agenda.

The more people there are who can be induced to cede their moral and intellectual authority to such an individual, group, organization, party or government, then the more powerful does the latter become. In fact, such power becomes one more tool in the arsenal of undue influence to broaden its sphere of control over other individuals who might not have ceded their moral and intellectual authority but whose ability to resist the exercise of that power that is rooted in ceded authority because the former is often severely attenuated and out-flanked.

Acquiring power through collecting the ceded moral and intellectual authority of others can never be justified even when constructive results might ensue through the use of such ceded authority. Such acquired power can never be justified because it is predicated on usurping the most essential dimension of what it means to be a human being, and sooner or later, the continued use of the power acquired through ceded authority will destroy not only individuals but the social setting as well, and history bears witness to this existential principle.

Working for a specific goal or purpose does not generally require anyone to cede his or her moral and intellectual authority to other human beings because the individual tends to be actively and directly involved with the goal or purpose being considered in a way in which that individual has full control over his or her moral and intellectual authority as they act. In other words, the goal or purpose gives expression to a person's moral and intellectual understanding of the way things should be, and, therefore, serves the given purpose or strives toward realizing a given goal in concert with that individual's direct exercise of his or her moral and intellectual authority.

One does not have to cede one's moral and intellectual authority in order to be able to work in co-operation with other people who also are operating in accordance with their own commitment to observing due diligence in relation to exercising their moral and intellectual authority as responsible agents in the world. Reciprocity is one of the key features of people who are in harmony with one another as they maintain control over their respective spheres of moral and intellectual authority while acting as independent agents in a social setting. The reciprocity is a reflection of the way in which the independent agents within the group or social setting tend to honor the right and responsibility of other people to exercise due diligence with respect to their respective capacities to serve as sources for moral and intellectual authority.

Agendas, on the other hand, are almost entirely devoid of considerations of reciprocity except in ways that have been reframed to make the relationship between a leader and the followers seem more equitable or appear more given to reciprocity than actually is the case. Those who push agendas rarely, if ever, are interested in working with people in order to ensure that the moral and intellectual authority of the latter is protected, preserved, and/or enhanced because doing this would tend to be counterproductive to and individual, organization, party, or government being able to push through an agenda.

To be able to successfully pursue an agenda, one needs: either raw power – in the form of brute force, or one needs the power that is acquired through inducing people to cede their moral and intellectual authority. The latter form of power seems more civilized than the exercise of brute force – whether in the form of an individual enforcer, or in the form of militaristic, legal, or governmental enforcement – but using the power acquired through inducing people to cede their moral and intellectual authority is, in the long run, every bit as destructive and unjustifiable as is the exercise of brute force to realize some given agenda.

When a person is not willing to cede his or her moral and intellectual authority, then such an individual recognizes and understands that the authority for any action issues from, or is rooted in, the person and does not issue from, nor is it rooted in, anyone else. When a person cedes her or his moral and intellectual authority, then such an individual is vesting that authority in another human being, group, institution, organization, party, or government to enable the latter to make decisions on behalf of the person who is ceding that authority. Furthermore, the individual who is ceding moral and intellectual authority to another human being tends to feel and to believe that she or he is no longer required to be a guardian over, or exercise due diligence with respect to, how such authority is actually being used.

Having moral and intellectual authority is a birthright. This is true from a spiritual, as well as a humanistic, perspective.

To have such authority means that one is responsible for exercising due diligence both intellectually and morally to ensure, to the best of one's capabilities, that what one is doing does not harm, undermine, or compromise anyone else's capacity for exercising similar authority in relation to her or his own life. To cede such authority to others means that one has been induced to abdicate the throne, so to speak, of one's own individual kingdom -- together with the authority that is, by birthright, vested in such a kingdom – and, thereby, to turn over that authority to another human being to dispose of as the latter individual judges to be appropriate.

When ceded moral and intellectual authority leads to empowerment of some other individual, organization, party, or government, such empowerment will inevitably be turned back upon the source from which that power originally was derived (i.e., the one who has been induced to cede moral and intellectual authority) in order to try to convince that source that she or he never had a right to such authority to begin with. Techniques of undue influence (involving the media, schooling, government policy, theories of jurisprudence, religious institutions, and various forms of social pressure) will be employed to keep individuals disengaged from their inherent right to observe due diligence with respect to the exercise of moral and intellectual authority.

Since the time of Max Weber, many people have been captivated by the idea of "charismatic leadership". A charismatic leader is someone who, supposedly, is to serve as a savior of some kind ... an individual who will solve the maladies of a tribe, group, or collective ... the one who will lead humanity to some mythical utopia.

When, historically speaking, so many 'charismatic leaders' turned out to be oppressive, self-aggrandizing, murdering, self-serving tyrants, then some people began to sour on the underlying traditional idea of leadership that was rooted in the notion that leadership is a function of personality traits of one kind or another that are inherent in the leader. Some of those who were dissatisfied with traditional approaches to the notion of leadership, went in search of some other, hopefully more fertile ground in which to plant the seed of leadership

For example, some people came up with the idea that the best leaders are those who give the impression that they are part of a set of people and, as leaders, are only really interested in helping people to get what they want and, as leaders, to act in ways that will allow people to realize that which the people actually desire. This is referred to as a "contingency model" because the concept of leadership is considered to be a function of the context in which a so-called leader operates.

Traditional models of leadership claimed that leaders were individuals who could overcome problematic circumstances through the manner in which they imposed their will on, or did their charismatic magic in relation to, such problems. Newer models of leadership maintain that it is the nature of the circumstances that will determine who will be a successful leader.

'Contingency model-approaches' to leadership maintain that every context involves one, or more, challenge for the exercise of appropriate leadership. Being able to successfully navigate such challenges suggests that there might be an optimum match between the nature of a contextually-based challenge and the qualities that a leader should exhibit in order for the latter for an individual to meet the challenge of leadership that is posed by a given set of circumstances. In other words, according to some of the newer theories of leadership, only a person with a certain kind of skill set will be able to succeed in any given set of circumstances involving a challenge of leadership.

To claim that every set of social or group circumstances poses challenges of leadership, is to frame discussion in a particular way. In other words, if one assumes that whatever problems arise in a group or social setting give expression to one, or more, challenges of leadership, then this is to automatically assume that all problems must be filtered through the idea of leadership in order to deal with those problems.

If, on the other hand, one were to argue that whatever problems arise within a social or group setting poses a challenge for the members of that setting, and in the process, one excluded any considerations of leadership from being part of possible proposed solutions, then one might begin to think about how to try to resolve such problems in ways that do not recognize the concept of a 'leader' in any traditional sense that requires one to make a distinction between leaders and followers with concomitant differences in assigned roles.

In the newer theories of leadership much depends on how one characterizes the nature of the leadership challenge that exists in a given set of circumstances. In addition, much will depend on how one believes those challenges might be best met ... or, even what one believes the criteria are for determining what constitutes 'best meeting' such challenges ... or, what one believes about whose perspective should be defining the criteria and methods for determining what might be meant by the idea of ' being best met'.

To say that circumstances or context provide the criteria for understanding the nature of leadership is to ignore the question of who gets to 'frame' those circumstances in terms of what the latter supposedly are about, involve, or mean. More importantly, and as outlined earlier, the new approach to leadership is predicated on the unquestioned premise that leaders are either necessary or even desirable in any given situation.

The authors of the *Scientific American Mind* article on 'leadership' believe that there is a symbiotic relationship between a leader and the followers who make up a set of social circumstances. This presumes that the dynamic involving: leaders and followers, is necessarily symbiotic rather than, for example, possibly parasitic in character, and this is a questionable presumption.

Newer theories of leadership give emphasis to the importance of having insight into the dynamics of group psychology. In other words, every individual participates in groups from which facets of identity are derived – namely, social identity. This aspect of identity is part of what makes group behavior possible since as different individuals identify with a given group and such a group acts in certain ways, individual behavior will be shaped by what goes on in the group.

However, what if someone raises the question of whether identifying with a group or permitting a person's behavior to be shaped by a group are necessarily good things? What if the self-realization of a person -- and, quite irrespective of whether one construes the idea of self-realization in spiritual or humanistic terms – depends on establishing an individual's sense of self quite independently of groups? What if the requirements of morality require an individual to swim against the currents inherent in the flow of group dynamics?

To be sure, human beings have a social dimension to them. We need other human beings to develop physically or emotionally in a healthy way, and we need other human beings to be able to, for example, learn to speak a language, and we need other human beings to be able to learn how to navigate through, and survive in, waters that are populated by the presence of other people. Furthermore, there is no doubt that many, if not most people, tend to filter their sense of self through the lenses provided by various groups.

Nonetheless, none of the foregoing admissions require one to say that one's sense of identity should be a function of groups.

Furthermore, none of the foregoing admissions requires one to contend that group dynamics is always a constructive force, nor do any of the foregoing admissions demonstrate that one does not have an obligation to oneself -- and, perhaps, even to the truth of things -- to resist the tendency of groups to want to impose themselves on individuals in oppressive, destructive ways.

To claim that group behavior is only possible when everyone in the group shares the same goals, interests, values, and understandings is a contentious claim. In many societies and groups there are an array of negotiated, mediated, adjudicated, and electoral modes of settlement that are accepted not because everyone shares the same interests, values and understandings, but because the participants have some degree of, at least, minimal commitment to a framework of rules and procedures through which agreements will be reached that while not entirely satisfactory, nevertheless, such agreements do have enough points of attractiveness that will enable the collective to proceed to interact in somewhat cooperative ways, despite whatever dimensions of friction and disharmony might be present.

How different people understand the underlying framework of principles, rules, and procedures that are being alluded to above and that govern such processes might be quite varied. Disputes and conflicts might arise because of these sorts of hermeneutical differences, and, as a result, problems tend to proliferate. At that point, groups might come together and try to utilize the underlying procedural framework, once again, as a way to try to sort things out ... not because everyone agrees on the meaning, value, or purpose of that framework but because they don't have an alternative to such a system ... unless , of course, a given community, society, or nation reaches a tipping point in which the participants believe that revolution – whether peaceful or violent – is the only way of trying to find a more equitable, logical, practical, and effective way of doing social things.

Leaders tend to be the gate-keepers of the different modalities for: mediating, negotiating, or adjudicating settlements within a given framework of group-dynamics. The power and authority of these leaders tends to be derived, in some sense, from such a system, and, therefore, leaders have a vested interest in maintaining that kind of system quite independently of whether, or not, that system actually serves the needs of the people whose behavior and ideas are being shaped, framed, and filtered by that system.

The reason why leaders often need to resort to an understanding of group psychology is so they can determine the fulcrum points in society that when leveraged will be capable of moving the members of a groups in directions that either will maintain the status quo or will advance the agenda of the leadership. If a leader can convince the 'followers' that he or she is one of them, and if the leader can identify the appropriate tipping points within such a group of followers, then the credibility that is derived from identifying oneself with the group's sense of self will permit a leader to leverage such credibility to move the group in a desired direction – not because this is what they group necessarily really needs but because the group is 'led' to believe that such a direction is what the group has wanted all along or is in the 'best interests' of the group.

Part of the process of the new approach to leadership involves techniques of persuasion that are designed to induce people to identify with particular groups and to induce such individuals to believe that the Interests, values, and beliefs of the group are their own interests, values and beliefs. These sorts of techniques permit leaders to gravitate away from using brute power to rule over people, and, instead, substitute's the willingness of someone to be led in various directions provided such a person can be persuaded that his or her interests, together with the interests of a given group, are co-extensive.

Thus, a person's desire for a sense of identity, together with that individual's desire not to be considered as an outsider relative to certain groups , become leverage points through which a person's life can be moved in certain directions. Moreover, once a person identifies with a group, the challenge becomes one of learning how to leverage the group, knowing that individuals within the group will simply follow along.

Leaders create a story line or mythology for the group. The people in that group follow the story line or give expression to the mythology, and in so doing enhance their own sense of identity.

In instances where there is a strong sense of group identity, those individuals within the group who best exemplify the sense of shared identity of such a group will tend to be the ones who, according to the new theories of leadership, will become the most effective leaders. There are a variety of assumptions inherent in such a perspective.

First of all, human beings tend to have varying degrees of allegiance with a number of groups that populate the larger collective. Some of these allegiances might be more important than others.

People are members of political parties, religious groups, families, neighborhoods, cities, states/provinces, ethnic groups, unions, management associations, socio-economic classes, professional groups, and so on. Consequently, situations rarely are: 'black and white' or 'us' versus 'them'.

There are cross-currents that run through our group affiliations. As a result, there often are divided loyalties.

Depending on the individual, some groups might have a stronger hold on one's loyalty than do others. Depending on the individual, a person might have more of his or her need to belong met by some groups more than by others.

Therefore, official or unofficial membership in various groups might, or might not, not contribute all that much to a person's sense of identity. Moreover, a sense of shared identity might vary from circumstance to circumstance and from time to time.

For example, going to sporting event and rooting for the 'home' side might create a sense of shared identity with all those other people who are cheering for the same team. However, once one leaves the sporting arena, then: whatever socio-economic class, or whatever party, or whatever ethnicity, or whatever religion one belongs to, might become much more important than any shared identity involving a sports team. Or, going to a specific church, mosque, temple, or synagogue might give expression to one kind of shared identity, but once one leaves such a place of worship and goes home to a particular neighborhood or goes into the voting booth, another sort of shared identity might take over.

In addition, those who look at the world through the lenses of social psychology often can't see the individual. Individuals might be committed to ideals, principles, values, purposes, interests, and goals that are not necessarily a function of a shared identity with others but are, rather, a function of the person's own search for truth, justice, morality, and life's purpose quite independently of what other people might believe or do.

Furthermore, even when there might be a certain similarity or overlap of interests, values, principles, and so on, between an individual and a given group, nonetheless, such overlap or similarity does not necessarily mean there is a consensus between the individual and group about what such interests, values, or principles might mean or how they should be translated into behavior. A group might not be a good fit for an individual or there might be fault lines of tension, friction, and disagreement that tend to color and shape a person's relationship with that group.

People might go from group to group looking for something that reflects or matches what is going on inside of those individuals. Such people might already have a vague or diffuse sense of identity and they are looking for other people who seem to share that same sense of things, so a group is not what gives the individual her or his sense of identity as much as it might confirm what already exists, and when people encounter such confirmation, then this is what makes them feel like they belong.

On the other hand, if a person feels that what is going on in a group no longer reflects or resonates with his or her sense of identity, then the person might withdraw from the group or move to its periphery, becoming relatively uninvolved in what is going on. Under such circumstances, it is not the group that provides the individual with her or his sense of identity but, instead, a group just serves as a means of validating that sense ... a means that might no longer be performing its function.

Within almost all groups there often are differences of understanding about what the group stands for, or what its purpose is, or what role the group should play in a person's life, or what its core values and principles are, or how those values and principles should be translated into action or behavior. Different people frame the group in different ways and such framings generate allegiances, loyalties, and fault lines.

Groups are not entities unto themselves. Groups are dynamic structures whose shape, character, and orientation are a function of what happens as different individuals and factions within the group play off against one another in order to determine whose perspective will tend to frame the group as being one set of things rather than some other set of things.

Therefore, to say that the person who best exemplifies a group's values and ideals is likely to become the most effective leader in such a group presupposes that the character of the group is clearly identifiable. Sometimes "leaders" from within a group are identified who exhibit certain qualities that, if correctly used, might be able to push the identity of a group in certain directions that are conducive to the agendas of people outside the group who wish to commandeer the group's energy and activity to serve the purposes of the external agency.

Finally, there is an unstated premised – something touched on earlier – that is running through virtually all of the talk about leadership. This premise maintains that leaders are necessary and, therefore, followers need to be created.

However, perhaps we should step back and ask a question. Why are leaders necessary?

A lot of answers might be given to the foregoing question. Leaders are necessary to keep society safe, or leaders are necessary to achieve human aspirations, or leaders are necessary to organize society, or leaders are necessary to ensure that resources are used wisely and properly, or leaders are necessary to help educate the unruly and unwashed masses, or leaders are necessary because human beings need moral guidance.

All of the foregoing ideas are predicated on the idea that only leaders know: how to keep society safe, or how to achieve their aspirations, or how to organize society, or how to use resources wisely, or how to educate people, or how to provide moral guidance. I have yet to see any proof of the foregoing contention that only leaders know how to do things or should be the ones who tell the 'followers' how to proceed in any given context.

Leaders tend to be individuals who are good at getting people to concede their moral and intellectual authority to such individuals in something akin to a process in which proxy votes are turned over to another agent at, or prior to, a stockholders meeting so that the one with the proxy votes has more power and control over things than otherwise might be the case. Leaders tend to be individuals who are good at framing life as a process that demands leadership so that the followers can be assisted to move in the right directions by ceding their moral and intellectual authority to act as individuals to the group leader. Leaders tend to be individuals who are good at convincing others that the latter people have a duty or obligation to cede their moral and intellectual authority to the leader ... that the leader has a sacred right to dispose of your intellectual and moral authority as the leader deems necessary

Even if one were to accept the foregoing idea – namely, that leaders are necessary – it doesn't automatically follow that every leader is capable of leading people in the right direction concerning the nature and purpose of life. So, there is a problem surrounding this issue of leadership – namely, even if one were to accept the basic premise that leaders are somehow necessary (which is, at best, debatable), one still would have to identify which leaders are actually capable of leading 'followers' in the appropriate direction with respect to truth, justice, moral qualities, purpose, education, security, economic activity, and the like.

According to some of the proponents of modern leadership theory, true leaders are those who are able to get people to act in concert with one another. This is done not through arranging for the people in a group to be watched by security forces or management groups or supervisors to ensure that the members stay true to the vision of the leaders, but, instead, it is accomplished by getting people to identify themselves with the values and purposes of a group, and, then, the members become their own watchdogs -- both individually and collectively.

Once a person has ceded his or her moral and intellectual authority to a group, then 'leaders' don't need anyone to oversee the behavior of the group members. The authority of the group, and, thereby, of the leader, has been internalized within individual members by the very act of ceding authority to another, and, therefore, those members will tend to operate in accordance with an internalized understanding which indicates that proper authority comes from without and not from within. In whatever way the group moves, the members will follow because the internalized authority of the leader – which has been acquired through the ceding of intellectual and moral authority by individual members -- and the group – which expects other members to cede their intellectual and moral authority in the same way -- will require this. If one wishes to continue to be a part of the group and if one wishes to continue to derive one's sense of identity from the group, then one must continue to cede one's moral and intellectual authority to the group and/or its leader.

One of the challenges of 'leadership' is to identify those members of a group who are beginning to indicate that -- through their words and behavior -- such individuals no longer wish to continue to cede their intellectual and moral authority to the group or to the leader. Such individuals tend to disrupt the efforts of the leadership to get the people in the group to work in a concerted manner and, consequently, those wayward individuals must be handled in some manner.

Thus, a second challenge for leadership is to try to find ways that are designed to work with, or work on, individuals who are wavering in relation to their sense of group identity and seek to reintegrate those individuals back into the values and principles that the leadership has assigned to the group as constituting the best way to move forward to give expression to the alleged purposes of the group … at least, as envisioned by the leadership. If such efforts toward reintegration should fail, then this would seem to lead to a new, perhaps irresolvable, challenge to some of the newer theories of leadership – namely, what does one do when people don't want to be led.

Social psychologists such as Solomon Asch, Stanley Milgram, Philip Zimbardo and others have shown that even one defector can influence other members of a group to act in ways that run contrary to group expectations, norms, purposes, and actions. Therefore, when the forces of internalized authority within individuals begin to falter or weaken, steps might have to be taken to prevent the spread of the 'virus' or 'malignancy' to other members of the group. In one way or another, members of a group seemingly need to be persuaded that re-acquiring the moral and intellectual authority that they previously ceded to leadership is not a morally, and/or spiritually, and/or religiously, and/or politically, and/or economically wise thing to do.

Thus, even in the context of newer theories of leadership, the indigenous leader of a group – that is, the one who supposedly best exemplifies the purpose, quality, or identity of a given group -- is still a watchdog who supervises group activity and looks for deviations from, or forces that run counter to, various group purposes, values, ideals, goals, and aims. As long as the leader's authority has been internalized by the other members of the group, then such members will carry the conscience of the group within them as they move about, but when such internalized authority begins to unravel, then the leader of such a group might have to begin to act just like leaders in traditional theories of leadership –that is, they might have to try to pursue tactics, techniques, and stratagems that will permit the leader to reassert his or her authority over, or impose her or his will upon, group behavior.

Authority comes in the form of at least two flavors. One variety occurs when an individual is competent – or more than competent – in relation to some ability, talent, skill, or form of expertise -- and, as a result, other people recognize the presence of such competence and are prepared, to varying degrees, to be influenced by such competence as long as being influenced does not require a person to cede his or her moral and intellectual authority in any way to the individual who is sharing her or his competence. This sort of authority helps to enhance everyone's potential, like tools enhance people's ability to do a variety of additional or extended tasks beyond the normal or usual abilities of such individuals.

A second species of authority involves the willingness of one or more people to cede their intellectual or moral authority to another human being. When such ceding occurs, the person(s) to whom such an important dimensions of being human is (are) ceded acquires authority over the ones who have ceded that dimension of being human. Under these circumstances, a leader can have no authority over anyone unless it is gained through such a process of ceding.

The first variety of authority is: co-operative, constructive, and is based on sharing experience and/or understanding, and/or abilities/talents. Most importantly, this mode of authority does not require the person who is benefitting through being influenced by such competence to cede anything to the individual who is influencing them.

I refer to this form of authority as 'authoritative consultation'. This is what an 'elder' – that is, a person who manifests some degree of socially recognized competence with respect to one, or more, facets of life -- contributes to any social setting in which the elder participates.

The aforementioned second variety of authority is: imposed, problematic, and is not about sharing but, rather, exacts a price for maintaining the relationship. That price is paid in the form of being required to cede one's moral and intellectual authority to another individual (or other individuals) in exchange for the 'service' of leadership.

I refer to this form of authority as 'pathological authority'. Such authority is rooted in a delusional system concerning how people see themselves in relation to others.

More specifically, anyone who believes that he or she needs to induce others to cede their moral and intellectual authority to a 'leader' in order for the leader to be able to accomplish his or her purposes fails to understand an essential dimension of human nature – which, in part, involves the ability and right to freely pursue due diligence in conjunction with life in relation to the constructive exercise of one's moral and intellectual authority – then such an individual is operating out of a delusional system that can continue to exist only by negating or being inattentive to certain existential facts concerning the nature of being human. On the other hand, anyone who believes that he or she must cede his or her moral and intellectual authority to other human beings in order to achieve one's purposes in life is also operating through a delusional framework.

The two sides of the delusion dovetail with one another. Together they give expression to the pathological form of authority in which one creates a system of 'followers' and 'leaders' that is maintained by, respectively, the ceding and acquiring of moral and intellectual authority during which one side loses authority while the other side gains authority by virtue of which the former individuals – the ones who cede – are shaped, oriented, directed and manipulated by the ones to whom such authority is ceded and who, thereby, acquire power.

Of course, a person might use brute force, torture, or threats to gain power over others. However, exercising such power is not the same thing as having authority over someone.

Gaining authority requires the participation of people who have moral and intellectual authority to cede. Such people co-operate with or comply with or are obedient to leadership by means of the act of ceding their moral and intellectual authority to the leader. If this were not done, the 'leader' would have no authority, even if that leader did have the power to bring about their desired ends independently of matters of authority.

People who exercise brute force or power often mistake this for exercising authority. Pathological authority – of whatever vintage -- is based upon essential human rights that, rightly or wrongly, have been ceded away, whereas the exercise of brute power is not rooted in the ceding away of such essential human rights but involves forceful attempts to negate the existence of such rights altogether – as if they never existed and did not constitute anything of an inalienable nature with respect to which an individual had a choice about ceding away or not.

Constructive co-operation does not presuppose any form of power or authority in order for such co-operation to occur. Not only can a person co-operate with other human beings without ceding away any moral and intellectual authority, but an individual's ability to truly and sincerely co-operate with others demands due diligence with respect to the exercise of his or her moral and intellectual authority in order to pursue co-operation in a fair and mutually reciprocal manner. Such co-operation ends when other people start trying to undermine, negate, or usurp my moral and intellectual authority for the purposes of pursuing an agenda that falls beyond the horizons of such a process of mutually reciprocal co-operation of two, or more, spheres of interacting sources of moral and intellectual authority.

Leadership, for the most part, is designed to short-circuit natural forms of co-operation among independent sources of moral and intellectual authority. Leadership is designed to co-opt such co-operation and re-frame it in terms of group activities that, in reality, are merely projections of a leader's agenda or vision for a given group of people.

Framing collectives into 'in-groups' and 'out-groups' is an arbitrary, artificial, and, ultimately, a destructive process. The truth of the foregoing is demonstrated by the many battles, skirmishes, and wars that have been fought to assert the superiority or priority of claimed rights of one group over the sovereignty of someone else's right to exercise their own moral and intellectual authority as long as such exercise does not undermine the sovereignty of another to do likewise.

Groups are not born into this world. Individuals are born into the world, and, so, the creation of groups after the fact is something that often is being imposed on individuals and not something that is necessarily required by the basic facts of individual existence.

There are different ethnicities, linguistic populations, as well as different physiological and intellectual abilities. However, these differences do not have to be translated into differences with respect to issues involving equality or rights. All people are born with the same rights until some 'leader' decides to reframe existence in order to explain: why not everyone is entitled to such rights in the same way, and why 'followers' have a duty to cede their moral and intellectual authority to those who wish to control how the narrative of being human unfolds in a manner that is conducive to the purposes of those leaders.

Nations are artificial creations introduced by leaders to provide a reason for why individuals should be willing to cede their intellectual and moral authority to serve the purposes of that nation – which really means the purposes of the leaders of that nation. Nations could not exist if people had not been induced to cede their individual moral and intellectual authority to a collective that was to be supervised and molded by a leader of some kind.

From the perspective of some of the newer theories of leadership, there is a dynamic relationship between social identity and social reality. In other words, the kind of social identity that has pre-eminence in a given locality will shape and orient the sort of society that will arise in that locality. Alternatively, the sort of social reality that exists tends to affect the sort of social identities that that might be acquired by people.

The foregoing way of looking at things tends to remove individuals from the picture except to the extent that those individuals either serve a particular social identity or are shaped by a specific social reality. However, individuals are expressions of a prevalent social identity or are shaped by a particular social reality only to the extent they those individuals cede their moral and intellectual authority to that social identity or social reality.

Because human beings are hard-wired with a network of inclinations toward the realm of the social, we are vulnerable, in a variety of ways, to forces of social identity and social reality. These vulnerabilities tend to induce or seduce individuals to cede away their intellectual or moral authority so that they become dominated by the authority and/or power structures that leaders tend to wield in relation to those concessions.

Any attempt to induce or seduce an individual to cede away his or her moral and intellectual authority to another human being is an instance of exercising undue influence and is a form of moral and/or intellectual abuse of the individual who is the target of such an exercise. Trusting others to help one to develop, and bring to fruition, one's capacity for moral and intellectual authority is not the same thing as being manipulated into ceding away such a capacity – unless, of course, one's trust is betrayed.

Trust is rooted in a deep-rooted sense that, among other things, involves the idea that another person: values, is sensitive to, and wishes to protect one's essential, existential capacity for exercising, as well as one's right to exercise, one's moral and intellectual authority. All violations of such trust give expression to a form of abuse – whether: physical, parental, familial, political, spiritual, economic, organizational, institutional, social, and/or governmental in nature.

Rituals, symbols, practices, and myths can be used to induce people to cede their moral and intellectual authority. Or, on the other hand, rituals, symbols, and so on can be used to help people explore and enhance the ability of individuals to learn how to not cede such authority but, instead, find ways of utilizing an individual's inherent authority to co-operate with others in mutually satisfying and reciprocal ways.

A shared identity that arises from assisting individuals to exercise their individual moral and intellectual authority in: co-operative, constructive, just, compassionate, equitable, charitable and peaceful ways is not the goal of a group that divides members into 'leaders' and 'followers'. A shared identity that helps individuals to realize their birth right as sources of sovereign moral and intellectual authority is an expression of a principle to which people in the collective are equally committed as individuals and not as members of a group, and to the extent that a collective or group seeks to thwart such an individualized principle, to that extent is the collective engaged in tactics of undue influence and practices of moral and intellectual abuse.

As such, individuals become willing participants in a group to the extent that the group continues to foster or nurture the moral and intellectual authority of individuals as sovereign agents. When the group stops serving this essential dimension of being human, then the individual needs to struggle toward re-acquiring whatever aspect of one's essential sovereignty has been compromised or undermined and withdraw from such a group, if not actively begin to work against the interests of that sort of group that is antithetical to the very nature of what it is to be a human being.

The people within a collective who can assist individuals to develop their essential sovereignty in constructive and beneficial ways are not leaders. They are elders or 'authoritative consultants'.

The source of such authoritativeness begins and ends with the degree of competency possessed by such a consultant with respect to helping someone to gain control over the latter's individual capacity for constructively exercising moral and intellectual authority. For example, helping someone to read should be an activity that is designed to enhance the constructive sovereignty of an individual's capacity for exercising moral and intellectual authority.

Learning how to read in a way that is free from forces of undue influence with respect to a person's essential right of sovereignty is something that can be done in conjunction with an authoritative consultant who is competent in relation to helping someone to learn how to read in this manner. When an authoritative consultant seeks to have influence beyond the horizons of that person's competency, then one begins to cross over into the realm of someone trying to be a leader for purposes of inducing someone to proceed in a direction that is not necessarily directed toward the healthy development of the latter individual's capacity to exercise moral and intellectual authority in a constructive fashion – both in relation to that latter individual and to the surrounding collective.

The individual who is learning to read does not have to cede any of his or her moral and intellectual authority in order to succeed. Rather, the task of the authoritative consultant is to find ways of co-operating with the sovereignty of the seeker after knowledge to help that individual to become competent with respect to being a reader who uses this competency to develop and enhance her or his own capacity for sovereignty.

Authoritative consultants can enter into dialogue with those who are seeking to benefit from such authoritativeness relative to some given activity. However, the moment when such dialogue seeks to induce the individual to cede his or her moral authority to the group, then such dialogue becomes a tool of undue influence, as well as moral and intellectual abuse.

Proponents of some of the newer theories of leadership maintain that if a person – a leader – can control how 'identity' or 'shared identity' is defined, then, one has a tool through which one can change the world. What such proponents say in this regard might be true to some extent.

However, anyone who seeks to control how others perceive or understand the idea of essential identity constitutes an exercise in undue influence and abusive behavior when it comes to the right of individuals to have control over their own sovereignty vis-à-vis the constructive exercise of one's moral and intellectual authority. Exploring such issues with another as a trusted equal in the process – that is, as someone who has the same rights of essential sovereignty – is not a matter of trying to control how the other comes to understand the character of that essential sovereignty, but, is, rather, an exercise in co-operative, reciprocal exploration concerning issues of mutual importance.

Based on the foregoing discussion, the following ten principles are intended as constructive axioms of leadership for anyone who is contemplating becoming a leader but who has not been successful in resisting such an inclination:

The first axiom of leadership is to resign. The rest of the axioms appearing below are contingent on someone choosing -- for whatever reason -- not to follow the first axiom.

The second axiom of leadership is to neither: seek control over others, nor to be controlled by them.

The third axiom of leadership is to always operate in accordance with principles of truth, justice, compassion, integrity, friendship, humility, nobility, honesty, patience, forgiveness, and charitableness;

The fourth axiom of leadership is to realize that true competence is authoritative not authoritarian;

The fifth axiom of leadership is to understand that actually helping: the poor, the hungry, the sick, the powerless, and the oppressed, tends to be antithetical to remaining a leader. Dialogue becomes a tool of undue influence, as well as moral and intellectual abuse.

Proponents of some of the newer theories of leadership maintain that if a person – a leader – can control how 'identity' or 'shared identity' is defined, then, one has a tool through which one can change the world. What such proponents say in this regard might be true to some extent.

However, anyone who seeks to control how others perceive or understand the idea of essential identity constitutes an exercise in undue influence and abusive behavior when it comes to the right of individuals to have control over their own sovereignty vis-à-vis the constructive exercise of one's moral and intellectual authority. Exploring such issues with another as a trusted equal in the process – that is, as someone who has the same rights of essential sovereignty – is not a matter of trying to control how the other comes to understand the character of that essential sovereignty, but, is, rather, an exercise in co-operative, reciprocal exploration concerning issues of mutual importance.

Chapter 3: <u>Leadership</u> – Part 2

When Iranian students occupied the American embassy on November 4th, 1979 and, in the process, took 52 employees of the embassy hostage – and would continue to do so for the next 444 days – the actions set in motion, among other things, a wide-ranging discussion. Included among the themes of the discussion were such questions as: Why did it happen? Who was responsible? What did the leaders of the event want? Could those leaders have accomplished their purpose(s) in some other way? Were international agreements concerning the sanctity of embassy employees violated? If so, could such violations be justified? Were human rights being trampled upon? Had the United States done anything to provoke the affair? What should leaders in the United States and around the world do in response to the situation?

All of the foregoing questions, and many more, could have been asked 26 years earlier – but, for the most part were not – when Kermit Roosevelt, grandson of Teddy Roosevelt and a member of the Central Intelligence Agency, helped orchestrate a coup d'état of Iran's democratically elected government of Mohammad Mossaddeq and appointed Mohammad Reza Pahlavi, the Shah of Iran, as the new ruler of Iran and, in the process, effectively assisted him to take millions of Iranians as hostages – and would continue to do so for the next 26 years. Those who control the media get to frame world events as they please, which is why depriving Iranians of their most basic right of self-determination has been depicted by most American media as being justified in 1953 because it was said, by various leaders, that over-throwing a democratically elected government was in the interests of the United States, whereas what happened in 1979 was described by various leaders as not being in the interests of the United States and, therefore, not justified.

People's human rights were trampled upon in both cases. People were taken hostage in both cases. International law was flouted in both instances.

There were a few differences in the two cases, however. First, none of the 52 embassy employees were tortured or killed by their Iranian captors (although some of the hostages were treated roughly and kept isolated for a time), whereas thousands of Iranians were tortured and killed by the U.S. supported regime of the Shah and his infamously notorious security force: SAVAK. Secondly, the Iranians voluntarily released their hostages after a little over a year had passed, whereas the United States was not prepared to ever release the hostages it had helped the Shah to take until the United States was forced to do so by the 1979 embassy incident in Tehran.

The foregoing scenario helps to introduce several issues that will figure prominently in the remainder of the present discussion. (1) Trampling on the rights of others and taking hostages, in one form or another, is a common practice of many so-called leaders within the Muslim (and non-Muslim) community; (2) the leaders for a variety of Islamic revival movements believe – incorrectly -- that they are justified in undermining, nullifying, or controlling the God-given sovereignty of both Muslims and non-Muslims to make individual choices concerning matters of spiritual and material welfare; (3) shari'ah and Divine justice are not legal issues but give expression to matters of ontology, metaphysics, morality, identity, essential potential, and spiritual development that are best handled individually and, when necessary (i.e., when problems arise), through seeking social – not legal – consensus or mediation.

The following discussion will briefly explore some of the ideas of a number of individuals who are considered to have played an important role in pioneering various species of social reform within the Muslim world and/or with respect to Islamic revivalism. While this exploration is not meant to be definitive, it is intended to be suggestive in relation to various issues of leadership among Muslims.

Sayyid Jamal al-Din al-Afghani was a nineteenth century proponent of employing so-called 'pan-Islamic unity' as a strategy for resisting and fighting against British imperialism. While all people have a right to be free from the oppressive tentacles of imperialism – whether this imperialism is: British, American, French, German, Chinese, Japanese, Russian, Christian, Jewish, Muslim or other – the character of the tactics that are used to fulfill such an intention tend to reveal a lot about the person using those tactics as well as about the sort of "leader" that individual seeks to be.

For example, although born in Iran and educated through a Shi'a perspective, Afghani often claimed to be a Sunni from Afghanistan. The issue here is not whether he was Sunni or Shi'a – or neither – but, rather, the point is that he was willing to alter his biographical narrative as a tactical means of promoting his overall strategy concerning anti-imperialism.

In fact, there is considerable historical evidence to indicate that Afghani was not much interested in being either a Sunni or Shi'a but was, instead, committed to certain philosophical and political ideas. Religious themes were considered by him to be merely useful tools to bring about the kind of non-spiritual end in which he was interested.

Afghani sought to blaze a path that was neither rooted, on the one hand, in a blind, unthinking commitment to the sort of theological tenets and practices that populated a great deal of the traditional Muslim landscape nor, on the other hand, was he interested in a slavish subjugation to Western values, ideals and practice. Afghani believed that the 'correct' use of rationality, political/military strength, and social activism would enable Muslims – both individually and collectively – to reinterpret Islam in a manner that would effectively unite Muslims against the onslaught of British imperialism, in particular, and Western imperialism in general.

Afghani was wrong. Islam doesn't need to be re-interpreted. Islam was, during the days of Afghani, what it always has been since the time of Adam (peace be upon him), and what it is today, and what it will continue to be in the future. Islam is the Deen or spiritual way given by God to humankind so that the latter might -- with appropriate effort and if God wishes. -- find their way to, and drink from, the water of Divine Truth, wisdom and knowledge in accordance with one's primordial spiritual capacity, or fitra, to do so.

Islam is not something that needs to be reinterpreted, reformed, or revived. What needs to be refashioned are the human attitudes, practices, and ideas that serve as obstacles to the discovery of Islam's actual nature.

Discovery is a process of learning, development, spiritual maturation, and, ultimately, of Divine Grace. This process of discovery is a delicate, fragile, challenge-laden struggle.

Such discovery is not something that can be imposed on or forced on someone ... either individually or collectively. The Quranic principle that there can be no compulsion in matters of Deen is a reflection of the complex and subtle character of the process of spiritual discovery.

Afghani was also mistaken in other ways. Islam is not something to which one can reason one's way ... although reason does have a role to play during the discovery process. Islam is not something that can be discovered or defended through political and military strength but, rather, Islam is eternally protected by Divinity ... although individuals do have the right to resist attempts by Muslims or non-Muslims to undermine one's ability to engage the discovery process concerning the nature of Islam. Moreover, social and political activism will not, in and of itself, lead to the discovery of Islam ... although social activism might be an appropriate means under the right circumstances and conditions to help protect and secure the rights of all human beings to have full sovereignty with respect to choice in relation to the process of spiritual discovery concerning the way or path or Deen that God has provided to humanity through which essential identity and capacity might be realized for purposes of learning how to worship Divinity.

In many ways, most of the foregoing points are moot as far as Afghani is concerned because he was not really interested in Islam per se. Afghani was committed to certain philosophical ideals – especially rationalism.

He believed that truth was capable of being apprehended through the scientific use of reason. However, only an elite was capable of achieving this, while the vast majority of Muslims were limited to – and should be constrained by – a form of religious belief that maintained that misdeeds in this world would be punished in the life to come and, by conforming to such a belief system, would cause no trouble in this world for the elites who would rule over the masses.

For Afghani, the populace should be induced to unify and, thereby, provide the elite with the power and strength the latter needed to pursue philosophical truths in relative freedom. Through social activism, the masses could be shaped and directed by leaders to serve an agenda that entailed something other than the discovery of Islam or the true spiritual welfare of Muslims. Through reason, Afghani hoped to demonstrate that certain aspects of Islam could be organized to form an effective ideological buffer against the encroachment of imperialism ... a buffer that would protect the elite and create the public space necessary to enable such an elite to pursue their own ends free from the oppressive intrusion of imperialism and without being bothered by Muslims who would be preoccupied with seeking to attain salvation in the next world by not transgressing in this world.

Afghani was skeptical concerning the potential of religion. He saw it as little more than a way of helping to console people's anxiety concerning what came after death and/or as a means of comforting people with respect to the problems of this world.

However, although skeptical about the value of Islam – or, really, the value of any spiritual tradition – Afghani felt that such sentiments could be exploited if one could convince Muslims that imperialism was a threat to their way of life. Furthermore, if one enhanced the foregoing threat with the idea that imperialism was the Trojan horse through which Christianity would be forced upon Muslims, then, one might have a very effective tool for manipulating and harnessing Muslim emotions and concerns to serve other political and social ends.

Although Afghani often would paint himself in the colors of an ardent defender of Islam, he was merely camouflaging his true intentions. He considered prophets to be wielders of a craft rather than true emissaries of God. He believed that Islam was antithetical to science even though through the Qur'an's guidance concerning the importance of empirical observation and critical reflection, the Muslim world had helped transform the face of scientific practice. Moreover, he had a fairly misogynistic view of women that did not reflect the actual esteem with which women were held in the Qur'an.

As noted previously, he felt that religion had little more to offer than as a way of consoling people concerning the difficulties of life and, consequently, as something that had no solutions to the problems of life. According to Afghani, only rationalism, military strength, and social activism could provide solutions to the challenges of life.

Apparently, Afghani was intelligent, charismatic, and had some oratory skills. He used these qualities to attract some followers, but in concrete terms he was able to accomplish very little except to be able to gain access to some of the more influential social and political circles in certain localities and, thereby, have the opportunity to ply his gift of gab.

In fact, Afghani got kicked out of a number of places when, among other reasons, he ended up on the wrong side of a political crisis despite his connections. These localities included: Iran, Istanbul, Afghanistan, and Cairo.

Interestingly enough, although various pronouncements of Afghani were considered to be heretical with respect to Islam, he was never killed for espousing his views. Instead, he was escorted out of the locality.

Afghani sought to be a leader. However, his desire to be a leader was almost entirely self-serving and predicated on a need to exploit others and to control them to serve his ends.

He tried to clothe his intentions in the language of Islam, but, in point of fact he had very little understanding of Islam. To the extent that he did speak some of the language of Islam, this was used as a tactical tool to bring about Muslim unity so that he would have a power base through which to fight against British imperialism and open up the sort of free space that would enable him to pursue his own – and that of others whom he considered to be among the elite – rationalistic approach to truth.

Some people might wish to cite Afghani as a pioneer of Muslim reform and Islamic revivalism. Nevertheless, I believe that anyone who takes a closer look at his life and teachings will see that he has nothing to offer to anyone who is sincerely seeking to discover the truth about Islam.

Unfortunately, there are all too many so-called Muslim leaders who are prepared to use the language of Islam to serve agendas that are not concerned with Islam or the spiritual needs of Muslims. Indeed, Afghani belongs to the lineage of would-be leaders who are willing to exploit, oppress and rule others for the ends of the alleged "leaders", and, perhaps, that is why some people try to invoke Afghani's name as a kindred, revolutionary spirit and, in doing so, unintentionally disclose something of their own underlying, self-serving agenda with respect to Muslims and Islam.

When Afghani was in Cairo, one of the individuals who was a part of Afghani's circle was Muhammad Abduh, a student at al-Azhar University. Afghani purportedly led the circle in discussions of philosophy, law, theology, and mysticism.

Whatever Afghani's facility with philosophy, law, and theology might have been, he knew next to nothing about mysticism because he had never been a practitioner of the discipline. However, when the people who are being led are relatively ignorant about a given topic, it is amazing how wise and informed someone with the gift of gab can sound to the uninitiated.

There is evidence that Muhammad Abduh had a passing acquaintance with some aspects of the Sufi path because he had spent time in the company of an uncle, Darwish Kadr, who was reportedly a shaykh and sought to teach the young Abduh about the principles, practices, and adab of the Sufi way. Nevertheless, Abduh's time among the Sufis was fairly short-lived and, in fact, later in life Abduh came to be quite critical of this mystical tradition.

Afghani was an activist. Muhammad Abduh was influenced by Afghani to also be inclined toward political and social activism, but Abduh was more interested in reform than revolution.

At one point, Afghani's activities became too problematic, and he was expelled from Egypt. Due to Abduh's association with Afghani, the younger activist also ran into difficulties, but new opportunities arose when Abduh was appointed to be one of the editors for 'The Egyptian Gazette', an official newspaper, and later went on to become the chief editor for the publication ... a position that permitted him to wield considerable influence in framing public discussion about a variety of issues.

Eventually, Abduh's criticisms of military and political leaders, as well as his writings concerning nationalism and the British occupation led to a three year period of exile. During this hiatus, Adduh reconnected with Afghani in Paris, and the two of them formed a society and publication whose primary objective was to sound the clarion cry concerning the dangers of European imperialism and interference in the affairs of non-western peoples.

Both the society and publication came to an end. Abduh returned to Beirut where he taught young children and, as well, wrote about a variety of issues.

In time, his exile from Egypt ended, and he was appointed to one of the law courts in Egypt. Subsequently, he became part of an administrative council at al-Azhar, and, then, later on he became the Grand Mufti for Egypt. While Grand Mufti, Abduh issued a number of fatwas for individuals who came to him with a variety of problems involving legal issues and matters of morality.

Abduh was aware of the allure that European civilization had for many Muslims. For instance, Western weapons of war were superior to anything in the Muslim world, and many Muslims felt they needed to acquire Western technology in order to be able to defend their lands against further Western encroachment. In addition, the economic wealth of the West was in stark contrast to the economic impoverishment of large parts of the Muslim world, and, again, many Muslims thought that if they imitated Western approaches to economics, that some of the 'magic' might rub off on Muslims.

War, technology, economics and politics were all fed and shaped by ideas. Some Muslims believed – quite incorrectly – that if the Muslim world would incorporate Western ideas into their lives, then perhaps, Muslims might ascend, once again, to the glory days of early Islam.

On the other hand, as much as many Muslims were dazzled and intrigued by the success of the West, it was also apparent that a considerable amount of that success was coming at the expense of Muslims whose lands and resources were being taken – through force, intrigue, or the co-opting and corruption of Muslim leaders – by Western powers. Muhammad Abduh was one of the individuals who understood that there was a basic disconnect between the lofty principles of freedom, democracy, technological progress, and economic growth espoused by the West, and the oppressive manner in which the West sought to induce the non-Western world to subsidize the materially expansive way of life that was being established in the West.

Muhammad Abduh also believed, however, that the West was not necessarily the primary reason for the problems of the Muslim world.

In fact, he laid the responsibility for those problems at the feet of Muslims themselves, and he maintained that the wretched condition of Muslims was a punishment from God for having strayed from 'true' Islam.

Abduh's solution was multifaceted. He urged Muslims to be guided by the authority of the salaf or spiritual forbearers of early Islam, but he felt that all such authority should be measured against the teachings of the Qur'an.

He argued that human texts were capable of being critically questioned to determine their degree of authoritativeness. On the other hand, he believed that the Qur'an did not contain any errors and, therefore, must serve as the source of criteria for judging the spiritual authoritativeness of the texts written by human beings – even those of the salaf.

Abduh believed, however, that there could be no disagreement concerning the teachings of the Qur'an. Consequently, the Qur'an would become the means of uniting Muslims and ridding themselves of their sectarian differences, and reason would be the essential tool for ascertaining the principles and values being given expression through the Qur'an.

Through discernment of the true teachings of the Qur'an, one could become spiritually united with the understanding of the followers of Muhammad (peace be upon him). Through the use of reason and, coming to understand the actual nature of the Qur'an, all schools of theology and law, according to Abduh, would come to share a common foundation, and, as a result, the ummah or spiritual community would become united once again.

Reason is something of a will-o'-the-wisp that seems to give off a kind of light but often tends to recede as one tries to approach it and determine its true nature. Oftentimes, one person's reason is another person's insanity or nightmare, and although we all make appeals to the importance of reason, we frequently have difficulty clearly stating, or agreeing upon, just what reason is.

Furthermore, trying to use reason in conjunction with understanding the Qur'an is fraught with problems. This is not to say that reason has no place in relation to the Qur'an, but one cannot start – or end -- with reason.

In a number of places in the Qur'an, one is told that if an individual will have taqwa, or piety, then God will teach that individual. So, the starting place is a matter of taqwa, not reason.

Taqwa is more of a spiritual orientation marked by an individual's openness to, or willingness to, go in whatever direction Divinity wishes to take a person. The use of reason might have played a role in helping to shape the condition of taqwa, but taqwa cannot be reduced down to a rationalistic process since taqwa is also informed by understandings that are fed by other dimensions of human existence ... such as faith – which is not a matter of blind belief but of informed, insightful experience that comes through Divine grace – and faith (as do God's blessings) has many levels and degrees ... the faith of a Muslim is not the faith of a Momin, and neither of these is the faith of a Mohsin – that is, one who practices ihsan.

Reason is only one of the mediums through which Divine teaching takes place. Moreover, Divine logic will not necessarily be reflected in what someone considers to be an expression of impeccable reason, and, therefore, although all Divine logic is eminently rational, not all human reason resonates with such rationality.

The mind, heart, sir, kafi, and spirit – all of which are referred to in the Qur'an – do not employ the same modes of understanding, and each of these faculties are taught by Divinity in accordance with the capacity of that faculty. Reason is a function of the mind, and the mind is capable of understanding some things while it is incapable of understanding other dimensions of truth.

Unfortunately, many Muslims erroneously believe that the Qur'an can be penetrated and circumscribed by what they consider to be tools of rationality or reason. As a result, they use reason to interpret the Qur'an instead of waiting for Divinity, if God wishes, to teach them about the principles and nature of the Qur'an. Interpreting the Qur'an is a sign of impatience and lack of humility.

So, Abduh was wrong when he believed that there could be no disagreement about the Qur'an. Many people (both Muslim and non-Muslim) have a tendency to bring their own agendas to the Qur'an and filter the words of the Qur'an through that agenda, and this can lead to nothing but distortion, misunderstanding and sectarian divide. They might use the words of the Qur'an, but the Divine meanings of those words often have been corrupted, sullied, and/or distorted by human ignorance.

The Qur'an gives expression to nothing but truth. However, the interpretational methodologies and disciplines through which the Qur'an might be engaged by human beings lead to nothing but problems since the Qur'an tends to close itself – unless God wishes otherwise -- to whomever seeks to touch the Qur'an in a condition of impurity – not just physical impurity but intentional impurity and emotional impurity and mental impurity as well ... and the desire to interpret the Qur'an is but one manifestation of such impurity.

Abduh spent a considerable amount of time writing about how what he considered Islam to be was superior to Christianity. Yet, the very book that he claimed as the ultimate authority – namely, the Qur'an -- indicated that Christians were people of the Book, as were Jews ... as were the followers of other Prophets who were alluded to in the Qur'an but were not specified.

He put forth his interpretation of Christianity just as many Christians put forth their interpretations of Islam. But, in the end, all such disputes are mired in the quick-sand of arbitrary speculations and musings in which so-called rational arguments are crafted through the tools of human rather than Divine logic ... although everyone involved in the quarrel seeks to claim -- in self-serving ways and, therefore, without reliable proof -- that Divine logic is on their side of the argument.

Rather than get on with the business of life's actual purpose, Abduh, at times, allowed himself – and in the process sought to induce others to do the same – to become preoccupied with irrelevant issues of which civilization – or spiritual tradition -- was superior and which civilization – or spiritual tradition -- was inferior. The coliseums in which such battles are waged are the playground of nafs, Iblis and fools.

It doesn't matter what someone else thinks of me, or whether someone else labels me as inferior. All that matters is what God thinks of me, and this is something to which no one else is privy and that no human being can establish.

Unfortunately, when the ego is caught in the vise of pride and self-esteem, Deen, fitra, and Divine assessment tend to be forgotten. Under such circumstances, everything of real importance tends to be relegated to the sideline before the childish concerns of nafs.

In trying to argue about the purported superiority of Islam over Christianity -- or, on another front, the importance of Semitic contributions versus Aryan contributions to the greatness of a given civilization relative to another – one becomes enveloped in a war of interpretations that are entirely man-made, and, as a result, quite distant from the truth of Divinity even as the respective antagonists seek to argue that their delusional systems reflect Divine truths. Yet, Muhammad Abdu's allegedly pioneering efforts in this regard have helped frame the way in which all too many Muslims today seek to engage the spiritual problems before us.

Motivated by a massive sense of inferiority because of the material success of the West and motivated by a deep sense of self-doubt that often asks the question of themselves as much as of God: namely, how could the alleged infidel be so powerful and dominant, while the true believers (i.e., Muslims) are so oppressed and unsuccessful, the quest of many Muslims – due to the teachings of so-called leaders like Muhammad Abduh -- becomes diverted by issues of wanting to feel superior, to feel powerful, and to recapture what they perceive to be the lost glory of a by-gone age ... they want to be victorious and defeat an external foe, while ignoring the internal foe (their own nafs) that is caught up in trivialities.

What many Muslims seem to forget is that Allah has promised in the Qur'an that people's faith will be put to the test in various ways. Sometimes the test will be through wealth and riches, and sometimes the test will be through privation and constraint.

Both the West and the East have been tested through historical events. Who comes out on top in a historical sense does not necessarily reflect the spiritual calculus that God uses to assess who passed and who failed such tests.

What many Christians, Jews and Muslims often share in common is an essential ignorance about the relationship between God and human beings. That ignorance is used to "reason" about life, the world, and what should be done in relation to a series of humanitarian crises that have been brought about by delusional interpretations that reflect agendas other than Divine purpose.

Samuel Huntington was quite wrong when he talked about an irreconcilable clash of civilizations involving the West and Muslims. What makes the clash irreconcilable are the delusional systems rooted in ignorance that populate both sides and that are driving the conflict … and Huntington, as well as people like Muhammad Abduh – each in their respective ways – has helped to perpetuate that problem of ignorance over the years.

Muhammad Abduh had been disappointed with his early encounters with education, feeling that too much emphasis was given to learning by rote and too little effort was invested in helping individuals understand the meaning and significance of what they were being required to memorize. He ran into the same kind of problem when he attended al-Azhar.

Consequently, one is somewhat perplexed when one reads about Abduh's approach to certain facets of education. For example, he maintained that the children of craftsmen and peasants should be given no more education than is necessary for them to follow in the footsteps of their parents.

According to Abduh, this meant providing such children with nothing more than summaries of Islamic teachings, along with outlines of ethical principles that indicated what was considered to be right and wrong. In addition, such children should be provided with a list of reasons as to why Islam became ascendant in the world.

Yet, we didn't come into this world primarily to become peasants or craftsmen or teachers. We came into this world to learn about and realize our relationship with Divinity, and, in effect, Abduh wanted certain classes of children to be subjected to little more than the very kind of rote learning with which he had been unhappy as a child.

Abduh believed that the curriculum for higher education should consist of, among other things, being exposed to the exegesis of the

Qur'an, as well as learning about the science of Hadith, and being taught to have a rational understanding of doctrine. Again, one is confronted with the specter of rote learning in which one must simply learn and accept someone else's ideas – the accepted beliefs of the time -- about exegesis, the so-called science of hadith, and what constitutes an allegedly rational understanding of Islamic doctrine. I don't really see any focus in Abduh's approach to learning that gave emphases to assisting students to learn how to become open to being taught directly by God rather than being taught through the intermediary of human interpretations, theories, and ideas about the nature of Islam.

In the realm of politics, Abduh maintained that the ummah or community is not only the fundamental source of authority for any ruler, but, as well, the ummah is the sole determiner of what is in the best interests of the ummah, together with being the sole determiner of the means that are to be used to realize such interests. Abduh also held that rulers are not permitted to interpret the Qur'an and that rulers are to be obeyed only as long as they adhere to the requirements of the Qur'an.

Elsewhere, Abduh argued that the final authority for everything is God and His Prophet. He further stated that in Islam, there is no authority except the call to do good and condemn the evil.

The foregoing several paragraphs -- although admittedly merely a summarized overview of Abduh's perspective – seem somewhat problematic. If God and His Prophet are the final authority for everything, then it would seem that the source of a ruler's authority might be something other than the ummah. Moreover, presumably, it is God not the ummah -- Who is the One that determines what is in the best interests of the ummah, as well as the One Who determines what is the best means through which things should be done. Is this not the whole point of revelation or guidance?

Moreover, just as a ruler is not to be obeyed if that individual deviates from the teaching of the Qur'an, so too, might one not suppose that the same principle applies to the ummah. In fact, one is a little fuzzy about just who it is, within Abduh's scheme of things, that is to establish what constitutes the true teachings of the Qur'an.

Abduh mentions that shura, or consultation, should govern the relationship between the ummah and the ruler. Yet, the precise character of this process of shura and how it is to govern the relationship between ruler and the ummah seems somewhat amorphous.

He claims that it is not necessary for people to have been trained in various disciplines of argumentation, investigatory research, or the like in order to participate in the process of shura. According to Abduh, all that is required is that people be committed to the truth and to the pursuit of what is in the public interest.

What it means to be committed to the truth is an issue of some contentiousness. Moreover, what constitutes the public interest or welfare also tends to be a very complex issue.

Does shura require unanimous consensus? Or, can shura be just a matter of simple majority? Or, is it enough that only certain elite groups be in consensus concerning such matters? And, can individuals – without prejudice -- opt out of, and not be part of, something to which others might agree? Finally, if a ruler consults with the ummah and, then, rejects or ignores the direction indicated by the shura process, has the ruler abided by the requirements of shura? Just what are the requirements of shura?

These matters are not straightforward. They have not been settled in a definitive manner – although there are some people who claim that the fundamental features of all of this were settled by the 10th century and, consequently, further deliberations were not only unnecessary but, according to such individuals, were, somehow, haram or forbidden ... although I don't recall that God said any such thing in the Qur'an.

The foregoing problems are not being raised in order to argue that the idea of a Muslim community is unworkable. Rather, the problems are being raised as a way of pointing out that a great deal of additional thinking, exploration, reflection and discussion needs to take place in order to be able to have a better understanding of the possible relationships among ummah, authorities, the Qur'an, God, welfare/public interest, truth, and Shari'ah.

Abduh – and this also is true of many other Muslims – seems to want to give the impression that everything is known ahead of time … that principles of right, wrong, truth, public interest, authority, and purpose are already known by everyone and have been agreed upon. Consequently, all we have to do is measure the conduct of a leader against the established standard and everyone will know where they stand.

The Qur'an enjoins human beings to obey the Prophet and those who have been placed in authority over one. What is less clear is whether, or not, for example what the Prophet said more than 1400 years ago should be obeyed today especially when the Prophet himself gave the order – on several occasions -- that all collections of his sayings should be destroyed. Indeed, if we are supposed to obey the Prophet Muhammad (peace be upon him) and if the Prophet indicated that one should not keep collections of Hadith, then why are we listening to Bukhari or Muslim or Dawood rather than the Prophet, and on what justifiable and convincing basis can it be argued that I am obligated to follow such sayings under such conditions?

Even if it could be undeniably established that we should consult the Hadiths, there are a great many questions about how to apply those sayings, teachings, and principles to the problems of today. When someone tells me that the Prophet, if he were physically with us today, would do things in a certain way and we can tell what that would be by consulting what he said some 1400 years ago, the question arises in me: Would I be obeying the Prophet or would I be obeying someone's interpretation of the Prophet, and if I were to obey the latter, would this necessarily be following the Prophet?

In addition, what is not clear with respect to the meaning of God's words with respect to the process of having someone placed in authority over one is just that: What does it mean to place someone in authority over another individual? The Prophets have been placed in authority over human beings. Therefore, when the former directly indicate – that is, when one is in their physical presence, or when one is given a veridical dream or spiritual encounter – that a specific individual ought to do something, then one should try to obey them.

Parents have been placed in authority over their children. But, even here, the Qur'an indicates that one is not obligated to obey one's parents if they depart from the teachings of Islam ... although there is an etiquette to such departures and, as well, there is much upon which to reflect with respect to trying to determine what it might mean to claim that one's parents had departed from the teachings of Islam.

Everyone and everything has certain rights over me. To the extent that I honor such rights, then people and things have authority over me, and I am obligated to obey such authority in relation to fulfilling the structural character of the rights that bind them and me.

My shaykh was placed in authority over me when I became his mureed. To the best of my ability, I sought to obey him.

Over the years, other individuals claimed to have been placed in authority over me. However, with time and experience I came to be skeptical concerning such claims.

Furthermore, I am much more cautious about whether, or not, what Divinity might have meant in relation to the idea of placing someone in authority over one is that this should extend to an assortment of would-be leaders and rulers simply because the latter individuals might have come to power in some way. After all, power and authority might not be co-extensive.

For example, one possible question is this: is coming to power through whatever means necessarily a matter of God having _actively_ placed such people in authority, or is it merely a matter of Allah having permitted such things to happen without investing any Divine authority in those individuals, and, as such, these individuals have power but not Divinely sanctioned authority? I am equally uncertain that what God meant in the Qur'an with respect to obeying those who have been placed in authority over one means that one is required to obey whatever religious clerics, imams, muftis, mullahs, and other such authorities say simply because they claim that they have been placed in authority over one.

Would-be leaders – both Muslim and non-Muslim -- make many claims concerning how things in society should be arranged ... about who should decide, and about how they should decide and in accordance with what criteria things should be decided and in relation to which goals decisions should be made and about what the obligations of people are with respect to such decisions. Nevertheless, it of essential importance that one not cede one's intellectual, moral and spiritual sovereignty or authority to such so-called leaders until one is completely sure – and this might never be the case -- that such a process of ceding, if it does take place, will not be betrayed, abused, or exploited ... and one only can become certain about such issues through a rigorous process of asking – and having satisfactory and complete answers be given – for an extensive variety of very pointed questions.

Besides studying jurisprudence and law in Qom, Iran, Ruhollah Khomeini also studied two other subjects, both of which were to have a tremendous influence in shaping how Khomeini understood Islam. These topics were (1) 'irfan' -- which has to do with the issue of gnosis or spiritual knowledge; and (2) 'hikmat' – which, as used and understood by Khomeini, is a form of wisdom that combines elements of, on the one hand, a system of thinking that is rooted in a form of logical scholasticism and, on the other hand, a way of seeking experiential understanding of ultimate reality.

For Khomeini, hikmat – wisdom – was the means through which irfan, or gnosis, was to be realized. By adhering to a discipline shaped by religious law as well as a set of spiritual practices, one would arrive, according to Khomeini, at a spiritual condition through which, if God wished, the individual would be 'opened' to spiritual truths.

Khomeini believed that irfan and hikmat were not antithetical to shari'ah but, in fact, were inextricably tied to Divine law. By following shari'ah one would be led to both hikmat (wisdom) and irfan (gnosis), and, as well, through kikmat and irfan one would be led to a deeper understanding of shari'ah.

There is no doubt that Khomeini was not only very knowledgeable with respect to traditional Shi'a poets, but he also knew about Sufi poets like Jalal-ud-din Rumi and Hafiz of Shiraz (may Allah be pleased with them). In fact, his familiarity with poets was such that it has been reported that a person could recite a line from almost any Sufi poet and Khomeini would be able to recite the following line. Furthermore, there is considerable evidence to indicate that Khomeini was fairly conversant with at least some of the writings of Ibn al-'Arabi (may Allah be pleased with him).

Like Ibn al-'Arabi (may Allah be pleased with him), Khomeini believed that the path to gnosis consisted of a process of purification. He broke this process down into four stages or modes of spiritual journey.

The first journey allegedly went from the human being to God. During this stage, the individual seeker of truth and ultimate reality attempts to transcend the realm of human limitations.

The second stage was said to be a journey with God through the Names and Attributes of Divinity. By means of this kind of journey, one supposedly came to understand how the Names and Attributes manifested themselves and governed different facets of reality.

The third facet of the spiritual journey involved the seeker's return to the material world and society. However, during this stage, the seeker is not separated from Divinity but is intensely aware of the Divine presence.

The fourth and final stage of the spiritual journey occurs when the seeker, after having acquired gnosis, uses that understanding and knowledge to assist others to struggle toward Divinity. According to Khomeini, one of the ways in which such assistance would be given is when the spiritually realized individual implements a government of Divine justice through which human beings will be guided toward perfection.

For Khomeini, the individual who had completed the four stages of the spiritual journey was the 'perfect' human being. Such people were the vicegerents of God and the ones who were to be placed in authority over the rest of humanity.

In essence, Khomeini's system of thought was an amalgamation of: (1) some of the teachings of ibn al-'Arabi, Rumi, Hafiz and other Sufi poets/authors (may Allah be pleased with them) concerning various aspects of transcendental mysticism; (2) Suhrawardi's philosophy of light (and this Suhrawardi is not to be confused with the Sufi mystic of the same name); (3) Avicenna's school of rationalistic philosophy, and, finally, (4) Shi'a theology. What is far less clear is whether, or not, Khomeini ever actually successfully traversed any of the four stages of the journey -- outlined previously -- to become a spiritually realized individual or perfect human being.

Many people who are intelligent can spout the theory of, say, mysticism ... and, indeed, academia is replete with these individuals. Such people can impress and dazzle many with their encyclopedic knowledge of poetry, doctrine, theory, and history, but none of this 'knowledge' necessarily means that such intellectually gifted people have realized the condition of gnosis concerning their relationship with Divinity. 'Talking the talk' of gnosis does not always entail 'walking the walk' of actually being spiritually realized.

Gnosis is not about genetically inherited intelligence. Gnosis is about the gift of experientially realized understanding that God gives to whomsoever Divinity pleases.

Furthermore, there are different modalities of human perfection. Human perfection is about the realization of primordial fitra or potential that defines one's essential nature.

There are as many different kinds of human perfection as there are created fitrahs or potentials. The perfection of the Prophets gives expression to 124,000 kinds of perfection. The perfection of the saints gives expression to countless other forms of perfection. The potential for perfection in each and every human being gives expression to still further modes of perfection.

Perfection is not about becoming God. Perfection is about fulfilling the potential that is inherent within us.

Happy is the person who is content with such perfection. Longing for any other kind of perfection will be a tawdry exercise in endless disappointment, frustration, and problems – for oneself and for others.

Consequently, even if, by the Grace of God, someone is able to realize her or his primordial potential or fitra, this does not mean such a person should assume that she or he has the right or duty to 'lead' others. To be God's vicegerent is to be a caretaker of creation, and having such duties of care does not necessarily mean one should become a political or social leader.

The individual who is a spiritually realized person has no need to seek to lead or guide others. By being who he or she essentially is, that person's mode of being a vicegerent is manifested through whatever that individual does or does not do. God uses that perfect 'tool' in whatever way Divinity pleases to serve God's purpose.

According to Khomeini, government can only be authentic when it acts in accordance with the rules of Divinity. Consequently, in order to be authentic, Khomeini believes that governments must implement shari'ah.

All too many Muslims have been brow-beaten into believing that shari'ah is purely a function of jurisprudence, legal doctrine, and legalisms. However, the Qur'an is not a legal document but a book of guidance, discernment, wisdom, example, balance, and knowledge that provides human beings with an opportunity to rigorously explore what it means to be a human being.

The Qur'an very clearly states that there can be no compulsion in matters of Deen, so just how does someone justify making government the medium through which shari'ah will be implemented and forced on the people in a given locality? The Qur'an also very clearly indicates that oppression is worse than killing, and, one wonders what could be more oppressive than when someone tries to force people to live in accordance with some given interpretation of shari'ah that reduces shari'ah down to little more than a narrowly conceived legal system.

Shari'ah is Divine Law, but this does not mean that such 'Law' must be explicated through legalistic doctrines and principles. Divine Law is the nature of the universe on all levels of Being ... material, emotional, mental, human, spiritual, and transcendental.

Shari'ah is the path that leads to a place where, if God wishes, one might be opened up to the truth – literally, to drink the waters of reality -- concerning the nature of the universe, including the nature of one's own essential self. To be sure, shari'ah is a path of purification, but there are many non-coercive, non-oppressive, and non-legalistic ways through which such purification might, God willing, be realized.

On the positive side, purification involves acquiring such qualities as: patience, courage, nobility, honesty, generosity, tolerance, integrity, friendship, forgiveness, repentance, love, steadfastness, humility, kindness, dependence (on God), longing (for God), and remembrance (of God). On the negative side, purification involves ridding oneself of such qualities as: jealousy, anger, envy, hatred, hypocrisy, deceit, selfishness, insensitivity, cruelty, resentment, arrogance, impatience, and heedlessness.

Can prayer, fasting, zakat, and hajj assist one with respect to the foregoing processes of purification? Of course, they can, but if one tries to compel people to pursue those practices, there is a very high likelihood that such compulsion and oppression will not only result in zero beneficial spiritual effects but quite possibly will have a problematic, if not destructive, spiritual impact on the people so oppressed.

Neither character nor morality can be legislated. One cannot be legally forced to develop character or to be moral since both character and morality are rooted in, among other things, having a purified niyat or intention, and methods of compulsion and oppression will never bring about such purification.

Outward behavior might be controlled through such methods, but the inner world of the heart and mind will not be so-controlled … indeed, it is human nature to be inclined to respond in problematic ways with respect to such oppressive attempts. Since spiritual progress is a matter of inward transformation not just changes in external behavior, seeking to compel people to follow a given legalistic path – even if it were correct (an assumption about which I am deeply skeptical) – is doomed to failure as a means of assisting people to realize their spiritual potential.

Does the foregoing perspective mean there should be no regulation of the public space … that there should be no attempt to protect our better selves against our lower selves? No, it doesn't, but the regulation of public space is not shari'ah. Rather, the regulation of public space is a process of creating conditions that are conducive to people being able to choose to pursue, or not, the actual path of shari'ah without adversely affecting the right of other people to make different kinds of choices concerning how to proceed in life regarding such matters.

One of the most precious gifts – and challenges – which God gave to human beings is the right to choose. Those who wish to make shari'ah a legalistic system of coercive rules seem to believe that they have the right to take away one of the most essential gifts that God has given to human beings.

Steps do need to be taken to ensure, as best as possible, that when the personal exercise of choice spills over into the public space in a problematic or destructive way, the possible deleterious ramifications of such choices for other human beings must be constrained and limited. However, the Qur'an offers up a tremendous variety of principles for dealing with such matters that do not have to be limited to legalisms ... and, in fact, a very good argument can be made that to insist on such legalisms as the only way of regulating public space is to be oppressive with respect to the guidance and teachings of the rest of the Qur'an.

What the Prophet did with respect to the regulation of public space when he was in this world physically is one thing. But, none of us is a Prophet, and, therefore, we should not suppose that we have the wisdom, gnosis, or authority to regulate public space in the same way he did.

We have absolutely no reliable insight into, or understanding of, what went on in the mind and heart of the Prophet when he was called upon to make different decisions. We have absolutely no reliable proof that if the Prophet were physically with us today that he would decide matters in this day and age in precisely the same way as he did more than 1400 years ago.

People who seek to use only part of the Qur'an to regulate public space are not following the example of the Prophet Muhammad (peace be upon him). The Prophet's character, understanding, behavior, insight, judgment and decisions were shaped by the entire body of the Qur'an – not just a part of it -- and there are very few, if any, people living today who can claim to know how all of this would come together to shape how the Prophet might seek to resolve any given problem involving the regulation of public space if he were physically living among us in today's world.

In the '70's Khomeini sought to convince students that they had an obligation to establish an Islamic state – that is, a government which was to be ruled by Khomeini's conception of shari'ah. During this time, Khomeini also sought to persuade clerics that they had a responsibility to assume control of such a state and to ensure that the state would be regulated through the enforcement of shari'ah construed as a legal system.

Khomeini's justification for seeking to establish an Islamic state was rooted in the doctrine of: 'Velayat-e Faqih'. This idea has been translated in a number of different ways including: 'the guardianship of the legal jurist' and the 'theological vicegerency of the jurist'.

In turn, the notion of 'Velayat-e Faqih' is rooted in Khomeini's ideas about the four stage spiritual journey to spiritual realization that culminates in a return to society through which the spiritually realized individual, or perfect human being, sets about leading other people to perfection. All of this is very presumptuous.

Khomeini seemed to assume that he was such a perfect man. He assumed that it is the right and duty of a perfect man to tell others how to live their lives. Khomeini assumed that it is the right and duty of such a person to impose shari'ah on others and to force them to pursue a particular way of life. He further assumed that a perfect person could lead others to perfection.

I believe that the Prophet Muhammad (peace be upon him) is a perfect human being, and, yet, the Qur'an clearly indicates that the Prophet cannot guide people to the truth. Only God can lead a person to realization of the truth. Only God can open up hearts to faith and knowledge.

The Prophet is the best of examples. He is a friend and supporter and one who prays for the forgiveness of his community and for all creation. He assists people – whether Muslim or Muslim – whenever he can and in accordance with the limitations of the sort of help that he has been permitted and enabled by God to offer. He gives counsel when asked, and, yet, he encouraged people not to ask him questions concerning Islam. Why did Khomeini believe that he could accomplish what the Prophet could not and, indeed, what was not even within the Prophet's mandate to try to do?

Ibn al-'Arabi (may Allah be pleased with him) – someone who Khomeini considered to be a perfect human being – never sought to establish an Islamic state nor did the former individual ever try to impose shari'ah (however he might have conceived it) on others. This is also true of Sufi mystics such as Rumi, Hafiz, and others (may Allah be pleased with them), and Khomeini looked favorably on all of these individuals.

However, somewhere along the line, Khomeini came to a very different conclusion than the spiritual predecessors whom he admired and quoted. This fact raises a lot of red flags concerning the legitimacy of Khomeini's understanding of many things.

Once Khomeini achieved power he proceeded to seek to purify society by ridding it of the alleged forces of evil that had been serving, in one capacity or another, as agents of the deposed Shah. The manner in which this allegedly perfect man sought to lead the evil-doers to a purified condition was not through counseling, guidance, dialogue, spiritual assistance, or the like, but, rather, he purified them by having them executed, and such executions were followed by similar purifications of other lesser officials and military personnel.

The Qur'an indicates that one is justified in killing those who spread corruption in the earth, but this doesn't mean that one must do this. Furthermore, one could engage in a rather lengthy discussion about who, exactly, was spreading corruption in the land with respect to the Iranian revolution ... especially given that the Qur'an says that if it were a matter of taking humankind to task for their transgressions against God, then not one living creature would be left on the face of the Earth (Qur'an 16: 61).

Once he ascended to power, Khomeini increasingly wanted everything under his control. He didn't do this because he was a spiritually realized individual and knew – via gnosis – what was best, rather he sought to control things because he apparently failed to realize that oppression and compulsion are not part of shari'ah.

Behavior sometimes is a good indicator of the intentions underlying it. In many ways and as the foregoing discussion suggests, Khomeini's behavior betrayed his apparent belief that he was a spiritually realized human being.

Unlike Khomeini, the example set by the Prophet Muhammad (peace be upon him) did not involve oppressively and forcibly trying to control the lives of people ... although that example did involve some instances of regulating public space in a way that resonated with the times in which, and circumstances under which, he and the rest of the community lived. Therefore, whenever a so-called leader presumes he or she has the right and authority to oppressively and forcibly control the lives of others, then one should observe due diligence in examining the theory of leadership out of which that person operates.

Hasan al-Banna, an Egyptian, was born in 1906 and passed away at the age of 43. Among other things, he founded the Muslim Brotherhood.

When he was approximately 12 years old, Banna joined a Muslim group that was concerned with issues of moral behavior. In fact, one of the primary purposes of the group was to induce its members to actively observe whatever the group considered to give expression to a strict code of Islamic behavior, and part of the inducement process was to levy fines on anyone who transgressed against that code.

A little later, he joined another group whose activities also revolved around issues of morality and bringing pressure to bear on anyone who might have erred – at least according to that group's leaders -- with respect to some aspect of moral behavior. One of the practices of this group was to send threatening letters to the alleged miscreants.

When he was thirteen, Banna became associated with a Sufi Order. This group was not only committed to following a strict code of Islamic behavior, but, as well, it had a charitable arm that sought to reform the morality of others, and Banna became actively involved with this dimension of the Sufi Order.

Although Banna developed an appreciation for certain aspects of the Sufi mystical tradition, he also had reservations about certain practices associated with some Sufi groups. On the one hand, he was attracted to what he felt was the tendency of Sufis to adhere to the moral dimension of Islam, but, on the other hand, he felt that too many innovative practices, or bid'a, had become intermingled with the Sufi path.

Without wishing to make a pronouncement one way or the other as to whether, or not, Banna was correct in his assessment of the Sufi path, a point does need to be raised with respect to the issue of bid'a or spiritual innovation. More specifically, while the Prophet Muhammad (peace be upon him) had issued warnings about the dangers of spiritual innovation, his warnings tended to be of a general nature and done without specifying that which constituted innovation.

Unfortunately, it is a common practice of all too many Muslims to try to claim that what the Prophet meant when he gave such warnings has to do with whatever the Muslims are against who are invoking the saying of the Prophet concerning spiritual innovation. If those Muslims are against music, then music becomes bi'dah, and the claim is made that this is what the Prophet had in mind when he talked about spiritual innovation. If those Muslims are against certain kinds of art, then such art becomes bi'da, and the claim is made that this is what the Prophet had in mind when he warned about spiritual innovation ... and so on.

Such Muslims might, or might not, be correct in their claims. The problem is that they don't really know what the Prophet meant when he is reported to have said what he did with respect to the issue of spiritual innovation.

The Prophet did indicate on a number of occasions that people should not make or keep collections of his sayings. So, is it an instance of spiritual innovation, or bi'da, when people seek to cite the authority of the Prophet's words to justify imposing beliefs or behavior on others?

While later in life, Banna never condemned the Sufi path, per se, he did argue that misguided Sufis should be reformed. Moreover, Banna indicated that Sufi writings should be rid of their impurities.

Determining who was a misguided Sufi and what writings needed to be cleansed were a function of Banna's judgment concerning such matters. Moreover, Banna believed that it was people such as himself who should be the ones who ought to have influential authority in relation to determining how misguided individuals and impure writings should be reformed.

Indeed, one of the facets of the Sufi path with which Banna was much enamored involved the relationship between a seeker and the shaykh or teacher. According to Banna, the connection was one of absolute obedience – a characterization with which I would take exception since I do not believe it reflects the actual nature of the relationship between a shaykh and a seeker. Banna wanted to extend this theme of absolute obedience to other kinds of relational arrangements involving so-called leaders (which he considered himself to be) and followers.

Obviously, if Banna was a leader, then the generality of people – who are defined by Banna as followers -- should obey what he, and others like him, said with respect to matters of bi'da, impure writings, and being misguided. According to Banna, it is the prerogative and right of the leader to decide, and it is the duty of follows to follow the prerogative of the leaders.

I have no problem with someone like Banna believing anything he likes. This after all is the right of sovereignty concerning the exercise of choice that God has bestowed on human beings.

I do have a problem when what someone like Banna believes spills over into the realm of behavior, and through this spill over, Banna begins to try to control me, or others, so that I, or they, become obedient to, and are compelled to serve, his vision of things. Banna presumes he has a right – nay duty -- to interfere in my life and rid me of whatever misguidance and impurities he believes me to operating through, and his justification for doing so is that he believes that he is right and that I am wrong.

Even if Banna were correct with respect to his understanding of the 'true' Islam – and this is not a foregone conclusion – there is a logical jump he is making that needs to be justified independently of being correct about something. This logical jump concerns the following question: under what circumstances, and to what extent, does someone have the right to interfere in another person's life even if one were to assume that the former person is correct and the latter person is wrong about some given issue?

The Prophet Muhammad (peace be upon him) was told through the Qur'an that it was not the Prophet's duty to guide others to the truth. Guidance belonged to Allah alone. Therefore, if the Prophet did not have the responsibility of guiding people, why does Banna believe he has the right and duty to do what the Prophet could not do?

When Banna was 21 years old, he wrote an essay to fulfill part of his educational requirements. In the essay he was critical of Sufis for withdrawing from society.

He believed that such a tendency limited their effective influence with respect to reforming society. Moreover, Banna argued that because regular teachers did not withdraw from society and, as a result, had a better opportunity to influence, change, and reform the lives of people, regular teachers were better than Sufi shaykhs.

Banna's essay was predicated on the presumption that: it is the job of a teacher or Sufi shaykh to influence, change, or reform other human beings. Perhaps part of the reason why some Sufis chose to withdraw from society is because they wished to remove themselves from the temptation of trying to interfere in the lives of other people rather than focus on reforming and changing their own lives.

Banna's essay is more than a little self-serving since, at the time, he was trying to satisfy the educational requirements for becoming a teacher. Moreover, his thesis seems not to reflect his earlier experience with a Sufi Order that did promote charitable acts with respect to the needy in society.

Of course, feeding, clothing, and housing people does interfere in the lives of people. However, this kind of interference is quite a bit different than trying to change, influence, reform, or purify the way people live their lives.

The former kind of interference has always been encouraged by both the exoteric and esoteric dimensions of Islam. However, there are many cautionary considerations surrounding the latter kind of interference … and one of these cautionary considerations is that the process of actively interfering in another person's life in order to reform or purify such individuals would seem to come in direct conflict with the Quranic teaching that there can be no compulsion in matters of Deen, and, as such, therefore, possibly qualify as an expression of bid'a.

One of the central principles in the Muslim Brotherhood that Banna established in 1928 revolved around the idea of restoring the caliphate. Banna, among others, had been appalled when earlier Kemal Ataturk had done away with the position of caliph in Turkey, and Banna believed that restoring the caliphacy would be an important means through which to reform and purify society so that it could be brought back to the true Islam.

Later on, Banna argued that politics should not be subjected to the divisiveness of a multiparty system, but, instead should be regulated through just one party. Supposedly, having just one party would be a means to unify the electorate or ummah, but Banna does not seem to have appreciated the fact that divisiveness comes from individuals not parties ... or said in another way, the divisiveness of parties is a function of the divisiveness of individuals as each, in her or his own way, seeks to find ways of controlling others to serve some agenda, and, therefore, the aforementioned divisiveness also can occur within single party systems as well as within multi-party systems.

Although Banna believed in holding elections, he believed that the people who ran for office should be restricted to certain classes of people. He felt that, on the one hand, only experts in religious law and public affairs, and, on the other hand, already established leaders of organizations, families or tribes, should be permitted to run for office.

Obviously, Banna was something of an elitist or oligarch and believed that power should be invested in a select group of individuals of whom Banna approved. Commoners, peasants, the un-empowered and women need not apply.

Indeed, Banna had a fairly repressive view of the role of women in society. He believed their activities should be restricted to motherhood, housekeeping, and staying out of sight. Consequently, he felt that women should not be taught religious law, technical sciences, or foreign languages but only those subjects that would permit them to be mothers, housekeepers, and invisible.

Apparently, among other things, Banna interpreted the Quranic ayat that men had been given a degree of superiority over women to mean that men had the right to take control of pretty much everything concerning the lives of women. However, although the Quranic ayat in question does not say in what way men had a degree of superiority over women, this has not stopped Muslim men from interpreting the passage in whatever way serves their interests, and, in the process, might be guilty of trying to introduce innovation, or bi'da into Islam.

For Banna, the government would manage all aspects of society. This control would extend from: ensuring that Islamic practices were correctly observed, to: censoring whatever books, films, songs, or ideas were considered to be antithetical to the 'true Islam'.

Banna is presuming that he and the other leaders of society know what 'true Islam' is. He also is presuming that even if he did know this that he has the right to impose such views on other human beings. What part of: 'there can be no compulsion in matters of Deen' doesn't he understand?

To be sure, society as a whole – not just government – has the challenge of determining how to proceed in a way that balances individual freedom with the need to protect the public space so that exercise of such individual freedoms do not adversely affect the capacity of others to pursue their own God-given right of sovereignty with respect to choice. This issue has a potential for being very problematic.

Nonetheless, acknowledging the existence of such a problem of social balancing does not mean that the government has the right or authority – although it might have the power to do so – to solve this problem for others and, in the process, impose its solution on the people.

Banna claims that leaders must listen to the will of the people. But, what does this really mean?

First of all, not every instance of the will of the people is necessarily in the best interests of the people, anymore than one can suppose that every instance of the will of an individual is necessarily in the best interests of that person. So, how does one decide between those expressions of the will of the people that should be listened to and those expressions of the will of the people that should not be listened to?

Secondly, if it is the will of the people that should be listened to, then, why is there any need for government? Can't people carrying out their own will? If it is the will of the people that should be listened to, then why are only government leaders in charge of educating, reforming, propagandizing and purifying that will?

The way in which Banna organized the Muslim Brotherhood reveals his intentions with respect to society if he should ever gain control over the reins of government. By 1946, Banna had established a hierarchical organizational model in which Banna had control over every facet and level of the activities of the Muslim Brotherhood.

Banna ran his organization in accordance with his erroneous understanding of the relationship between a Sufi shaykh and a mureed or seeker. Namely, Banna believed that everyone in the organization owed absolute obedience to him. While he did establish a smaller and larger body of members with whom he would consult concerning matters, the final decision would be his.

The process of becoming initiated into the Brotherhood is also very revealing. Candidates were required to take an oath of commitment to Banna's conception of jihad in which a person should be willing to seek out death and martyrdom as he sought to convert the world to Banna's ideological stance concerning Islam.

The foregoing oath of commitment was taken in a darkened room. During the ceremony, the would-be initiate had to swear secrecy concerning the Brotherhood while his hand was on a Qur'an and a pistol.

The pistol is a multi-faceted symbol. On the one hand, it implies a willingness to use force to carry out the agenda of the Brotherhood, and, on the other hand, it implies what lays in store for anyone who violates the oath of secrecy or the demand for absolute obedience.

Considered from another perspective, the use of both a pistol and the Qur'an in the initiation ceremony suggests a deep-rooted lack of faith in God. Among other things, the presence of the pistol tends to indicate that Banna seemed to believe that the Qur'an, by itself, was not considered a sufficiently adequate focus of loyalty, commitment or solution to life's problems.

According to Banna, the purpose of the Brotherhood was to offer assistance to the rulers. The form of this assistance concerned advising the ruler how to run the country in accordance with the ideals of 'true Islam'.

Nevertheless, Banna also indicated that the Brotherhood should be prepared to use force if the rulers proved to be intransigent with respect to the 'advice' or 'counsel' that was being offered through the Brotherhood. In other words, his position seemed to be: 'listen or else', and as someone once told me, if you can't hear no, then, what one is asking is not a request or a mere giving of advice and counsel.

The fact of the matter is that at times violence was employed by the Brotherhood, not only with respect to the government but, as well, in relation to individuals with whom the Brotherhood considered to be purveyors of something other than the 'true Islam'. This willingness to resort to violence if one doesn't get what one wants is a very slippery slope that very quickly ends up justifying all manner of acts of cruelty, brutality, and oppression.

Banna wanted to return to the teachings of the salaf, the spiritual forbearers of early Islam. However, his motives for wishing to do so are somewhat muddled.

On the one hand, he blamed the condition of the Muslim world -- vis-à-vis being in a position of degrading subjugation to Western imperialism and colonialism -- on the fact that Muslims had strayed from the teachings of 'true Islam'. Banna argued that the salaf adhered completely to 'true Islam' and, as a result they were rewarded with control of a large part of the known world at that time.

Banna believed that if Muslims were brought back to the 'true Islam', then Muslims would, once again be rewarded by God – as he believed had been the case in relation to the salaf -- with control of the world and, in the process, would be permitted to throw off the shackles of Western oppression. Unfortunately, by thinking in this manner, Banna has muddied the waters of intention in which what is done by a Muslim should be done for the sake of Allah and not for the sake of any advantageous rewards or ramifications that might come from this.

The Muslim Brotherhood might have accomplished any number of good things such as: assisting the needy, feeding the poor, building schools, physically cleaning up neighborhoods, and helping the sick. However, such good deeds always had a hidden price and cost in which sooner, or later, people would be expected to pay for those good deeds by ceding their moral, intellectual, and spiritual authority to the leaders of the Brotherhood.

If God wishes, true Islam teaches individuals how not to cede their moral, intellectual, and spiritual authority to anyone but God. If God wishes, true Islam teaches individuals that one does not need to commit oneself to the way of God with one's hand on a pistol and that the Qur'an, alone, is more than adequate. If God wishes, true Islam teaches individuals that while we have duties of care to others, nevertheless, seeking to fulfill such duties does not entitle one to absolute obedience from others. If God wishes, true Islam teaches individuals that trying to convert others to Islam is not one of the pillars of Islam and that the inclination of hearts to Islam is the business of God, not of human beings. If God wishes, true Islam teaches individuals that one should have some degree of humility with respect to the correctness of one's understanding of the truth and that just because one believes one is right, this does not justify one's trying to impose one's beliefs on others. If God wishes, true Islam teaches individuals that there can be no compulsion in matters of Deen, and, therefore, to whatever extent one uses compulsion, force, and oppression in order to induce someone to adhere to one's interpretation of the 'true Islam', then, one is violating one of the basic tenets of Islam.

Given the foregoing, I am of the opinion that there is a great deal about the 'true Islam' with which Banna was not familiar. Given the foregoing, I am inclined, God willing, to be prepared never to cede my intellectual, moral, and spiritual authority to would-be leaders like Banna who tend to filter reality through their own high opinion of themselves and believe they have been given Divine sanction to proceed in a direction that, unfortunately, seems far more likely to take people away from the 'true Islam' than toward it.

Chapter 4: <u>Constitutional 911: 9/11 and the Constitution</u>

Many people have criticized both *The 9/11 Commission Report* and the various NIST (National Institute of Standards and Technology) reports concerning the collapse of three buildings at Ground Zero in New York for lacking qualities such as: thoroughness, rigor, accuracy, and integrity. What I have not seen to date – although someone, somewhere might have said something on this topic – is that the very processes through which the 9/11 Commission and NIST were permitted to produce their reports were unconstitutional.

In other words, neither the 9/11 Commission nor NIST had constitutional authority to do what they did. More specifically, Congress did not have the Constitutional authority to pass legislation to create the 9/11 Commission, and the Department of Commerce -- the parent body of NIST -- did not have constitutional authority to enable NIST to conduct its research and produce its reports in relation to 9/11.

No matter what one's theory concerning 9/11 might be, I believe there is indisputable evidence that the events of 9/11 have been used as a pretext for eviscerating the Constitution – and, actually, some of these issues [for example, torture, extreme rendition, warrantless wiretaps, the Patriot Act, and undeclared wars) already have been explored and analyzed by a variety of people Yet, many of these same individuals who have been critical of the government in the ways noted previously seem to be of the opinion that although the 9/11 Commission and NIST had the right to do what they did, they just did it badly, and, as a result, such critics seem to have failed to understand that the 9/11 Commission and the NIST reports were part of the Constitutional evisceration process that ensued from 9/11.

Great tragedy occurred on September 11th, 2001. Obviously, the nearly 3000 lives that were lost on 9/11 -- along with the many families that, as a result, were adversely affected -- is near the top of the list.

However, the damage that has been done, and is being done, to the Constitution is enabling many more such tragedies to unfold. The patriot Act, the wars in Iraq and Afghanistan (where hundreds of thousands more people have died), torture, extreme rendition, crimes against humanity, warrantless wiretapping, hundreds of billions of dollars that have been wasted on war, crippling indebtedness, a failing economy – these are all the bastard children of countless incestuous affairs being illicitly conducted (that is, which are unconstitutional) within, and through, the federal government.

The following discussion outlines the underlying issues. In addition, this essay will explore a few of the ramifications that have arisen through the unconstitutional processes at issue.

The Constitutional basis for my contention concerning the 9/11 Commission and NIST are rooted in four provisions of the Constitution and after listing these roots, I will elaborate upon them in greater detail through much of the remainder of this essay. (1) *Article IV, Section 4* of the Constitution states that: "The United States shall <u>guarantee</u> every state in the union, a republican form of government." (2) The *Preamble to the Constitution* stipulates that the purpose for which the Constitution has been created is: "to establish a more perfect union, establish justice, insure domestic tranquility, provide for the common defense, promote the general welfare, and secure the blessings of liberty for ourselves and out posterity." (3) *The Ninth Amendment* indicates that: "The enumeration in the Constitution of certain rights shall not be construed to deny or disparage others retained by the people." (4) The *Tenth Amendment* stipulates that: "The powers not delegated to the United States by the Constitution, nor prohibited to it by the states, are reserved to the states respectively, or to the people."

----

(1) The promise of republican government in Article IV, Section 4 of the Constitution has nothing to do with the Republican Party. In fact, although I am not a Democrat, nor do I belong to any other political party, nonetheless, one might easily argue – and quite plausibly I believe (and this will be elaborated upon shortly) – that the current Republican Party is the complete antithesis of the actual meaning of "republicanism" being referred to in the Constitution ... although to be fair about the matter, one quite justifiably could say the same thing of the existing Democratic Party – namely, that when its candidates are

elected they usually do not properly observe the fiduciary responsibilities that are entailed by a republican form of government.

The idea of guaranteeing every state in the union, a republican form of government could be read in, at least, two ways. (a) The federal government is guaranteeing that every state will have a republican form of government, and, (b) the federal government is guaranteeing that the federal government will provide a republican form of government in its relations with the various states.

Interpretation (a) is both oppressively tyrannical and runs contrary to the whole revolutionary and constitutional history of America. Therefore, the guarantee of republican government being issued through Article IV, Section 4 is about the quality of government that the central government will offer to each of the states of the union.

Unfortunately, the sad fact of the matter is that almost every administration in the federal government that has taken office since the inception of the United States of America has failed to realize the Constitutional requirements of Article 4, Section 4 – which is not a promise, but a guarantee -- concerning the matter of a republican form of government. Consequently, almost from the very beginning of this country as a constitutionally constructed entity, virtually every federally elected government has conducted its administration in an unconstitutional manner.

When the Constitutional Convention was in progress in Philadelphia, much of the discussion was done through a spirit of republicanism. Indeed, republicanism was part of the ideology of the Enlightenment that influenced the Framers of the Constitution, and, as such, republicanism was: a way of life; a way of thinking; a way of behaving.

Moreover, the theme of republicanism was so close to the hearts of the Framers of the Constitution they held that no one should govern others unless such leaders were completely governed by republican principles. This was so much the case that it was enshrined in the Constitution in Article IV, Section 4, and was probably one of the primary reasons why individuals such as Madison and Monroe initially felt there was no need to create a separate Bill of Rights since the guarantee of republican government contained in the Constitution should – they believed – satisfactorily accommodate such concerns.

So, what is republicanism? It encompasses a set of core values such as: being benevolent; having integrity; demonstrating character; showing judiciousness; displaying egalitarianism; possessing and giving expression to qualities of virtue; being truly disinterested in personal gain or profit while serving others; having the capacity to be impartial arbiters in all matters and, therefore, never serving as a judge in one's own cause; showing tolerance and modesty in all matters; exhibiting unfailing honesty; manifesting honor and reasonableness in every affair; being willing to sacrifice oneself for the good of others; being unbiased and independent when evaluating and judging any situation; having high-mindedness guide one's thoughts and actions in relation to the public good.

In an ideal republican world, a person in government would not receive a salary or profit for one's labors on behalf of the public. This is one of the reasons why many of the individuals who stayed for the entire Constitutional Convention struggled financially throughout the process, and it is also one of the reasons why others who had assembled for the Constitutional Convention had to leave before the process had been completed – namely, they could no longer afford to survive in Philadelphia and be away from their means of generating income.

Given the foregoing set of republican values, one could understand how people like Monroe and Madison believed that a Bill of Rights was unnecessary. After all, if government officials lived in accordance with the requirements of republican values then all of the protections of human rights that are given a voice through the Bill of Rights could be satisfied by individuals who operated through republican values ... or, so, the theory went.

Fortunately, there were many other individuals in the Colonies who, although they admired and sought to abide by the values inherent in the republican spirit, they, nevertheless, had a less sanguine – or, perhaps, more realistic -- view of human potential. They realized that not all individuals who achieved elected or appointed office in the Federal Government could necessarily be counted on to abide by the requirements of a republican philosophy.

Consequently, these more far-sighted members of the fraternity of Framers had the guarantee of republican government written into the Constitution. In addition, they insisted that unless there was a separate Bill of Rights that would be added to the main body of the Constitution very soon after the ratification process had been completed, then there would be no ratification of the Constitution as written ... the issue was, in a sense, a deal-breaker.

The republican spirit prevailed. A gentleman's agreement on the Constitution had been brokered, and soon after the Constitution was ratified, a process for developing a Bill of Rights was instituted, and the results of that process were subsequently ratified in 1791.

Article VI of the Constitution states:

"This Constitution, and the laws of the United States which shall be made in pursuance thereof; and all treaties made, or which shall be made, under the authority of the United States, shall be the supreme law of the land; and the judges in every state shall be bound thereby, anything in the Constitution or laws of any State to the contrary notwithstanding.

"The Senators and Representatives before mentioned and the members of the several state legislatures, and all executive and judicial officers, both of the United States and the several states, shall be bound by oath or affirmation, to support this Constitution."

Among other things, the foregoing excerpt from the Constitution – the beginning portion of which is referred to as 'the Supremacy Clause' – indicates that all laws must be in compliance with the Constitution. This means, among other things, that all laws must be in compliance with the guarantee of republican government.

In short, one of the primary filters through which everything in the Constitution must be understood is encompassed by the "guarantee of republican government". If one wishes to talk about the intent of the Framers, then everything that they did, said and wrote was a function of republican values and principles because that is the philosophy and understanding which essentially shaped their perspective concerning government and social affairs.

Anything that does not satisfy the guarantee of republican government is unconstitutional. Furthermore, all Senators,

Representatives, members of the state legislatures, as well as all executive and judicial officers are bound by the requirements of the guarantee of republican government to acknowledge as much.

Unfortunately, for most of the history of the United States the aforementioned guarantee has not only been unacknowledged, but, as well, it has not been properly enforced with respect to the actions of any of the branches of federal government. Consequently, many of the Congressional laws, executive orders, and judicial decisions that have been generated over the years are unconstitutional for when those laws, executive orders and judicial decisions are critically and rigorously examined, they usually are not capable of passing the litmus test entailed by the guarantee of republican government.

Furthermore, this means that many of the decisions and practices of: Congress, the Executive Office, and the Judiciary that are cited as precedent to support or rationalize their judgments actually often constitute invalid forms of reasoning. This is so because such precedents are frequently the result of processes that could not satisfy the guarantee of republican government that is stipulated in Article IV, Section 4 of the Constitution and that all governmental officials are required by Constitutional authority to support through affirmation or oath ... as is said in another context, such precedents are the fruit of a poisonous tree (the failure to satisfy the conditions of republican government) and, as such, are, therefore, Constitutionally unacceptable.

To name just a few of the fruits of such a poisonous tree, one might mention: The Federal Reserve Act of 1913. The entire Act was put together in a secret meeting on Jekyll Island, off the coast of Georgia, by a group of seven individuals (Charles, Norton, Paul Warburg, Nelson Aldrich, Benjamin Strong, Abraham Andrew, Henry Davidson, and Frank Vanderlip) who represented a variety of private banking and financial interests and, then the Act was guided through Congress by people (such as Nelson Aldrich, who was the Republican Whip for the Senate) and who knew that the proposed Federal Reserve would not be a Federal institution but a corporation that served the interests of a consortium of private member banks rather than the interests of the vast majority of the people of the United States and which, for the most part, would be beyond the control of the Federal or State governments.

The foregoing was a clear violation of the guarantee of republican government. This is so not only in relation to the influence that special interests had in constructing the legislation concerning the Federal Reserve (and, there are many, many cases in which private lobbyists and special interest groups write the legislation that is voted on – often unknowingly -- by members of Congress), but the failure to observe the requirements of republican governance also reflects how many people in Congress failed to exercise reasonableness, integrity, honor, impartiality, honesty, judiciousness, impartiality, and benevolence (to anyone but the bankers) during the process of passing the Federal Reserve Act.

In fact, much of the legislation that deregulated the financial industry – e.g., the Glass-Steagall Act of 1933 – and which laid the groundwork for the creation of intentionally complex and mystifying financial instruments, such as derivatives, is unconstitutional. This is because the manner through which many, if not most, of the deregulatory laws came into existence violated the peoples' right to republican governance ... that is, many individuals who were involved with the passage of such legislation were not people with: honor, integrity, honesty, judiciousness, benevolence, impartiality, egalitarianism, independence, and high-mindedness that was free of all self-interest and private passions concerning such legislation.

Another example of the fruit of the poisonous tree concerns corporations. In today's world, corporations possess great power, have most of the rights and protections of actual human beings, and, yet rather ironically, often don't have any of the responsibilities of biological persons.

This current state of affairs has turned the understanding and concerns of colonists and the Framers of the Constitution upside down. In colonial days, corporations were, for the most part, loathed by the colonists – except, of course, for those individuals who stood to gain money and power through their cohabitation with one of the predominant corporations of colonial days – namely, the East India Company.

The Boston Tea Party was an act of rebellion not only against King George, but it was also a statement of protest against the East India Company that had been given an unfair advantage in commerce by being largely exempt from the taxes that were being levied on colonial tea entrepreneurs through the Tea Act of 1773. The East India Company, which had English government office holders and royalty among its stockholders, used the leverage provided to it through the Tea Act to drive smaller tea suppliers out of business by undercutting the prices charged by the latter who had to pay a tax from which the East India Company was largely immune.

The Framers of the Constitution had no intention of, either explicitly or implicitly, delegating rights and powers to corporations. Corporations are not mentioned in the main body of the Constitution nor in any of the amendments for a very good reason – corporations were considered to be malevolent forces intent on denying people the right to have control over their own lives.

However, despite the provisions of the Constitution, corporations have continued to seek ways to undermine democracy and usurp the powers of: the people, states, and the federal government. They have sought to accomplish this through a variety of venues, many of which involved the corporations who owned railroads.

For instance, consider the 1886 Supreme Court decision involving Santa Clara County versus Santa Fe Railroad. Over the years since that decision, corporations have tried to use what they have incorrectly portrayed as the substantive character of that decision as a precedent for treating corporations as persons. However, the attempt of corporations to push for such recognition violates the essential spirit of what is meant by republican governance in several ways.

First, the Santa Clara County decision did not acknowledge or stipulate that corporations were persons. Instead, the impression that such a precedent had been established was created by a court reporter – J.C. Bancroft Davis, a former executive for the railroads, and who, while employed as a court reported for the Supreme Court, earned money on the side by publishing Supreme Court decision with annotated introductions of his own thoughts. It was those annotated comments of the court reporter – not the actual legal decision -- which made the claim that the aforementioned decision had stipulated that corporations were persons under the law.

Secondly, the idea that corporations were persons under the law and, therefore, were entitled to the same rights or powers as biological persons would have been rejected by the vast majority of colonists, as well as by the Framers of the Constitution. To try to argue otherwise would require one to rewrite America's revolutionary history, and, as a result, one has no problem in ascertaining the Framers' intent in relation to corporations like The East India Company – such corporations were predatory capitalists and to whatever extent they were permitted to exist, they should not be given any powers or rights that could not be completely controlled or revoked by the people.

Since then, corporations have used money, economic power and collusion with their corporate partners, the banks, to corrupt the political process in America and everywhere else in the world. Consequently, all of the powers and rights that corporations have acquired through the process of government have been gained by ensuring that the guarantee of republican government is ignored and corrupted.

In fact, one can take the issue further. Any attempt to consider corporations as anything other than legal fictions with respect to the very circumscribed category of artificial persons in order to provide civil liability protection with respect to monetary debt or damages in relation to investors of such artificial entities cannot pass the litmus test concerning the Constitutional guarantee of republican government. Moreover, all attempts to claim 14th Amendment protection for corporations are also unconstitutional because the 14th Amendment clearly stipulates that its provisions are specifically for: "all persons born or naturalized in the United States" and corporations are neither born nor naturalized.

Indeed, corporations are not citizens at all – born or naturalized. Thus, when one reads a bit further down in the 14th Amendment that: "No state shall make or enforce any law which shall abridge the privileges or immunities of citizens of the United States", this does not prevent laws being made that do abridge any privileges or immunities which corporations might believe themselves to have – and this is so, because corporations are not citizens.

Finally, the last part of Section 1 of the 14th Amendment states that no state might: "deny to any person within its jurisdiction the equal protection of the laws." A corporation is not a person in the sense of a being who has come into this world through biological birth and is a citizen of the United States by either birth or a process of naturalization, and, therefore, corporations are not entitled to equal protection under the law.

The entire history of corporations seeking to be legally identified as actual persons or being recognized by certain jurists as actual persons is predicated on a failure to comply with the requirements of the guarantee of republican government. This is so because all such efforts have been rooted in desires and qualities that are the antithesis of the sort of republican values and principles that are alluded to in Article IV, Section 4 of the Constitution – in other words those efforts have not exhibited properties of: benevolence, disinterest in personal gain, being unbiased, honesty, virtuousness, having integrity, and not possessing self-interest or private passions.

One could extend the foregoing sort of reasoning to a wide variety of other issues. For instance, passage of the Patriot Act -- along with so many other Congressional Acts – is unconstitutional because most of the members of Congress did not read the Act before passing it. This is a violation of the guarantee of republican government.

One could add other examples of violations of the Constitutional guarantee of republican government. Conflicts involving Vietnam, Panama, Grenada, Nicaragua, Iraq (twice), and Afghanistan were -- and are -- unconstitutional ... irrespective of what Congress, the Executive Office, or the Judiciary claims. All those conflicts involved demonstrable: deceit, dishonesty, injudiciousness, unreasonableness, bias, and, as well, all those conflicts lacked: character, honorableness, integrity, benevolence, and impartiality. Consequently, all of those conflicts have failed to comply with the Constitutional guarantee of republican government that the federal government owes to the states.

The requirement of republican government is the lens through which all issues of national security and interests must be assessed. No war can be declared and no conflict can be fought unless one can demonstrate that the war and the conflict comply with republican principles and values.

Moreover, if, either after the fact or before the fact, a given war or conflict can be shown to be based, or to have been based, on lies (as say, Vietnam, Iraq – twice -- and Afghanistan have been so exposed), then the perpetrators of such essential breeches of the Constitution need to be impeached, if still in office, convicted, and then, whether, or not they hold elective or appointive office, held accountable for having committed: war crimes, crimes against humanity, and treason in relation to the very principles and purposes for which America came into being.

Or, consider the following. All government treaties and policies involving Native Peoples have been unconstitutional because they all violated, in one way or another, the Constitutional guarantee of republican government to the states and their people.

Nothing that the federal government has done in relation to Native peoples can be characterized as being: honorable, reasonable, impartial, unbiased, honest, tolerant, virtuous, benevolent, or disinterested. Throughout its history, the Federal Government has consistently and continuously violated Article IV, Section 4 of the Constitution by failing to provide citizens of the various states with republican governance in relation to a proper treatment of Native Peoples – some of whom provided ideas that helped shape and orient the thinking of the Framers of the Constitution.

Every rider that is added to a Congressional Bill – riders that seek some sort of special entitlement for a given state, district, region, or group as an implicit price for passing the bill in question -- is a violation of Article IV, Section of the Constitution. The very existence of such riders is demonstrated proof that the Bill to which they are attached lacks: integrity, independence, impartiality, honor, character, honesty, judiciousness, and virtuousness.

This might be how Congress operates. However, to the extent that this is the way Congress operates, then all such activities are unconstitutional since they are a violation of the guarantee of republican governance that is owed to the citizens of all the states in America.

Furthermore, many of the laws encompassing: elections, the unfair advantage that the Republican and Democratic Parties have in most jurisdictions, the way in which votes are recorded in many places (e.g., the newer electronic devices that leave no paper trail to verify the integrity of the process), campaign financing, and the use of public airwaves in relation to candidate debates and coverage are in violation of the Constitutional guarantee of republican government for all citizens of the respective states. This means that the elections arising out of such processes are also unconstitutional, for the latter are functionally related to the former activities – activities that lack often lack: integrity, honor, equitability, judiciousness, impartiality, egalitarianism, virtuousness, and character.

How the legislation is worded, or what might be said by various jurists in their decisions concerning this, or that, precedent in any of the foregoing matters, is often irrelevant. This is because the process through which the legislation has been generated or the judicial decisions that have been reached concerning such legislation give expression to numerous violations of the guarantee of republican governance.

Thus, even if one wanted to argue that Congress had constitutional authority to pass a law through which the 9/11 Commission was created (which I do not believe they had and will argue as much shortly), and even if one wished to maintain (which I do not believe can be done in a plausible way ... again, more on this shortly) that the Department of Commerce had constitutional authority to direct NIST to undertake a series of reports concerning the collapse of the three buildings at the World Trade Center (although one might wonder why their alleged mandate did not include the Pentagon as well), there is a wealth of evidence to indicate that neither Congress, nor the 9/11 Commission, nor NIST, nor the Pentagon conducted themselves in accordance with the specifications of Article IV, Section 4 of the Constitution which stipulates that the Federal Government is under Constitutional obligation to guarantee republican government for all of the states and their respective peoples in such matters. Indeed, a litany of questions and charges (that I won't reiterate here and might easily be found in a variety of references) have been raised concerning the: honesty, integrity, independence, judiciousness, character, virtuousness, impartiality, reasonableness, and disinterestedness of: Congress, the 9/11 Commission, NIST, and the Pentagon in relation to their respective investigations into 9/11.

In other words, neither Congress, nor the 9/11 Commission, nor NIST, nor the Pentagon, nor the Office of the President, nor the judiciary have met the litmus test of republican government in relation to 9/11. This is not a matter of officials making promises and, then, not living up to them, but, instead, this is a matter of all branches of the Federal Government having failed to meet the conditions of Article IV, Section 4 of the Constitution that guarantees a republican form of government in all matters.

Guarantees are not about giving a good faith effort – and, even this is questionable concerning the way the Federal Government handled the events prior to, on, and following 9/11. Guarantees are about the absolute fiduciary responsibility of all branches of government to ensure that republican values are instituted in everything that is done by any of those branches of government.

There is only one place in the Constitution in which any guarantees are given. This concerns the manner in which all activity – no matter which branch -- of the Federal Government must be conform to the principles, values, and spirit of republican governance.

There are no exceptions to Article IV, Section 4. This is the very heart of the Constitution, and if that provision is disregarded, then, all ensuing governance will be corrupted and become corrupt due to the absence of republican principles and values.

All one has to do is look at the current situation in the United States politically, economically, socially, educationally, financially, militarily, judicially, and internationally and one can see the effects that have ensued as a result of the United States persistent and pervasive disregard in relation to the central importance of republican government to a constitutionally viable democracy. The Framers of the Constitution understood this issue, but most of us have written off the guarantee of republican government as a quaint artifact of ancient history, and, as a result, we are suffering the consequences.

The 9/11 Commission Report, the various NIST reports, as well as *The Pentagon Performance Report* were all conceived in, and dedicated to, the proposition that they did not have to comply with the requirements of Article IV, Section 4 of the Constitution. This was a continuation of the acts and policies that the federal government had begun perpetrating before, during, and after the events of 9/11.

As a result, we have been graced with such things as: torture, extreme rendition, militarism, imperialism, enemy combatants, military tribunals, destruction of foreign countries, financial meltdowns, economic exploitation, loss of civil liberties, corporate malevolence, increasingly unmanageable debt; a failing infrastructure, Congressional gridlock, and the loss of hundreds of thousands of lives (including some that were our own). Irrespective of how one might feel about what might, or might not, have occurred on 9/11, the fact of the matter is that the Constitution has been eviscerated by a succession of federal administrations who have failed to keep faith with the Framers' guarantee of republican government for the citizens of all the states in America.

------

(2), (3) and (4).

All of the Framers of the Constitution, along with most of the colonists, believed that rights were extra-governmental. In other words, rights were inherent in their status as human beings and were not derived from, or gifts bestowed by, government.

The foregoing belief is given unmistakable expression in the second paragraph of the Declaration of Independence. Indeed, the idea of democratic government presupposed the existence of human beings who had the sort of naturally endowed rights that would enable them to come together and fashion a form of governance that would protect those rights within a framework that would help advance the common welfare along with all of the other principles mentioned in the Preamble to the Constitution.

Article I, Section 1 of the Constitution stipulates that" "All legislative powers herein granted shall be vested in the Congress of the United States, which shall consist of a Senate and a House of Representative." The legislative powers that are alluded to in Article I, Section 1 are specified in Section 8 of the same Article.

More specifically, in Section 8 of Article I of the Constitution one finds the following enumerated powers to which Congress is entitled. These powers include the ability to: (a) collect and lay taxes; (b) borrow money; (c) regulate commerce; (d) establish conditions for naturalization and bankruptcy; (e) coin and regulate the value of money; (f) provide for the punishment of counterfeiting; (g) establish post offices; (h) promote science and useful arts through copyright protections; (i) constitute tribunals inferior to the Supreme Court; (j) define and punish crimes committed on the high seas; (k) declare war; (l) raise and support armies; (m) provide and maintain an army; (n) make rules for the government and regulation of the land and naval forces; (o) provide for calling forth the militia to execute the laws of the union, suppress insurrections, and repel invasions; (p) provide for organizing, arming, and disciplining the militia; ; (q) exercise exclusive legislation in relation to the District of Columbia and all places purchased by the consent of the legislature of the various states for erection of forts; magazines, arsenals, dockyards, and other needful buildings; and (r) make all laws that shall be necessary and proper for the carrying into execution the foregoing powers by this Constitution in the government of the United States, or in any department or officer thereof.

The foregoing powers are not absolute. They are constrained by: the Preamble to the Constitution and the guarantee of republican government.

In other words, powers cannot be executed in just any way Congress wishes. Those powers must be exercised in accordance with republican principles – which are guaranteed – and must be done to further the purposes set forth in the Preamble to the Constitution ... namely, "to form a more perfect union; establish justice; insure domestic tranquility; provide for the common defense; promote the general welfare, and secure the blessings of liberty to ourselves and our posterity."

Furthermore, the Preamble is not a piece of rhetorical fluff. Without it, the Constitution has no direction or purpose.

Just as the guarantee of republican government gives expression to how government is to conduct itself, so too, the Preamble touches on why pursuing a union of people through government is important and what government is supposed to accomplish.

Unfortunately, there is a great deal that goes on in the three branches of the Federal Government that does not serve the purposes for which the Constitution was created. If one took almost any piece of legislation, executive order, or judicial decision and asked for a rigorous defense be given as to how such legislation, orders, or decisions advanced the causes of the Preamble to the Constitution, much of the former could be shown to be: arbitrary; problematic; inconsistent; unnecessary; ill-conceived; biased; ineffective; and injurious to justice, domestic tranquility, the common defense; the general welfare, and securing liberty for ourselves and posterity.

To the extent that the foregoing claim is true, then all legislation, executive orders, and judicial decisions that cannot be shown to be able to rigorously and demonstrably further the purposes of the Preamble really are unconstitutional. If one's legislation, orders and decisions cannot be shown to serve the purposes for which the Constitution was created, then, such legislation, orders and decisions are really antithetical to why the Constitution was originally created.

For instance, one might ask: How did the Congressional law that formed the 9/11 Commission advance the purposes inherent in the Preamble to the Constitution?

Did the 9/11 Commission help "form a more perfect union"? No, it didn't. The Commission and its executive director were riddled with conflicts of interest, and such conflicts of interest are an anathema to the idea of forming a more perfect union. Furthermore, *The 9/11 Commission Report* is also riddled with errors of many different kinds encompassing problems of both omission and commission, and, once again, it is very difficult, if not impossible, to understand how error is ever going to lead to the formation of a more perfect union.

Did the 9/11 Commission establish justice? No, it didn't because the Commissioners, researchers, and executive director went out of their ways not to establish justice except through statements, arguments, and inferences that were lacking evidential credibility and intent on promoting a conspiracy theory favored by the government. In fact, a terrible injustice was perpetrated on the 9/11 families, the

American people, and the rest of the world through the 9/11 Commission and its report.

Did the Commission insure domestic tranquility? No, it didn't, and in fact it had exactly the opposite effect since a number of polls now indicate that well over a hundred and twenty million people (including a number of 9/11 families, as well as an array of professional pilots, architects, engineers, ex-military and intelligence offices, and scientists) in the United States now believe that the 9/11 Commission did not do a credible job in relation to its investigation of 9/11.

Did the Commission provide for the common defense? No, it didn't since it actually undermined the possibility of such a common defense through its many errors of commission (e.g., the Commission intentionally left out the testimony of scores of people who had evidence that ran contrary to the government's conspiracy theory) and, as a result, made certain that many truths about 9/11 would never see the light of day – and, you cannot provide for the common defense by hiding the truth.

Did the Commission promote the general welfare? No, it didn't because the Commission was a body that was engaged in something other than a thorough and rigorous search for the truth -- which is the only thing that could have promoted the general welfare under the circumstances. Instead, America, 9/11 families, and the rest of the world have been fed a steady diet of misinformation, disinformation, and an invented mythology by *The 9/11 Commission Report*.

Did the Commission secure the blessings of liberty for either ourselves or our posterity? No, it didn't but, instead, the Commission placed our liberties at risk through promoting and propagandizing a conspiracy theory that the government had advanced, without credible evidence, within days following the events of 9/11 – a conspiracy theory that *The 9/11 Commission Report* could not defensibly or plausibly maintain and, yet, a conspiracy theory that has been used by all too many people who should have known better to help rationalize and justify the dismantling of civil liberties in America, Iraq, and Afghanistan.

Since the 9/11 Commission, its researchers, its executive director, and its report were not advancing the principles of the Preamble to the Constitution, then they must have been advancing some other agenda.

In other words, whatever was going on with the 9/11 Commission was unconstitutional.

In addition to the constraints imposed on Congressional legislative power by the Preamble to the Constitution and the guarantee of republican government, there are several amendments to the Constitution that are intended to remind everyone – government and citizens alike – that Congress is not entitled to extend its activities beyond the limits that are specified in the Constitution – almost all of which are contained in Section 8 of Article I and that have been outlined earlier. These two amendments are the ninth and tenth amendments.

Colonists, in general, as well as many of the people who were most active in the constitutional and ratification processes, in particular, were concerned that the federal government might try to extend its authority beyond the enumerated powers of Article I, Section 1 in the proposed Constitution. Therefore, they insisted that the Constitution be amended to reflect such a concern -- namely: "The enumeration in the Constitution of certain rights shall not be construed to deny or disparage others retained by the people," and this is known as the Ninth Amendment.

This meant that the powers and rights of Congress were fixed and limited by the Constitution. Moreover, whatever those powers were, they could not be extended in such a way as to deny or disparage the rights and powers that people retained beyond the enumerated powers and rights of Congress.

The protections of the Ninth Amendment were further strengthened through the Tenth Amendment. This amendment states that: "The powers not delegated to the United States, nor prohibited by it to the states, are reserved to the states, or to the people."

The Tenth Amendment accomplished two things. First, it reiterated an important principle, initially introduced through the Ninth Amendment – namely, citizens or the people have constitutional standing quite independently of the federal government or state governments.

If this were not the case, then the Ninth Amendment would have talked about how the enumeration of rights or powers belonging to the federal government should not be understood to either deny or disparage other rights and powers retained by the states. However, the Ninth Amendment did not mention state rights or powers. The amendment only referred to the rights and powers of the people.

Moreover, the Tenth Amendment affirms that the constitutional standing of people or citizens is independent of the federal governments when it adds the phrase: "or to the people." If the Framers of the Constitution had wanted to reserve all powers for the states that have not been delegated to the federal government or that have not been prohibited to the state governments, then the Tenth Amendment would have ended with the words: "are reserved for the states," but this is not what the Tenth Amendment says.

When the issues underlying the Tenth Amendment were being discussed, Roger Sherman from Connecticut suggested that the phrase "or to the people" be added to the wording of the amendment. This suggestion was accepted without objection or debate.

One cannot read the Tenth Amendment as if the phrase: "or to the people," is just a literary device that offers another way of referring to state governments. Constitutionally speaking, state governments are one thing, and the people are quite another.

There was much suspicion among colonists concerning any kind of government, and this was a direct result of their collective experiences either in Europe and/or through the tyrannical manner in which the British (and their colonialist agents) sought to control things in America. This meant that not only was the idea of a central, federal government to be approached with caution and with respect to which citizens should have protections and relief, but the aforementioned suspicions concerning governance extended to both state and local governments as well.

The Bill of Rights is almost entirely dedicated to protections of people and not of states. The Tenth Amendment does offer protection to states, but, simultaneously, that amendment also extends protection to the people by clearly indicating that: people were to have constitutional standing along with states and that citizens had a choice as to whether they wished those powers that were not delegated to the federal government or prohibited to the states to fall within the purview of the people or the purview of state governments that, theoretically, represented citizens.

The people insisted on a Bill of Rights because they did not trust government – any government. The people insisted on the Ninth and Tenth Amendments because those amendments gave the people a constitutional standing that neither the federal government nor the state governments should deny or disparage.

Unfortunately, states historically have continuously sought to usurp the rights and powers of people that were granted to people under the Ninth and Tenth Amendments. States, in this respect, have tried to do to the people what the federal government has attempted to do in relation to the states and the people – that is, to extend the sphere power, influence, and control of the central government.

For example, let's return to the list of enumerated powers that are listed in Article I, Section 8 of the Constitution and that have been stated earlier. Nowhere in that list of powers is there anything indicating that Congress has the right and power to create legislation concerning a 9/11-kind of investigation.

The closest that the enumerated list comes to such a possibility is in relation to the power of tribunals. The primary root meaning of the idea of a tribunal is in the form of a court or forum of justice.

In fact, Article I, Section 8 indicates that the power at issue involves the capacity "to constitute tribunals inferior to the Supreme Court." This infuses the notion of tribunal with a thoroughly judicial flavor.

The 9/11 Commission did possess the power of subpoenas, and this is similar to what happens in relation to tribunals. Moreover, most witnesses had to swear an oath under possible penalty of perjury, and, again, this is somewhat similar to what occurs within tribunals.

Nonetheless, despite the foregoing surface similarities between the investigation of the 9/11 Commission and the idea of tribunal, the 9/11 Commission does not really satisfy most of the criteria that might justify calling such a process a tribunal. For instance: (1) the Commission was not constituted with a judicial purpose in mind but, from the beginning, was treated as an investigation; (2) there was no special prosecutor appointed; (3) there were no defendants; (4) there was no attempt to observe the laws of evidence or follow normal court procedure; (5) the entire process of research was kept hidden and was not subject to rules of disclosure or cross-examination; (6) there were witnesses (e.g. George W. Bush and Richard Cheney) who did not have to swear an oath before giving testimony; (7) no judge or judges were assigned to the investigation; (8) although there were witnesses who gave false testimony, no one was held accountable; (9) although the power of subpoena was available to the Commission, it was almost never used, and as a result, even if justice were the point of the exercise – which it wasn't – justice could never had been served by Commissioners who were, for whatever reason, unwilling to exercise the subpoena power in anything but a perfunctory and very limited manner; (10) there were no sanctions associated with the findings of the commission; (11) the findings of the 9/11 Commission were not subject to review by the Supreme Court that is clearly a requirement entailed by the Congressional power to be able to constitute tribunals that are "inferior to the Supreme Court".

One cannot try to claim that something is a tribunal when it ignores, or tramples upon, most of what a tribunal requires. Furthermore, even if one were to concede the idea that 9/11 Commission was a tribunal (which the foregoing points indicate is not the case), then, at the very best, such an individual is faced with the prospect that the 9/11 Commission was unconstitutional in the manner in which it violated the principles inherent in the Preamble to the Constitution, as well as unconstitutional in the way in which it violated the guarantee of republican government set forth in Article IV, Section of the Constitution.

The fact of the matter is, the 9/11 Commission was not a tribunal in: intent; name, form, principle, process, or results. Therefore, in passing legislation that created the 9/11 Commission, Congress exceeded its constitutional authority.

None of the powers that are enumerated in Article I, Section 8 of the Constitution entitle Congress to form a 9/11-style investigation. Congress could have created a tribunal that would have been required to pursue the issues surrounding 9/11 in a very different way than the 9/11 Commission did, but Congress didn't do this, and, therefore, the

9/11 Commission as constituted and realized was in violation of the Constitution.

According to the 9th Amendment, "the enumeration in the Constitution of certain rights shall not be construed to deny or disparage others retained by the people", and, yet, this is exactly what Congress did through the formation of the 9/11 Commission – deny and disparage rights that are retained by the people. According to the 10th Amendment, "the powers not delegated to the United States by the Constitution, nor prohibited to it by the states, are reserved to the states respectively, or to the people," and, yet, by passing legislation for the 9/11 Commission, Congress transgressed into areas that are clearly the preserve of, and reserved for, the states or the people.

By passing legislature to form the 9/11 Commission, Congress not only violated the 9th and 10th Amendment rights of the people as pointed out in the foregoing comments, but, as well, Congress violated the 5th Amendment rights of people. Among other things, the 5th Amendment introduces the idea of a "grand jury".

Normally speaking, grand juries are formed when a district attorney or attorney general wants to prosecute someone whom he or she believes has committed a crime. During the grand jury proceeding, the prosecutor puts forth an array of evidence that she or he believes strongly indicates that a given individual has committed a certain crime.

The members of the grand jury are free to ask whatever questions they like concerning such evidence. They also are free to ask for additional evidence and witnesses to be presented.

Once all the witnesses and evidence have been presented, the prosecutor leaves the room where the grand jury has been convened. The jurors then discuss and explore the issues among themselves as to whether, on not, they believe sufficient evidence has been presented to underwrite an indictment of the accused individual.

The understanding of many people – including that of some lawyers and prosecutors – concerning the idea of a grand jury tends to end at this point. In other words, once the grand jury reaches a decision concerning whether, or not, to indict someone, then supposedly the work of the grand jury is complete.

However, a grand jury does not serve the state or its legal officials. The grand jury serves the people, and the reason that the idea of a grand jury has been enshrined in the 5th Amendment is to preserve the civil liberties of citizens.

Consequently, on the one hand, grand juries are the last outpost of protection for citizens against arbitrary and unwarranted prosecution by the government. However, on the other hand, grand juries also are a constitutionally authorized forum to ensure that the government is not undermining the civil liberties of citizens in ways that might extend beyond the interests of any given district attorney, attorney general, or other legal representative of the government.

Once the immediate reasons for which some level of government has convened a grand jury have been served, a grand jury is free to pursue any other issue that is of interest to the members of that jury that carry implications for the civil liberties and rights of citizens. Many district attorneys and attorney generals who actually know about this dimension of the power of grand juries are often not inclined to share such knowledge with the members of a grand jury and, thereby, help those members understand the full potential of their power under the Constitution.

The powers of grand juries are entailed by the guarantee of a republican form of government for the states. The powers of grand juries are entailed by the rights inherent in the 9th and 10th Amendments – rights that belong to the people and not to the central government. The powers of grand juries are entailed by the principles given expression through the Preamble to the Constitution. The powers of grand juries are entailed by the priority that people have over governments through the natural, inborn rights of human beings and from which governments derive whatever authority they have.

By passing legislation that created the 9/11 Commission, Congress usurped the rights and powers of grand juries to make determinations and judgments in such matters. By passing legislation concerning 9/11, Congress attempted -- in contravention of the amended Constitution -- to deny and disparage the rights and powers of the people ... rights and powers that could be exercised through venues like, but not restricted to, a grand jury.

Furthermore, by participating in a commission that was without constitutional authority, each of the Commissioners, as well as the executive director of the Commission, and all of the Commission researchers did also effectively deprive the American people of the latter's 5th, 9th, and 10th Amendment rights. I do not call what the various participants did a conspiracy, but, rather, each person acted individually and, probably without any real understanding of the nature of their unconstitutional behavior. However, whether done unknowingly or knowingly, all those individuals were, nonetheless, still denying and depriving American citizens of their Constitutionally established rights by working with and on the 9/11 Commission.

Article II, Section 2 of the Constitution indicates that the President shall: "appoint ambassadors, other public ministers, and counsels, judges of the Supreme Court, and all other officers of the United States whose appointments are not herein otherwise provided for, and that shall be established by law." In conjunction with the 9/11 Commission, the President did appoint, first, Henry Kissinger, and, then, Thomas Kean to serve as Chairman of the 9/11 Commission.

However, the 9/11 Commission was created through Congressional legislation. It was not a Presidential body.

Thomas Kean was assigned to the Commission as the President's representative on a legislatively created body. As such, Thomas Kean had no special authority apart from what Congress had enabled (unconstitutionally) the Commission to have in the first place.

By appointing the chairman for the 9/11 Commission, the President violated the 5th, 9th, and 10th Amendment rights of the people because he was co-operating with a body – namely, the Congress – which had exceeded its Constitutional authority in relation to the powers that it had, and had not, been granted. Consequently, in the process, the President also exceeded his authority even though under other circumstances the President does have the Constitutional authority, as noted earlier, to appoint various individuals as ambassadors, Supreme Court judges, counsels, or officers of the United States.

In addition to Congress and the President, there is another facet of government that also violated the 5th, 9th, and 10th Amendment rights of the people. The facet of government to which allusion is being directed here concerns the Department of Commerce that authorized NIST (National Institute of Standards and Technology) to conduct an investigation into the building collapses at the World Trade Center.

NIST came into being in 1901 and is under the auspices of the Department of Commerce. It is a non-regulatory agency whose stated mission is: "to promote U.S. innovation and industrial competitiveness by advancing measurement science, standards, and technology in ways that enhance economic security and improve the quality of life."

Whatever technical facility NIST might have, neither the Department of Commerce nor NIST had Constitutional authority to investigate the World Trade Center building collapses. The investigation of those collapses was not about, on the one hand, regulating commerce, nor, on the other hand, was such an investigation a matter of promoting innovation and industrial competitiveness, or advancing: measurement science, standards, and/or technology.

Even if one were to concede that the Department of Commerce and, therefore, NIST had Constitutional authority to conduct the investigation it did with respect to the World Trade Center (which I do not concede and that they cannot justify under the Constitution), overwhelming evidence exists through the work of people such as: Richard Gage, Steven Jones, Judy Wood, Kevin Ryan, and many, many others that NIST did not conduct itself in accordance with its Constitutionally mandated obligation to go about its activities in compliance with republican principles of: honesty; integrity; honor; impartiality; judiciousness; character; independence; or reasonableness.

Moreover, it seems rather odd that NIST was given authority to investigate the collapse of the World Trade buildings, rather than, say, the National Transportation Safety Board or the FBI. Of course, in many ways, neither the NTSB nor the FBI is really equipped with the resources and expertise to examine the collapse of three buildings at the World Trade Center except in very restricted ways.

Unfortunately, almost from the very beginning, the FBI failed to treat the World Trade Center as a crime scene. The FBI permitted evidence to be taken away without consideration for the possibility that its theory concerning the nature of events on 9/11 might be incorrect or incomplete, and, consequently, as an agency of the central government, the FBI violated the Constitutional guarantee of a republican form of government for the states – a possibility that assumes more ironic proportions given that the FBI has, since, publically stated they have absolutely no credible evidence capable of tying 'Usama bin Laden to the events of 9/11.

One might also add that the FBI has acted unconstitutionally in the manner in which it has handled potential evidence about 9/11 involving, among others, Sibel Edmonds, Indira Singh, Robert Wright, and David Schippers. In the first three cases, the FBI has put a gag order on the people in question and, as a result, has prevented those individuals from sharing what they know with the American people.

The provisions of Article IV, Section 4 of the Constitution are quite clear. The federal government – including all of its agencies – are under an absolute guarantee to provide a republican form of government to the states of the union, and, yet, based on what <u>has</u> been said by Edmonds, Singh, Wright, and Schippers, the FBI has not acted with: impartiality; honesty; honor; integrity; judiciousness; character; or reasonableness in relation to 9/11.

The cry of 'National Security' does not trump a constitutional guarantee of republican government. This is especially so when there is prima facie evidence provided by, at least, four individuals, acting independently of one another, that the FBI has not conducted itself in accordance with the Constitutional requirement of republican government with respect to the events of 9/11.

In addition, the mantra of "National Security" also does not justify the use of torture water-boarding, extreme rendition, the invention of categories such as "unlawful enemy combatant", or maintaining captives without due process. The military and all intelligence agencies are under the auspices of the federal government, and, therefore, they are subject to the requirements of Article IV, Section 4 concerning the guarantee of republican government to all states – and this remains true whether, or not, the country is at war or engaged in some military conflict.

If the federal government in any of its manifestations does not comply with the Constitutional guarantee of republican government, then national security has been violated because there is nothing more vital to the national security of America than the requirements of republican government. There is nothing more important or essential to Constitutional stability and viability than the requirement that all federal employees (whether members of Congress, members of the military, members of the so-called intelligence community, members of the judiciary, or members of any department or office within the federal government) act with: integrity, character, honesty, impartiality, judiciousness, benevolence, independence, honor, self-sacrifice (not the sacrifice of others), and virtue. Moreover, if federal employees cannot act in the foregoing manner, then everything they do is unconstitutional.

Currently, despite whatever successes and good features might be present, the United States is a failed state. It is a failed state because it gives expression to all the characteristics of a failed state.

More specifically:

(1)   Failed States do not honor the provisions and guarantees of their constitutional documents – and the foregoing discussion has shown that the United States federal government has done this again and again.

(2)   Failed states are unwilling or unable to protect their citizens – e.g., 9/11; Katrina; the BP/Deep Water Horizon catastrophe (along with many other environmental disasters); the financial meltdowns involving derivatives; the banking industry; endless wars for contrived reasons.

(3)   Failed states tend to regard themselves as beyond the reach of domestic and international law – e.g., America's opting out of the World Court, as well as its undermining the United Nations by continuing to support Israel's illegal occupation and confiscation of Palestinian property, as well as Israel's illegal wall, settlements and violation of Palestinian human rights.

(4)   Failed states feel free, if not entitled, to carry out aggression and violence against other countries and peoples – e.g., the United States' acts of unprovoked aggression against Iran, Guatemala, Cuba, Vietnam, Lebanon, Nicaragua, Chile, Grenada, Panama, Haiti, Iraq (twice), Afghanistan, Pakistan, and the Palestinian people.

(5)   Failed states suffer from a deficit of democratic institutions –
e.g., America's legal system Is broken and disadvantages the poor in all
too many ways; congress is deadlocked and almost completely under
the influence and control of lobbyists and special interests; the
military is used as a tool for imperialistic and corporate agendas; the
electoral process is deeply dysfunctional; the executive office often
behaves as if it is a monarchical, imperial presidency that does not
have to serve anything but its own agenda.

(6)   Failed states usually have no, or little control, over their
central banks or actively collude with such banks to the disadvantage
of the vast majority of their citizens so that the latter are enslaved by
the banking system rather than empowered by it – e.g., the Federal
Reserve system is a consortium of private banking interests that was
unconstitutionally legislated into existence and has never once been
able to avert any of the crises (such as the Great Depression or the
current near-Depression and the recent meltdown in the financial
markets) for which it, allegedly, was created.

(7)   Failed states are characterized by a media whose behavior
and potential for objectivity and integrity have, in many ways, been co-
opted -- e.g., if the American media had been objective and acted with
integrity in relation to the events of 9/11 – which they did not—then
America's present situation might not be so dire.

(8)   Failed states terrorize their own citizens and the citizens of
other countries – e.g., the persistent evisceration of the American
Constitution that has been perpetrated by all three branches of the
federal government over the last several hundred years is nothing less
than a series of terrorist attacks upon successive generations of
American citizens, and such terrorist attacks have permitted other
terrorist activities by the federal government to spill over into
America's treatment of many other countries and peoples around the
world.

In view of the foregoing, I believe that there are roughly five
choices facing the American people:

(a)   Acknowledge that the 9/11 Commission was an
unconstitutional usurpation of the rights of citizens under the 5th, 9th
and 10th Amendments of the Constitution, as well as a violation of both
the Preamble to the Constitution and Article IV, Section 4 of the

Constitution that guarantees republican government to all of the sates of the union, and, as a result, permit American citizens – not the government – to pursue a new investigation into the events: leading up to, occurring on, and ensuing from 9/11. This could be a first, and very necessary step that permits Americans to reclaim and reassert their right to a constitutional democracy that has integrity and other qualities of republican governance.

(b)   Convene a new Constitutional convention in which the American people have an opportunity to correct all the things that currently help make the United States a failed nation.

(c)   Permit states to secede and make their own arrangements – alone or in concert … and I might point out that although I consider much of the recent discussions concerning secession by various states (e.g., Texas) to be of a frivolous and ill-conceived nature, states do have the right to secede from the Union if the federal government breaks the Constitutional contract that binds states together. In fact, secession is one of the rights and powers that is entailed by the 9th and 10th Amendments, and, therefore, Lincoln was wrong when he sought to force states to remain in the Union. However poorly conceived a move to secede might be, it is neither necessarily an act of insurrection, nor is it an act of sedition or treason, and, therefore, the federal government has no power to prevent it. When the federal government, or any of its agents, no longer complies with the requirements of republican government, then the federal government has lent justification to the desire that people or states might carry with respect to the issue of secession.

(d)   Enter into a series of bloody, chaotic rebellions, insurgencies, and insurrections through which multiple parties all vie to control other human beings and deprive the latter of their natural, inherent rights as human beings.

(e)   Go with the status quo and be sucked down by the whirlpool in the toilet of an increasingly failed state.

The first option noted above – that is, holding a new, rigorous, independent investigation into the events surrounding 9/11-- is the easiest and least problematic choice facing the American people. Moreover, pursuing that choice might be the best chance America has of pulling back from the precipice of destruction on which the country is teetering.

The second option – that is, convening a new constitutional convention – might serve as a very constructive complement to the foregoing option. Although there is a great deal about America that is right, there also is far too much about America that is dysfunctional and destructive (with respect to ourselves and others), and, therefore, there is a deep need to revitalize and rededicate our democracy through establishing methods and principles that might permit America to be better than it has been over the last several hundred years.

Although the last three options noted above are actual possibilities that are staring us in the face, I don't see any of them as being able to constructively solve the problems with which Americans are currently confronted even as I see different groups within the general population who seem to be increasingly advocating some form of secession, insurrection, or rebellion. Moreover, I feel that those individuals who believe that America will somehow stumble through the current Constitutional crisis without being required to change, in any essential way, the nature of governance or without having to change what is currently going on within government, are suffering from a form of thinking that is seriously delusional in nature.

We can choose to rid ourselves of our current failed state status, and I believe the first step in this process involves either: initiating a new, citizen-controlled but constitutionally authorized investigation into 9/11, and/or convening a new Constitutional convention. The alternative to the foregoing is that we can choose to become an increasingly failed state through secession, insurrection, rebellion, or maintaining the status quo.

America is at a tipping point. The fracture lines are running in all directions, and although just as no one can predict when a major earthquake will occur, all the indices are present to point to a coming cataclysmic social and political event or series of such events in our collective futures.

Time is running out. Important choices need to be made now, or very soon the capacity to choose might be ripped from our hands by social, political, and economic events that could inundate us in an irreversible fashion.